THE MAKING OF
PRIDE (AND) PREJUDICE

SUE BIRTWISTLE & SUSIE CONKLIN

PENGUIN BOOKS
BBC BOOKS

PENGUIN BOOKS
BBC BOOKS

Published by the Penguin Group
Penguin Books Ltd, 80 Strand, London WC2R 0RL, England
Penguin Putnam Inc., 375 Hudson Street, New York, New York 10014, USA
Penguin Books Australia Ltd, 250 Camberwell Road, Camberwell, Victoria 3124, Australia
Penguin Books Canada Ltd, 10 Alcorn Avenue, Toronto, Ontario, Canada M4V 3B2
Penguin Books India (P) Ltd, 11 Community Centre, Panchsheel Park,
New Delhi – 110 017, India
Penguin Books (NZ) Ltd, Cnr Rosedale and Airborne Roads,
Albany, Auckland, New Zealand
Penguin Books (South Africa) (Pty) Ltd, 24 Sturdee Avenue,
Rosebank 2196, South Africa

Penguin Books Ltd, Registered Offices: 80 Strand, London WC2R 0RL, England

www.penguin.com

First published 1995
33

Printed in China
Colour reproduction by Saxon, Norwich

$\mathcal{C}$ONTENTS

The Bennet family.

$\mathcal{I}$NTRODUCTION

In the autumn of 1986, I was invited to a preview screening of *Northanger Abbey*. Andrew Davies, a writer with whom I'd worked several times before, was there and we sat together. He remembers the evening well: 'It was an interesting, quirky adaptation and afterwards Sue turned to me and said: "I know what I'd like to do: *Pride and Prejudice* and make it look like a fresh, lively story about real people. And make it clear that, though it's about many things, it's principally about sex and it's about money: those are the driving motives of the plot. Would you like to adapt it?" It's a favourite book of mine, so I said, "Yes," and that was that.'

Producer Sue Birtwistle.

Well, it wasn't quite as easy as 'that was that'. From that evening until our version of *Pride and Prejudice* is broadcast in the autumn of 1995, nine years will have elapsed. Why did it take so long? What were we doing for all that time? Other projects, of course (in Andrew's case, many other projects!).

He and I met the following week and talked about our passion for the book. We were clear from the beginning that we wanted to make it on film so that it would have an energy and vitality to match the book. People often ask: 'Why make a new version on film when the BBC had made one on videotape in 1980?' Although videotape is the dominant medium for television and works for current affairs and documentaries, I don't feel it serves drama well. It always looks undernourished; it's too present, too literal. Unpoetic, if you like. We wanted scenes to have a freedom that is just impossible to achieve recording on video in the studio.

Writer Andrew Davies.

We decided not to offer it to the BBC at this stage but to try instead to sell it to ITV. This struck many people as odd, since the BBC is usually seen as the natural home for 'classic drama'. Our reasoning was that, as the book is apparently the most read novel in the English language in the world, we should try to make it available to the widest possible audience. We felt that, if it were shown on the BBC, then the ITV audience might not even give it a chance. Whereas we knew that a BBC audience would probably at least try a Jane Austen serial wherever it was scheduled.

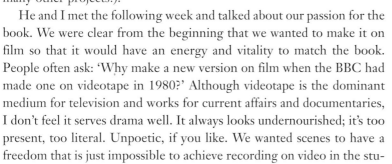

I knew that if I contacted the ITV companies and said, 'Would you like to do *Pride and Prejudice*?' I'd probably have received a short, sharp 'no.' So, instead, I telephoned Nick Elliott, who was then Head of Drama at LWT and with whom I'd worked before, and said: 'Andrew Davies and I would like to take you to lunch and sell you a six-part adaptation of simply the sexiest book ever written.' We refused to name the book. He was so keen that we met the following day and we told him the story as if it had just been written: 'Well, there's five girls aged from 15 to 22 years old and their mother is desperate to get them married to rich men because, though some are very beautiful, they are poor' and so on . . . He became rather excited and asked if the rights were free. When we finally confessed it was *Pride and Prejudice* he was stunned. But Nick, typically, made a quick decision: 'I thought it was a thrilling idea. I was certainly carried by the argument that it could be popular drama, and I decided there and then to commission the first three scripts. At that time in ITV companies, there was a wider range of possibilities for drama. It wasn't as ratings-driven as it later became. When the first scripts were delivered, I thought they were terrific: some of the most exciting scripts I've read. Unfortunately, others there felt that six years was too soon after the last BBC version and so the project was put on hold.'

The project may have been 'on hold', but the publicity wasn't. Andrew had been asked in an interview what he was currently writing. He mentioned *Pride and Prejudice* and, in the same sentence, the words 'sex and money'. The tabloid newspapers needed no further encouragement. 'SEX ROMP JANE AUSTEN' hit the headlines. This new version, they confidently asserted, would have full frontal nudity and daring sex scenes. The broadsheets picked up the story. We even featured in the cartoon on the front page of *The Guardian*. Jane Austen experts were consulted and were quick to condemn this 'spiced-up' version. No one, of course, bothered to telephone me to check if the story was accurate. It wasn't. No doubt, we made a mistake when we described the novel as sexy; what we meant, of course, was that Darcy staring at Elizabeth across a room is exciting, that Darcy and Elizabeth touching hands the first time they dance is erotic. What we did not mean was naked bedroom scenes. But this story, it seems, will run and run.

In early 1993, the ITV network was again becoming interested in *Pride and Prejudice* and Nick Elliott felt he had a real chance of getting it made at last. It was at this time that Michael Wearing, Head of Drama/Serials at the BBC, stepped in. As he says: 'There was a real wish for the BBC to return to making the classic serial, and reading the first three scripts led one to believe that this was potentially a splendid and vigorous interpretation. There will always be debate about whether the BBC should have redone *Pride and Prejudice* but, after all, there will be a fifteen-year gap between the two versions and I do feel that a great

LET'S SAVE THE BODICE-RIPPING FOR THE TV ADAPTATION, MISS AUSTEN.

From *The Guardian*, 1990.

Michael Wearing.

book like this one can bear revisiting. What attracted me about this version was that the idea of doing it wasn't executive-led; it didn't come from within the BBC, but came directly out of the passion of the people involved. I decided to commission the final three scripts.'

In November 1993 I was asked to prepare a budget based on the scripts and discussions with Gerry Scott, the production designer, and casting director Janey Fothergill. By Christmas we had been given the go-ahead and in January '94 director Simon Langton joined and pre-production (the arrangements that are necessary before filming can start) began. Suddenly, the project had a dozen or more people working on it full time. The numbers grew steadily until, in June, on the first day of filming, I drove to the location and saw at last the whole unit in place in a large field. It was like an enormous circus: large trucks for equipment, lights, props, catering, caravans for the actors, make-up and wardrobe, a double-decker dining bus, horses and carriages, dozens of actors in costume and make-up and the entire crew busy at work preparing for the first shot of the film while trying to introduce themselves to each other. After all, they knew this was the beginning of five months of intensive work together. This was my private moment of anxiety when I asked myself, 'What have I started?'

Filming in Wiltshire.

We began in Grantham and finished in Warwick on 1 November. Post-production continued until mid-May 1995, and the last remnants of the team then disbanded. In early autumn, the BBC publicity department will take over, the programmes will be shown to the press and the actors will be re-called for interviews. By Christmas 1995, it will all be over and I'll be left alone, fountain pen at the ready to face the 'Dear BBC, Why, oh, why . . . ?' letters. I hope there won't be too many about anachronistic teacups or coach wheels. We have tried during the production to be as accurate as possible, but we always felt it was more important to go for the spirit of the original book. We decided to write *this* book because we were always asked the same questions about the filming process wherever we went. I hope it will answer some of those questions.

The process of making *Pride and Prejudice*, though very hard work, was hugely enjoyable. There were many treasured moments. Perhaps one from early pre-production days will serve here to give a flavour: there was much interest from America in investing in the project and I was telephoned by one potential backer (it was not, I hasten to add, Arts and Entertainment Network, New York, who did eventually become our welcome co-producer). The call went like this:

'We're very interested in putting £1 million into *Pride and Prejudice*. Can you tell me who's written it?'

Assuming that, if they were prepared to invest so much money, they would have already read the book and just wanted to know who had adapted it, I said: 'Andrew Davies,' and then added as an afterthought: 'from the novel.'

'Novel? What novel?'

'Er . . . the novel. By Jane Austen.'

'How are you spelling that?'

'A.U.S.T.E.N.'

'Is she selling well?'

'Er . . . yes. Very well.'

'How many copies has she sold?'

'You mean altogether?'

'Yeah. Since publication.'

'Since . . . er . . . 1813?'

There was a long pause. 'You mean she's dead?' (Another pause.) 'So she wouldn't be available for book signings?'

Sue Birtwistle
May 1995

chapter 1

*T*HE SCRIPT

Writing a six-part television serial is difficult and time-consuming work, but for Andrew Davies adapting *Pride and Prejudice* was a particularly enjoyable experience: 'The novel itself is actually my favourite novel and has been for ages. I've re-read it simply for pleasure so many times, and I think I like it better than any other Jane Austen novel, largely because, like everybody else, I'm in love with Elizabeth. I find her kind of joyful energy and sassiness just so beguiling. Later on Jane Austen tried to do rather more complex things with her heroines. For me just this book, just Elizabeth, has these qualities, which are really very modern. She's fiercely moral, she's got a terrific sense of humour, she makes fun of people, she doesn't take herself seriously, but she doesn't put herself down either. She needs to marry money but she's determined she's going to love the man she marries. She is a great character.'

Before Andrew could sit down and enjoy the process of writing the scripts, he had to determine the length of the adaptation. 'Of course, *Pride and Prejudice* has been done as quite a short movie, but you leave out some very important things doing it at that length. Because the book is so tight – her plot works just like a Swiss clock and doesn't have any flabby bits in it – everything counts. Originally I thought I could do it in five episodes but, because the needs of television scheduling make four, six or seven episodes a much more convenient thing, this was not a popular idea at all!

'I must confess that I think her as delightful a creature as ever appeared in print' (Jane Austen on Elizabeth Bennet).

'So I looked again and found that if we did it in six episodes, we'd be able to be really filmic with the letters, and show those events that Jane Austen alludes to as little flashback or invented scenes. And I found that it fitted very neatly into six episodes. I say "very neatly" in comparison with *Middlemarch*, which was like trying to get an elephant into a suitcase in some ways. One would have liked more, and it was a struggle deciding what to leave out. With *Pride and Prejudice* I was jolly pleased we were able to get it all in.'

At this stage there was much discussion to ensure that each episode opened as vibrantly as possible and ended as strongly as possible – ideally at a key turning point in the story. Overall the first three episodes

Darcy and Bingley have their first view of Netherfield.

'Bingley looked at and into Netherfield for half an hour and took it immediately' (Jane Austen).

Inspired by the galloping horses, Lizzy runs downhill towards Longbourn.

lead us to Darcy's arrogant first marriage proposal, which Elizabeth rejects; the last three episodes lead up to his heart-felt second proposal, which a chastened Elizabeth joyfully accepts.

The process of adapting a book for television is not as straightforward as some might assume. All too easily an adaptation can lovingly copy a book scene by scene only to find that the final product is too literary and undramatic. Important scenes in the book suddenly don't seem to make sense on screen, or time-jumps, which are explained beautifully in prose, make for a fragmented narrative in the film, or memorable dialogue on the page turns to lead in the actor's mouth. This can happen for a number of reasons.

Usually there is no central narrator (or voiceover) who can point out the intricate state of mind of a particular character, or describe a new character when he or she appears, or relate the back history of a character's life for the audience. And though occasionally a voiceover is used in an adaptation, it tends to work best when the original book is written in the first person – *Brideshead Revisited*, for example. The narration then becomes an integral part of a known character in the story rather than an omniscient presence that can distance the audience and prevent it from getting fully involved.

Andrew Davies taught literature for many years and has a thorough understanding of the structure of the novel but, when it comes to television and film, he is a full advocate of the 'show, don't tell' approach to scriptwriting. In other words, the camera can tell you a great deal that a narrator would, but in a different and quicker way. Of course, dialogue is terribly important – and Jane Austen has written some of the most delightful dialogue in literature – but good visual storytelling is at the heart of a memorable film. The goal therefore was clear – to remain true to the tone and spirit of *Pride and Prejudice* but to exploit the possibilities of visual storytelling to make it as vivid and lively a drama as possible.

'The advantage of writing for film [as opposed to traditional studio drama on videotape] is that it just frees it up tremendously. For example, I wrote in a little opening sequence, which isn't in the book at all. It shows Bingley and Darcy riding their horses, and Bingley deciding to take Netherfield. It then moves to Elizabeth seeing them from perhaps half a mile away, and thinking, 'Oh, there are two chaps on horses!' Of course, she doesn't know who they are but, almost as if inspired by the galloping of their horses, she turns and runs downhill towards Longbourn. So right at the beginning one's trying to express some of this vitality. That's something you couldn't possibly do in a studio.

'With scenes I've included in the dramatization which aren't in the novel, people sometimes ask, "What is the justification for that?" and I would have to say, what is the justification of spending money if you're just going to produce a series of pictures alongside the dialogue of the novel? You have to offer an interpretation of the novel. There's this nonsense which some people say about adaptations that you've "destroyed" the book if it's not identical scene by scene. The novel is still there for anybody to read – and everybody has their own "adaptation" in a sense when they're reading it.

'In something like that opening scene, part of the justification for showing Bingley and Darcy at that moment when Bingley decides to take Netherfield is to show them as two physical young men. They are young animals on their big horses; that's one of the things they are. We also see in that brief exchange that Bingley, as he's described in the novel later on, is impulsive because he makes a quick decision, and that Darcy views life with a rather critical eye and is a little contemptuous of country manners. Of course, very importantly, you also get the sense of the kind of income level we're dealing with. We see Netherfield, which is a seriously big house and so anyone thinking of renting it must have a lot of money. And almost immediately afterwards you see Elizabeth walking up to her own house, which most of us nowadays would consider very desirable, but it's about a twentieth of the size of Netherfield. That indicates that the income of the Bennet family is about a twentieth of the income of the guys they hope to marry. And you can convey all of that without any ponderous dialogue.'

GENERAL PRINCIPLES OF THE ADAPTATION
Darcy and Elizabeth

'One of the first things that struck me about *Pride and Prejudice*, and which I decided to bring out very clearly, is that the central motor which drives the story forward is Darcy's sexual attraction to Elizabeth. He doesn't particularly like her, he's appalled by the rest of her family, her general circumstances, the vulgarity of her mother and some of her sisters and he fights desperately against this attraction. But again and again, he is drawn into conversation with her because she's a sparky woman, who resists him and is cheeky to him, whereas almost every other woman he's met tries to flatter and appease him – notably Miss Bingley. Unable to fight against this attraction, he proposes to her in a very arrogant and disagreeable manner.

'At this stage of the story, she still doesn't like him at all, and doesn't recognize her unconscious attraction to him. Ever since he snubbed her at the Meryton assembly she has fixed him in her mind as a very proud and disagreeable man, and so she actually refuses him. He is angry, amazed and wounded by the things she says, but eventually he overcomes his anger and his sense of humiliation, and proceeds to show her that he can be thoroughly nice and helpful, and eventually she comes to see his true character.

'I realize in telling this story that I've really been telling it rather as if it's a story about Mr Darcy, whereas the book is definitely a book

'He is such a disagreeable man that it would be quite a misfortune to be liked by him,' says Mrs Bennet.

Elizabeth hears herself described by Darcy as 'tolerable; but not handsome enough to tempt *me*'.

about Elizabeth. In the novel Darcy is a mysterious, unpredictable character, whom we only really begin to understand right at the end. I haven't done a version about Mr Darcy, but I suppose in showing that his desire for Elizabeth is the motivation of the plot, I've perhaps pushed it a bit more to being a story about Elizabeth and Darcy, rather than a story about Elizabeth.'

DRAMATIZING ELIZABETH

Despite this decision to bring Darcy more into the foreground, most of the action is still seen from Elizabeth's perspective, and she is still the one with whom we most clearly identify and with whom we must get totally involved. Andrew's task, therefore, was to ensure that the character so well known and loved in the book was equally vibrant when she was brought dramatically to life.

'To walk three miles above her ankles in dirt, and alone, quite alone!' (Miss Bingley).

'Elizabeth is so perfectly done in the book, there isn't very much to do really, besides let her be herself. Although I must say we were all keen to grapple on to an aspect of her that is very vivid and clear in the book, but often ignored by critics, commentators and interpreters of Elizabeth, which is that she is a very active, lively girl, not just mentally but also physically. Again and again she is described as running out of the room, or rambling through the countryside, and so on. So there is this kind of tomboyish, almost gypsy-ish quality to her, which we wanted to get across.

'Her eyes were brightened by the exercise' (Darcy).

'I'm not sure how far people would agree with me, but I almost think that this is a coded way of Jane Austen telling us she's got lots of sexual energy. This is probably what appeals to Darcy, unconsciously at any rate, who is used to some very artificial females. Here's a natural one, who runs round, gets her feet muddy, says what she thinks, sticks up for herself and it turns him on! When she arrives at Netherfield on foot Miss Bingley actually comments, "She really looked almost wild!" But the men respond differently. Bingley says, "I thought she looked remarkably well!" and Darcy comments that her eyes were "brightened by the exercise". We all know the benefits of going to the gym and things like that – so she's full of whatever chemicals are released by healthful exercise and the chaps unconsciously respond to it.'

'BACKSTAGE' SCENES

'Jane Austen famously never included any scenes in which a young lady could not be present, so that you never get conversations between men on their own – most of the conversations are "on stage" as it were, on occasions where everyone is fully dressed for a social occasion. There are some private conversations between Jane and Elizabeth in their bedrooms, but these are the exception rather than the rule.

'In the adaptation, however, I felt free to go backstage, partly to show that these are real human creatures, who have bodies and have to get dressed up. In fact, the bodies and faces of the Bennet girls are their only assets in the marriage market, and so we see them dressing themselves up, borrowing each other's clothes and trying to present themselves as well as they can in this struggle to get well married. So we do have a lot of little backstage scenes.

'I particularly wanted to show backstage scenes with Darcy and Bingley because in almost any version of Jane Austen I've seen, everyone seems terrifically stiff and buttoned up the whole time; you get no sense that they are living, breathing, feeling people inside. So I thought, "What do they do in their spare time?" and decided to show them going riding, and shooting and fencing. Darcy goes swimming at one point and it's partly a way of showing him as a real human being.'

Darcy fencing.

The swimming sequence at Pemberley is a good illustration of how visual storytelling can communicate as much about a character as a literary description, though in a different way. During their tour of Pemberley the housekeeper takes Elizabeth and the Gardiners into the gallery where Elizabeth is shown a portrait of Darcy. Elizabeth stares at it a long time – trying to put the picture of the formal but smiling Darcy together with the portrait she has made of him in her own mind. We then cut to Darcy riding towards Pemberley. From a distance he looks every bit like the formal Darcy we are used to. But then we cut in close and see that he is actually travel-stained and sweaty, his breathing heavy from the exercise. He heads to the lake and decides to dive in – 'a brief respite from duty, and from the tumult of his tormented and unhappy feelings', Andrew writes in the stage directions. We then follow Darcy underwater – not absolutely vital, one might think, but again it was a visual way of communicating a different picture of Darcy 'cleaving through this other element, a natural man, free of the trappings of culture'. In that brief moment, one is reminded that Darcy, for all his responsibilities as the owner of Pemberley, is actually a young man. And, by intercutting Elizabeth staring at his portrait with the flesh-and-blood Darcy the audience sees, one is able to point up the idea that there are many portraits of Darcy being formed in the story, as Lizzy tells Darcy herself at the Netherfield ball: 'I hear such different accounts of you as puzzle me exceedingly.'

Darcy dives into the lake: 'a brief respite from duty'.

We, the audience, are also forming a portrait of Darcy, and are given glimpses of him denied to Elizabeth, thereby making us more actively involved in the story: 'I wanted the audience to get a sense fairly early on that there is a lot more to Darcy than Elizabeth sees,' says Andrew. 'Some people might see that as a mistake, as giving away something in advance, but I think the richness you can get out of it makes it, at any rate, a very interesting way of looking at the book. And, of course, we were careful not to give too much away.'

These scenes also help to build the transition from the proud and arrogant Darcy we meet at the beginning to the thoughtful and loving Darcy we come to know at the end of the story. This seemingly sudden change in character has been much discussed by critics and lovers of the novel and is one that poses particular challenges for an actor. (See Colin Firth's discussion of playing Darcy in Chapter 9.) At the script stage, inventing a few moments in which to bridge the transition was crucial: 'It's easier to believe in this complete change in character which Elizabeth has brought about if you can see glimpses of him, say with his friend, in which he's being completely open and friendly and is just what a good friend ought to be.'

BUILDING ON EXISTING SCENES: THE MERYTON ASSEMBLY

The Bennet family is first introduced to the Netherfield party at the Meryton assembly. It is here that Jane and Bingley first set eyes on each other and that Darcy's character is fixed as proud and disagreeable by all of Meryton society and, most importantly, by Elizabeth, who is stung by his refusal to dance with her. Yet Jane Austen devotes just three pages to describing this crucial event in the book. The only dialogue she gives us is a short exchange between Darcy and Bingley. It soon became clear that this event was pivotal in setting up the story, and so the decision was taken to build it up substantially in the adaptation.

Dramatically it was the ideal place in which to introduce the audience to new characters and to make the relationships between those we'd already met better understood. When Bingley is introduced to Mrs Bennet, she points out her daughters to him. We see Jane and Elizabeth having fun but behaving with decorum; we see Mary sitting out another dance, destined to remain a wallflower; and we see Lydia and Kitty cavorting about with 'the youth-club element', as Andrew calls them. The fact that Mr Bennet is not there tells us something about his character too.

We meet the other prominent family in the area – the Lucases. We see that Charlotte Lucas is Elizabeth's close friend and that her father, Sir William, is a likeable buffoon. By being the first to greet the Netherfield party we understand that he is a leading figure in Meryton society.

Andrew also wanted the dance to be a bit of a knees-up, with energetic and not tremendously skilful dancing, lots of heavy drinking and coarse male laughter going on around the refreshment table. 'We wanted to show the difference between what is, in effect, a rather rowdy village hop and a very formal ball, which we will see at Netherfield in Episode Two. The idea was to contrast the kind of behaviour that is permissible at these events.' This was done not only by choosing faster dances but also by contrasting the bands we see at each event. At the assembly there are only three rough-looking musicians, whereas at

'Come, Darcy, I must have you dance. I hate to see you standing about by yourself in this stupid manner.'

'A single man of large fortune. What a fine thing for our girls!' (Mrs Bennet on Bingley).

Netherfield we see an elegant eight-piece band. The quantity and quality of food are also contrasted. At the assembly we see a few food and drink tables at the edge of the room, while at Netherfield there is a dedicated supper room with lavish dishes.

This issue of money and class is further accentuated when the Netherfield party enters the assembly room. They look rather horrified by what they find and the room goes painfully silent for a moment. Thereafter it is clear that getting through the evening will be a case of stoical endurance for everyone in the Netherfield party except for Bingley, who proceeds to have a whale of a time. This contrast allowed us to recognize the differences in Bingley's and Darcy's characters early on in the story.

Visually the differences in class are clearly pointed up as well. The Bingley sisters' frocks are made of rich colours and expensive-looking fabrics, whereas the Bennet girls wear simple muslin. We don't see them dance with anyone from Meryton, which suggests that they see themselves as socially superior to anyone else in the room. And finally through Mrs Bennet, who works hard all evening in an attempt to pair off the girls with eligible men, we learn about Darcy's considerable wealth and social position.

Elizabeth and Charlotte wait for dancing partners at the assembly rooms.

DRAMATIZING LETTERS

Jane Austen was a prolific letter writer and, possibly as a consequence, letters form an important part of *Pride and Prejudice*, particularly in the second half of the book, where crucial and complex pieces of information are conveyed in this way. Dramatically, however, it can be unexciting to see someone reading or writing a letter, even if the information it carries is vital. For Andrew, therefore, the challenge was to dramatize these letters in as visual a way as possible.

'I think there is some evidence to suggest that *Pride and Prejudice* actually started off as an epistolary novel. While the first half of the novel is full of scenes, in the second half the characters all go off to different parts of the country and write each other rather long letters. That was the biggest technical difficulty in adapting the book. I had to use a variety of just about every device going,

Sir William Lucas introduces the Netherfield party to Meryton society.

The Netherfield party arrives at the assembly rooms.

ABOVE: 'Mr Bingley thought Jane quite beautiful and danced with her twice' (Mrs Bennet).

ABOVE RIGHT: Miss Bingley impresses Meryton with 'her air of decided fashion'.

Lizzy receives a letter from Jane with the latest news from Longbourn.

with voiceovers and flashbacks, people actually sitting down and reading them, people reading them to each other, voiceover commentary and a mixture of all of these.

'In the book, for example, Mr Bennet sits at the dining table and reads aloud a letter from Mr Collins announcing that he's going to visit Longbourn, and a fortnight later he arrives. What I've done is start off with Mr Bennet reading this letter. We then see Mr Collins coming out of the church, where you get a sense of the kind of sycophantic clergyman he is. Then, as his letter continues, we hear Mr Collins's voice reading it and we actually see him enacting the journey, and describing his means of transport in ridiculous detail, and finally, we cut to him at Longbourn, laboriously climbing out of the carriage. That is all done in the space of this single letter, or a rather cut-down version of Mr Collins's letter.'

This sequence is not only a neat and visual way of dramatizing Collins's letter but also a useful way of introducing and describing new characters. We see the formidable Lady Catherine, who will play such a crucial part in the story later on, and her sickly daughter, Anne. In addition, we get our first glimpse of Collins's parsonage, which, combined with seeing him both fawning over Lady Catherine and being rather rude to his servant, helps us to form a view of his character before he even arrives at Longbourn.

Dramatizing letters can also be used to point up irony. When Jane, who always sees the best in everyone, writes to Lizzy about her visit with Miss Bingley in London, she says matter-of-factly: 'I was very eager to see Caroline again and I thought that she was glad to see me, though a little out of spirits.' What we see, however, is the two sisters coldly receiving her and very anxious to see her gone. Our suspicions

TOP: Mr Bennet learns of Mr Collins's plan to visit the family.

ABOVE: Mr Collins arrives at Longbourn.

LEFT: Mr Collins attends his noble patroness, the formidable Lady Catherine de Bourgh.

are confirmed when Jane describes Miss Bingley's promised visit some weeks later. We see her carriage draw up outside the Gardiners' house in Cheapside and her getting out, nose in the air. 'Miss Bingley goes slumming,' Andrew wrote in the stage directions!

DARCY'S LETTER TO ELIZABETH

By far the longest and most important letter in the book is Darcy's letter to Elizabeth after she rejects his first proposal of marriage. In it, he defends his actions in breaking Bingley's attachment to Jane, and relates his long and painful association with George Wickham, a revelation that is so authoritative and detailed that Lizzy is forced to believe Darcy's account and face the humiliating fact that she has been utterly deceived by Wickham.

Jane Austen tells us that Darcy gave Elizabeth 'an envelope containing two sheets of letter paper, written quite through, in a very close hand. The envelope itself was likewise full.' In the book it runs across six densely packed pages. But in the script, where the opportunity was taken to dramatize the scope of the letter fully, it accounts for the first twenty minutes of Episode Four – and that with some careful pruning beforehand!

Darcy writes his letter to Ellizabeth and gives it to her the next morning. 'Will you do me the honour of reading that letter?'

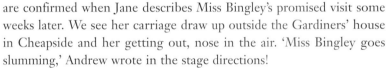

Miss Bingley and Mrs Hurst are not pleased to receive Jane in London.

In dramatizing this letter, Andrew employed a complex sequence of flashbacks and invented scenes. At first, they simply serve to help us visualize events Darcy describes in his past, such as his playing with Wickham when they were children, their Cambridge days and finally his discovery of the relationship between Wickham and his sister Georgiana. Both the audience and Lizzy believe in the authority of these events.

Then there are flashbacks to events both Darcy and Elizabeth witnessed (such as the Netherfield ball), except that this time Lizzy is forced to see her family's embarrassing behaviour from Darcy's perspective. As a consequence, Andrew wrote heightened flashbacks to exaggerate the humiliating spectacle of, for example, her mother bellowing to Lady Lucas that if Bingley marries Jane it will 'throw the girls into the paths of other rich men'. This over Darcy's damning commentary: '. . . the situation of your family, though objectionable, was nothing in comparison with the total want of propriety so frequently betrayed by your mother, your younger sisters, and even your father.' Again, Elizabeth is forced to accept that Darcy has got a point.

But Lizzy is not totally won over by his letter: there are moments when she imagines events to which Darcy alludes, but which she hasn't witnessed herself. She sees them with comic exaggeration, as she is convinced he behaved worse than his letter suggests. For example, Lizzy reads that once Bingley went to London, Darcy followed and 'engaged in the office of pointing out to him the certain evils of his choice of your sister as a prospective bride'. Andrew's stage directions indicate that Lizzy imagines the worst.

It was also decided to swap the two halves of the letter and begin first with his account of Wickham. Because Andrew wanted to start with Darcy writing the letter in the night, it was more dramatic to intercut this section with the Wickham flashbacks, as this is the most painful part of the letter to Darcy. We can see the torment Darcy feels in remembering these events, thereby suggesting to the audience that the revelations about Wickham must be true.

'I felt that when Darcy first sits down to write that letter it is in anger and then later, I think, it turns to something else – mainly because he can't bear to be misjudged by Elizabeth. We start off with Darcy and see he's taking a long time to write the letter – he goes on for hours into the night in his bedroom, describing the history of his relations with Mr Wickham.

'In order to do that, I've gone into a series of flashbacks which show both the childhood and the university days, and finally an incident which is lightly alluded to in a way (it's never dramatized in the book) but is terribly important in terms of Darcy's character and what has made him as he is, and why he's so wary and suspicious of other people. That is that his 15-year-old sister Georgiana, to whom he was almost a

Mrs Bennet's loud conversation embarrasses Elizabeth at the Netherfield ball.

father, was virtually (though I don't think technically) seduced by Wickham. They were about to elope together, which would certainly have meant her ruin, when Darcy arrived for a visit at what, he tells Elizabeth, "turned out to be the vital moment".

'I decided to show this in a flashback so we could see this innocent girl, and view Wickham in a completely different light from how we've seen him before. We see that he is scared of Darcy and gets paid off and more or less thrown out of the house – all this in a series of quick flash-backs. When reading the book, Georgiana often seems hardly in it at all, but I think in this flashback she'll stick in our minds. And we realize that Darcy is a very caring brother who rebukes himself for his carelessness. It also signifies how highly Darcy thinks of Elizabeth that he's prepared to reveal this very private and painful piece of history, simply because he doesn't want her to misunderstand him. He thinks she herself will have the discretion not to gossip about it – he trusts her.

Darcy tries to convince Bingley of the 'certain evils' of his choice of Jane as a wife. Bingley's natural modesty makes it an easy task.

'We then cut to the morning and Darcy giving Elizabeth the letter, shots of her as she sits reading it and then Darcy continues in voiceover talking about why he dissuaded his friend Bingley from pursuing his love for Jane. He describes the scenes at Netherfield from his point of view, commenting that he didn't believe Jane's affections were passion-ately engaged. We see that it was possible for him to think that, but then we cut in closer and see Jane as we have come to know her, and we are reminded that Darcy was wrong.

'Then when he talks about the really rather awful conduct and behaviour of the Bennet family, Elizabeth remembers events in an exag-gerated way, as one does – and she comes to the conclusion that she can scarcely blame Mr Darcy for wanting to have nothing to do with this dreadful bunch of people!

'And so there are touches of humour in there, although it's mainly a very painful letter – both for him to write and and for her to receive – and as it begins to sink in, she still thinks, "Well, I don't like Mr Darcy much, but I'm going to have to admit that he's right in some respects – that he has some justification for his behaviour."'

LYDIA'S AND WICKHAM'S ELOPEMENT

In the book it's clear that Lydia's elopement means not only her own social ruin, but the impossibility of either Jane or Elizabeth marrying well, or even respectably. The consequences of the elopement would have been clear to an audience in Jane Austen's time but is more diffi-cult for a modern one. So we have added an extra line where Elizabeth comments: 'Our whole family must partake of her ruin and disgrace.' It was decided that it would be useful to see something of Wickham's and Lydia's situation once they arrive in London, which could be intercut with the Bennet family waiting desperately at Longbourn for news of their whereabouts.

Wickham follows Georgiana to Ramsgate to persuade her to elope. Darcy arrives in time to save her.

Lydia and Wickham elope: 'What a good joke it will be when I write to them at Longbourn and sign myself Lydia Wickham!'

Wickham starts to regret the elopement.

'I thought that this was one of the little liberties we could allow ourselves in the adaptation – let's see what this "poor disgraced girl" is like. We've got the clue from how she carries on when she comes back to Longbourn after getting married – she's not at all chastened. I liked the idea of seeing Mrs Bennet wailing, "Oh, my poor girl, my poor Lydia!" and then cutting to her with Wickham in London and seeing that she doesn't look at all miserable. She's a bit bored and wishes they could go out more, but she's very proud of her catch and can't see what she's done wrong.

'I imagined that Wickham, on the other hand, is possibly regretting the passionate impulse that caused him to run away with her because they haven't got any money, and she's saying, "When can we go out and see the sights?" and such things, and he's worrying about his debts and people coming after him and thinking, "Maybe I didn't do the right thing this time."'

DARCY AS THE 'AVENGING ANGEL'

The other advantage of seeing Lydia and Wickham in London is that it provided an opportunity to dramatize Darcy's key role in making them marry. 'I took a bit of a chance in a way, and decided it was worth letting the audience guess that Darcy was on a mission of mercy. In the novel we learn about Darcy's role in putting things right much later, and again only through a letter (this time from Mrs Gardiner). But we thought it would hold up the narrative action if we had to go into another letter so near the climax of the story.

'I also thought that it was worth dramatizing because he's actually going on a sort of Heroic Quest, like heroes in fairy stories and folk tales. There is something heroic about his decision to seek out and pay off this man who nearly ruined his sister – all because he loves Elizabeth. It's a terrific part of the story really – the Avenger on the trail. So we see him travelling to London, and searching through it for Wickham. I thought it would be good to see Darcy as a man of action, which we know he is, although there are no scenes in the book which show it. I thought, "Let's see him really intervening; let's see that he's somebody who can change things and make things happen," which indeed he is. There was a lot of discussion about how much to show but I think it was a risk well worth taking.'

APPROACH TO DIALOGUE

'Jane Austen writes wonderfully dramatic dialogue, so I was reluctant to cut it, but it was necessary in places to do so. This was not just to make it fit into the allotted fifty-five minutes, but more importantly because there can be an almost musical quality in the way scenes dovetail – a kind of rhythm and pace which one strives for – which scenes that are too dialogue-intensive can disrupt. And because we can communicate so much visually – for instance, by the expressions on people's faces – you don't need quite so many words as you do in a novel, where so much is carried by the dialogue.

'On the whole I treated different characters in different ways in using the dialogue. With Mr Collins, for example, who's a pompous, pedantic character, I left his dialogue rather as it was represented. My own belief is that Jane Austen, like every other novelist, doesn't write completely naturalistic dialogue. She's writing something that is like real speech, and alludes to it, but is more elegant and more pointed. I actually believe that most of those characters, especially the Bennet sisters when speaking together, would say "isn't" rather than "is not" – although it's shown as "is not" in the book. I wanted to make the dialogue sound like something that could be spoken in the early nineteenth century, but also something you wouldn't think terribly artificial if it were spoken now. Occasionally we'd find in the book Elizabeth saying something that sounds a bit too self-consciously arch – but I certainly didn't go into much rephrasing or paraphrasing. I'd sometimes substitute one word with another if I thought a modern audience would more readily understand it, but that's about it.'

Darcy as the 'Avenging Angel'.

ON LEARNING THE DIALOGUE

Jennifer Ehle:
'It's the hardest dialogue I've ever had to learn. Shakespeare is a doddle compared to Jane Austen. I think this is essentially because the sense of the line comes at the end of it and also the lines are much longer. When I get to the end of a sentence I usually say, "Oh, I see!" and then I have to go back and read it again. Sometimes the thoughts are quite convoluted – you do all these hairpin bends – so it takes some getting used to. But it's like anything – by the end I found it much easier to learn. It's like learning another language.'

Alison Steadman:
'I haven't done a lot of period drama, so at first I found the language very difficult. You think you've learned it and then, when you come to run it, odd lines and phrases are completely wrong. Because we speak in a completely different way I kept wanting to put in modern phrases. It was a nightmare at first. I thought, "I'll never get on top of this; I'll never get the hang of it." And what was worse was that I imagined I was the only one who was having problems. But then I found everyone was finding it extremely difficult to learn. Then I felt

better and once you get over that feeling, you get into the rhythm of it and the speech patterns suddenly all begin to make sense.'

𝒫RE-PRODUCTION

With the scripts completed and the go-ahead given by the BBC, the producer was then ready to bring on board the other key production staff, the most central of whom is the director. Pre-production is an immensely busy time when all the details of the filming, from location hunting and casting, to budgeting and scheduling must be immaculately planned.

DIRECTOR SIMON LANGTON: FIRST IMPRESSIONS

'Six hours of solid reading is a daunting prospect, especially since you want to concentrate on the language so much, but I was fascinated by the characters and was never bored. I sensed the sort of enthusiasm and real love for the piece that Andrew had himself. His dialogue was imbued with energy and his whole approach was to make the characters real. I was sure that the first people to recognize this would be the actors. I suppose I was expecting something more archaic and literary, closer to the previous productions, which never seemed very naturalistic.'

Another key ingredient that convinced Simon to direct the programme was that it would be made entirely on film rather than on videotape in the studio.

'We used to work this ridiculous system in the Seventies when you had eight days' rehearsal and then you had two hours in which to record the entire thing. The result of this studio-based filming was everything I didn't like about classic drama. It always looked slightly forced.

Simon Langton and Lucy Scott.

'And there's a whole new generation of young people who have been brought up watching drama on film, which is structured and shot in such a different way. I think film is more authentic and adds up to the kind of production Andrew had in mind; the scripts are written with a filmic sense of rhythm. It is more expensive than studio but it does affect the actors.'

During pre-production the director's life breaks down into two areas. One is approving the main locations found by the production designer and location manager. The other is casting.

CASTING

Casting all the parts in the production was a huge task. Although the director and producer will have their own ideas, it is vital that a casting director is brought in to oversee the whole process.

JANEY FOTHERGILL TALKS ABOUT CASTING

'I know the book very well – for a start, I did it for A level! But I love Jane Austen anyway. It's just brilliant to be able to work on something you really like because it engages your heart as well as your mind. But, of course, knowing the book so well means you have a very strong preconception of what the characters are like, which can make casting it harder. Most people who are familiar with it will know just what Elizabeth and Darcy should look like, and there is no way in which we can satisfy all these differing notions. But obviously the first step for me is to make sure that the director, producer and I are all thinking along the same lines.

'Then we list the people we've all thought of as possibles for each part. We started with Elizabeth and Darcy, and then went on to the Bennet family. Now Darcy, I feel, is such a specific type – in a sense he really is what Mills and Boon heroes are, the naughty, arrogant, difficult man who underneath has great charm and sensitivity and is – oh, yes, most important – *rich*!

'The five Bennet girls are a problem to cast because of their ages, which range from 15 to 22 years. And they are all important parts. In fact, three of them – Elizabeth, Jane and Lydia – are leading parts and it's very difficult to find people of the right ages with sufficient experience and enough serious work to their credit. There are a lot of other young women in *Pride and Prejudice*, so we decided to see every actress between the ages of 15 and 28! Absolutely everyone, whether they had been to drama school or not. But finally, I think, in the case of Elizabeth, there were probably only about half a dozen serious candidates. It came down to the classical actresses because you have to have someone who can hold it together. It's a play-carrying part and that in itself takes a lot of stature and a sort of gravitas.

'The other important thing with *Pride and Prejudice* is getting people who are witty enough. I have a real bee in my bonnet about this. If people don't have that light touch, watching it can seem interminable. So we were looking for wit, charm and charisma, but also for the ability to "play" that period. Some people simply can't do it; everything about them is too modern. It's a difficult thing to analyse; there are a lot of good young actors and actresses around, but they are just very twentieth-century and don't have the right sort of grace. I don't think that can be instilled any more than you can train someone to be funny. People like Colin Firth are quite unusual in that they can play most decades quite easily; there is very little that he can't tackle.'

Colin Firth.

The Bennet girls.

Jennifer Ehle

(Elizabeth Bennet)

Susannah Harker

(Jane Bennet)

Julia Sawalha

(Lydia Bennet)

Polly Maberly

(Kitty Bennet)

Lucy Briers

(Mary Bennet)

Alison Steadman

(Mrs Bennet)

Benjamin Whitrow

(Mr Bennet)

Joanna David

(Mrs Gardiner)

Tim Wylton

(Mr Gardiner)

Adrian Lukis

(Wickham)

Colin Firth

(Darcy)

Emilia Fox

(Georgiana Darcy)

Crispin Bonham-Carter

(Bingley)

Anna Chancellor

(Miss Bingley)

Lucy Robinson

(Mrs Hurst)

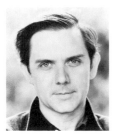

David Bamber

(Mr Collins)

Barbara Leigh-Hunt
(Lady Catherine
de Bourgh)

Christopher Benjamin

(Sir William Lucas)

Lucy Scott

(Charlotte Lucas)

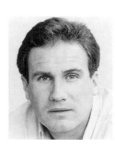

Rupert Vansittart

(Mr Hurst)

AUDITIONS

'We narrow down our lists and are then ready to invite people to come and see us. For the main parts, we would send a full set of the scripts to the relevant agents. In this case, the wonderful thing was that the scripts were so good, the agents would ring and say, "Great, fantastic scripts, they'd love to meet for it." Add to that the fact that the whole project is so high-profile and there's no problem getting actors interested.

'They would come in to meet the producer and director and we'd chat before they read a couple of scenes. This can be very nerve-racking for the actors, but where the script is such a joy to read it can be a hoot too. You may just let them read it once cold, and then say, "Let's try it again, but do this, or that," if only just to see if they've any range apart from what they've shown first time. After the readings, if people were witty enough with the right presence, then they went on to be screen tested.'

Casting chart.

SCREEN TESTS

'Two or three contrasting scenes are chosen and sent ahead to the actors, who'd be expected to learn them so that when they test, their eyes aren't locked down on to a piece of paper. We arranged for the costume and make-up designers to kit them out, so they'd be properly made-up and have their hair done and be wearing some sort of costume of the period.

'They then performed the pieces in a television studio, with people reading in the other parts, and we recorded it all on video. During the tests, they were asked to move around and to sit, and we'd make sure that the camera recorded close-ups of them from all angles, as well as full-length and mid-shots. There was perhaps twenty minutes of material of each test to view afterwards, when we all compared performances and looks. It really is important to check all this out when the part is a leading one and the actor may not be very experienced. The other benefit of screen tests is to see how different people go together. For the Bennet girls, we'd say, "Would that person look right? Or do the actresses look too similar? Will we get confused as to which one's which? Or do they look ludicrously different?" With Darcy and Bingley it was important to get a physical contrast. Having already cast Colin Firth as Darcy, we deliberately looked for someone very different in both looks and manner for Bingley, and I think we found him in Crispin Bonham-Carter.

'Mr Bingley was good-looking and gentlemanlike; he had a pleasant countenance, and easy, unaffected manners' (Jane Austen).

'Sometimes an actor will audition for one part and we might offer something else. This happened with Lucy Davis who, when we first saw her, had not really worked much professionally. She auditioned for Lydia and, liking her very much, we offered her a screen test. It was obvious when she came to test that she'd done a tremendous amount of work on the scripts we'd sent and we were very impressed with her. We

Julia Sawalha
as Lydia
Bennet.

Emilia Fox as Georgiana Darcy and Joanna David as
Mrs Gardiner.

seriously considered casting her, but she was too inexperienced. It's an enormous part; Lydia has to be very witty, and naughty, attractive, feisty and with knock-down energy. In the end, we decided to offer it to someone we'd not even tested, but who is very experienced – Julia Sawalha. We needed to feel confident that we had a Lydia who could deliver the goods, as she's such a driving force in her scenes. But we were also very keen to have Lucy, so we offered her the part of Maria Lucas. This was a bonus for us because she brought the same commitment to this smaller role. And, of course, for young actors it's important to work with experienced actors, directors and producers as much as you can. If you do a small part well, it will always lead to more work.'

CASTING GEORGIANA
'Georgiana Darcy was difficult to cast. She has to be 16, but a very young, innocent 16, completely untouched by the world. As Darcy's sister, she has to have class. She's described as looking proud and haughty, but only because she's painfully shy, which meant we needed someone who could act, while in the scripts she also plays the piano beautifully. So we were looking for all these things in one young girl!

'We did a huge trawl. We'd already seen hundreds of girls for the other parts and none of them was our Georgiana. So we went to ordinary schools and asked if they had anyone they thought could do it. After seeing about seventy girls, we were getting desperate and ended up going through our own address books to see if any friends had daughters who might be suitable – preferably the offspring of an actor in the hope she might have inherited some talent! In the end, Simon suggested Emilia Fox, who is the 19-year-old daughter of Edward Fox and Joanna David and who is passionate about acting. He knew her slightly and felt she had the right looks and the class. So we phoned and asked if she'd come to meet us. Her father was very against this idea, as she'd just started at Oxford, but she came in to read and felt just right for the part. In fact, we auditioned her twice, just to make sure – and this gave her time to convince her dad!'

LUCY DAVIS ON BEING CAST

'I was so pleased, so happy, to audition for Lydia and very nervous. I was sent one scene from the script, which was great because you don't often get that. I had only two days to prepare. You're not expected to learn the piece but it does make a great difference if your face isn't glued to the script while you audition. I felt really happy after the audition; I thought it had gone well but, because I'd had no previous experience of anything big, I didn't realize what the next process was. So when I got a message from the agency saying: "We've got some good news for you – please ring," I just thought, "I've got it!"

'The agent said, "Good news; you've got a screen test." I said, "Great. What's that?" It was a few weeks before the test and I was sent several scenes, this time to learn. I did so much work on those scenes! I know it sounds pretentious to outline your lines in bright orange pen, but that's what I did. And I wrote lots of instructions for myself down the side of the script to remind me of how I wanted to play the part. Not things like "She feels really happy here", but odd words like "Burst" or "Wow" or "Giggle". At the screen test, I was really anxious in case anyone saw my script and thought, "She's weird!" (In fact, I've still got my scripts – I think it'll be interesting in years ahead to look at them). Considering how nervous I was, the test was actually good fun. Being in costume and having the make-up and hair done helped more than you could imagine.

'First, I had a couple of rehearsals in the studio and the first assistant director laughed when it was supposed to be funny, which gave me a real boost, and Maggie Lunn, one of the casting directors who was reading opposite me, was so encouraging that even if you feel they are just being kind, it helps you to relax.

'I was really disappointed not to get the part of Lydia, but I was pleased to be offered Maria Lucas. I mean, if I'd auditioned for Maria in the first place and been given it, I'd have been thrilled. It's just that, having had a chance to try for Lydia, I was sad because I thought, "I'll never play her now. By the time the play is cast again, I'll be too old!" I realize it would have been a huge responsibility and I could have made a mess of it. And the brilliant thing about playing Maria Lucas is that not many people know who she is, as she's usually cut out of other versions, so I didn't have anyone else's performance to follow. It was all new territory and I thought, "I can have fun with this!"'

Lucy Davis as Maria Lucas.

OFFERS

'With established actors like Colin Firth, Alison Steadman or Barbara Leigh-Hunt, whose work you know well, there's no need to screen test or, indeed, audition. You just make a straight offer of the part to the agent and send the scripts. With a major series like *Pride and Prejudice* you would expect an answer within the week.

'Once the part has been accepted, the actual deal is done between the BBC's contracts executive and the agent. I might advise at this stage and give the bookers more information about what the actor has just done. Casting directors have to keep up with this. We go to drama schools to see the students in plays, as well as going to the professional theatre as much as possible and watching endless video cassettes. It's our job to know who's around and whose star is rising.'

BILLING

'The deal is usually "subject to billing", which means the credits the audience reads at the beginning or end of the film. The agent negotiates this directly with the producer. With some actors and agents this is of major importance, and disagreement can be a deal-breaker, particularly when there are a lot of high-profile actors in the same project. Occasionally actors will turn down a plum part, even if the money is right, if the billing isn't good enough. So it's up to the producer to balance out the credits and make sure everyone is satisfied before the contracts are finalized.'

LENGTH OF CONTRACT

'The main difficulty in casting something like this, which films over five months, is that some actors may be used for only parts of the filming. It won't be a problem if this is, say, for two consecutive weeks' filming, but some of the characters appear in different parts of the story that might be filmed in varying locations at different times of the year. This could mean that an actor is booked for two weeks in June, five days in July, eight days in August, three weeks in September and four days in October, making it very difficult for him or her to fit in other work. I explain to the agents that the producer will be as accommodating as possible if their clients are offered other work during filming, though obviously their primary commitment has to be to the project in hand.'

'The whole process of casting is very enjoyable; it's such a lovely job. The pleasure of it is in working with like-minded people, especially if it's a project like this where I loved the scripts and the parts are such gems to cast. If all these things gel, then the process is great fun!'

Alison Steadman: 'When I was offered the part of Mrs Bennet, it was like being given a huge box of chocolates – you know, when you can't wait to dive in. I just couldn't, couldn't resist.'

Alison Steadman on Mrs Bennet and Lydia: 'I think Lydia shows us exactly what Mrs Bennet was like in her youth. Lydia is obviously her favourite child. She is an anarchic, wild, loving, bright-eyed young girl who's full of fun and spirit. She's attractive, flirtatious, and finds the soldiers irresistible. As Mrs Bennet admits herself, "I remember the time when I liked a Redcoat myself very well — and indeed so I do still in my heart."'

JENNIFER EHLE ON WHY SHE WANTED TO PLAY ELIZABETH

'Elizabeth is such an incredible part. I first read the book when I was about 12, and it was the first grown-up romance or classic that I read. I had tried to read *Wuthering Heights* but I couldn't understand it – the passion in that is very grown-up. With *Pride and Prejudice* I was able to fall in love both with Darcy and with Lizzy. I didn't have any concept of being an actress at that time, so I didn't want to play Lizzy, I wanted to *be* her very much. In fact, I probably pretended I was for a couple of days.

'She's a wonderful role model. She's independent. She manages to be a free spirit in a society that doesn't encourage free-spiritedness, which is something that I think appeals to young women today because they can sympathize with her. So she's quite easy to identify with. I love her wit and her intelligence. There aren't that many female role models in literature or film who are as bright as she is. She is certainly no victim.

'It's so lovely to read a book by a woman that one is able to understand at the age of 12 and to know that it was written in 1813. You realize that you're not the first person to feel all those things. And it's wonderful to go through the fantasy of falling in love – it's so flirtatious and yet so safe; nothing really sexually threatening happens in it. It's a lovely fantasy to have.

'When I was called for a screen test I had no idea how many other potential Elizabeths were being tested. I was nervous, of course, but I really enjoyed it. I'm afraid the costume didn't help me much because it was far too small so the back wouldn't fasten and I had to have the microphone wire tied round the middle! But the wig and make-up were a great help. I've never confessed this before, but I cheated a bit. I knew that everyone was worried about the fact that I am blonde because they felt that Lizzy should be dark. So the night before the screen test, I dyed my eyebrows darker and deliberately didn't wash my hair that morning so it wouldn't look as fair. Everyone kept saying, "We didn't realize how dark your eyebrows were. It's great! You'll look fine in a darker wig!"

I could tell things had gone well, but waiting to hear was an anxious couple of days. It was so exciting when my agent called to say that I'd been offered the part. My parents took me out to dinner to celebrate. I thought I was the luckiest person in the world to be able to spend an entire summer being Elizabeth Bennet.'

Jennifer Ehle as Elizabeth Bennet.

Sam Breckman returns from location hunting with a few photos.

Luckington Court, Wiltshire, as Longbourn.

LOCATION HUNTING

'Choosing locations is a collaborative process,' says Simon Langton. 'I didn't have an overall vision of how the piece would look at this stage, though I did have a very strong idea of what some of the locations should look like.'

Finding locations is time-consuming work, and the process of negotiating a contract with the respective property owner can involve many hours of discussion and planning. This task was put in the hands of the location manager, Sam Breckman, who had detailed discussions with the production designer, director and producer early on in order to prioritize the location hunt and set a brief as to what was required.

'Our main location for *Pride and Prejudice* is the Bennet family house, Longbourn,' says Sam. 'We would be filming in it for ten weeks, for both interior and exterior scenes, so it had to be very special. We would be making a lot of demands on it. We needed a drawing room, dining room, library, large hall, staircase, landings and three bedrooms, as well as extensive gardens. We would also be making demands on its owner, as we knew we would need at least five weeks to prepare the house before the filming. We wanted to split the shooting so we could film there during the summer, but then return for two weeks in October, to register the changing seasons.'

Finding a suitable Longbourn was designer Gerry Scott's biggest concern. 'I remember saying to Sam that Longbourn was going to be very difficult to achieve. It has to be a very specific size but can't be too grand; it mustn't threaten the social levels that we were hoping to establish. It also needed to sit in its own grounds and be from the correct period. We had no idea where we would find such a house, and one's heart sank at the thought of asking some owner to move out for three months while we shot there!

'The other problem with these smaller period houses is that a lot of the original features will have been replaced, central heating and fitted carpets put in everywhere and generally a lot of changes done to make them more comfortable for a modern family to live in it. This makes it well-nigh impossible for us to start turning it back into a period location because the costs are just prohibitive.'

STARTING THE SEARCH: Sam Breckman

'Gerry Scott had a memory of Lacock village in Wiltshire and thought it might serve as Meryton, which is the small town near to Longbourn. She and I took Sue and Simon for an early visit and we all agreed it would be ideal, if we could persuade the National Trust (which owns the village) and all the residents to let us use it. So I then looked at the Ordnance Survey map to try to find a house for Longbourn near Lacock. You have to understand the topography to know where houses

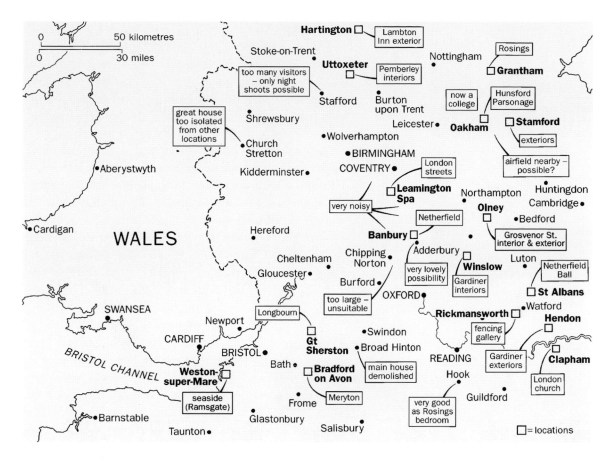

like that might have been built. Then I drove and drove. You get a sense of where to look, an instinct of which roads to travel down. I saw a flash of ochre in the distance and thought, "What's that?" and I arrived at Luckington Court. I thought, "I've found it!" I knocked on the door and introduced myself to the owner. She invited me in and it seemed that everything we needed was there. We were fortunate to find it all in this one place and even more fortunate in its owner, Angela Horn, who positively welcomed the idea of our filming there.'

Gerry takes up the story. 'The fact that Sam found the right house, in the right place, with a welcoming owner was a miracle! But Mrs Horn had not had experience of a film crew before, and Sam and I like to make it very clear to location owners what filming means. We both believe that it would be desperately unfair to imply to an owner that our coming to their house would not be a major disturbance because it will be. You can't move upwards of sixty or seventy people in and out of a house on a daily basis without this being an enormous upheaval. So I think you really have to be clear about the disadvantages. If the owner is still happy about it, then it's fine – we all know where we stand. Mrs Horn was absolutely wonderful with us. She understood what our problems were likely to be; she anticipated what we might need to do.'

Sam's map: 'I try to pinpoint the most difficult location first and then try to find the other ones as near as possible because travel time for a film unit costs money. Sometimes you will find a wonderful location, but there's nothing else near by, so it's not a practical proposition, and you have to start the search again.'

Derbyshire landscape.

Pemberley.

PEMBERLEY TO HUNSFORD

We were all keen to establish a relationship between the sites and grandeur of the houses. Pemberley, which is Darcy's house, has to be the grandest. Then, in descending order of importance, we placed Lady Catherine de Bourgh's house, Rosings Park, followed by Netherfield, which Bingley rents, Longbourn and finally Hunsford Parsonage, where Mr Collins lives. Having found Longbourn, we decided to look for Pemberley next and then fit the other houses in between. So Sam set off again: 'Houses on the scale of Pemberley are few and far between. It is supposed to be in Derbyshire, which would give it a distinctive northern look, and it has to be very big and set in stunning scenery. It has to say, "I am powerful, I am wealthy, but I have taste."

'Some people think Jane Austen was thinking of Chatsworth House as Pemberley, but in fact Chatsworth is referred to in its own right in *Pride and Prejudice*. We finally settled on Lyme Park, which is situated on the Cheshire/Derbyshire border. Unfortunately, due to a

Rosings.

changeover of management during our filming period, we were allowed to film only the exterior of the house. This caused great problems, because we had to find interiors that would match but in another location. On our travels Gerry and I had seen some striking interiors but, for various reasons, it was impossible to use the exteriors. Sudbury Hall in Derbyshire was one and, fortunately for us, it was not too far from Lyme Park. So we decided to have what is called a "split location" and film all the exteriors of Pemberley at Lyme and all the interiors at Sudbury.

Netherfield.

'This can create problems, of course. If there is a scene where a group of people walk up the steps and into the house, we have to finish the scene in another location, perhaps several days later and several miles away. Yet it is essential that all the details of the costume, make-up and performance match. Another difficulty while we were shooting at Lyme Park was that we had no "weather cover". If it rained, there were no alternative scenes to film inside. And, if production falls behind schedule, it costs money. The team knew they were taking a big risk. Fortunately, the summer of 1994 was blessed with sunny weather and the risk paid off!'

Longbourn.

Hunsford Parsonage.

ANGELA HORN – OWNER OF LUCKINGTON COURT

'You have to be willing to go the whole hog. Filming takes over your life and, if you agree to do it, you have to honour your side of the bargain.

'When I first decided to have the film crew here I expected to suffer a lot from being displaced. After all, I've lived here undisturbed for the last forty years. But instead, I've never been happier. Everyone in the crew works from dawn to dusk, but they're always cheerful.

'It's the numbers I can't get over. It's nothing to have seventy people

to lunch in the catering truck, then there's another for make-up and costume, and a rest van for the artists and an enormous quantity of large generators. Luckily they can all park in the drive and the church car park and not damage the garden.

'They bring in real period experts, you know. Even the flowers in the garden have to be right. I wasn't allowed to have my busy lizzies or my blue petunias.

'I'd advise anyone contemplating this to find a separate wing to live in. Luckily they didn't need all the house, so I was able to keep my lovely kitchen with its Aga, which is the centre of the house. And there's the housekeeper's room behind the kitchen which Sam had completely redecorated as a sitting room for me and moved in some of my furniture. Upstairs, my bedroom was to be used for Mrs Bennet's room, so I was moved to the nursery wing and bathroom. All my

other furniture was moved out and put into storage for the duration and the house was transformed from Luckington to Longbourn. All this was done very smoothly, the only mishap being that I'd put all the bills I was about to pay in the "dumb waiter" I have. Because of changes they were making, this had been pulled to the top floor and jammed there for all the filming, so I couldn't pay my bills for five months!

'They did offer me a role – as an extra – but I declined. I'm very fussy now about being photographed. I don't mind so long as I can hide under a hat. It works a treat. Otherwise I look the age I am.

'I will miss the film crew. They really were awfully nice. They became like a family. I cried at the thought of them leaving. It was like a ghost town when they went but I cheer up by reminding myself that I now have enough money to re-roof the west wing.'

ROSINGS, HUNSFORD, NETHERFIELD, LONDON STREETS
Sam Breckman:

For Lady Catherine de Bourgh's house, Rosings, we eventually chose Belton House in Linconshire, our fourth National Trust property. It's a splendid Restoration country house with wonderfully formal gardens to the front and rising parkland to the side. It also has its own attached small church, ideal for Mr Collins. We needed now to find the Parsonage in the same area. It had to be more modest than Longbourn, next door to a church that matched the one at Belton House (as they were supposed to be one and the same) with pretty gardens for Mr Collins to look after. The Old Rectory at Teigh in Leicestershire, owned by Barry and Tor Owen, fitted the bill perfectly and we all received a warm welcome there.

The last main location, Netherfield, was found near Banbury, and in the schedule we wanted to link this with the scenes of Darcy in the

Lord Leycester Hospital – used as a coaching inn.

ABOVE: Parkland at Rosings.

ABOVE RIGHT: Spanish chestnuts: the location for Darcy's second proposal.

streets of London. We'd had great difficulty finding what we needed in London itself. Period exterior town scenes are always a problem. As Gerry Scott says: 'My heart sinks whenever I read something like EXT. LONDON STREET in the script.' The money involved in just taking a camera out to an exterior townscape is phenomenal because you have to do so much 'negative' work: you may have to remove signs, aerials, alarm boxes, door knockers, telephone cables and cover the roads – and this is before you start to design. We only needed it for one day's filming so we couldn't afford to spend money or travelling time. We finally found what we needed in Warwick in Lord Leycester's Hospital. We were also able to film one of our coaching inns here, which made it economic. The scenes are all night scenes, which is fortunate for, although the building is lovely, it would have been a bit 'chocolate box' for our purposes if filmed in the daylight.

NEGOTIATIONS

Once the locations are approved, Sam Breckman has to discuss in detail with the Art Department what is required at every property and then go back to the owners or custodians and negotiate the deal. At Lacock village, for example, the discussions took five months. Once the National Trust, as the freeholders, had given their consent for the main street to be closed during filming and for the tarmac surface to be covered in soil and grass, the council and the police had to be consulted. At this stage Sam wrote to all the residents explaining what would happen and inviting them to attend a meeting to discuss all the implications. After this, there was further information by letter and house-to-house calls to answer questions. Once all this is agreed, he has to arrange workshop space for the design team, carpenters and painters. A tool store has to be organized, car parking arranged, plans to divert traffic in the village worked out, security people hired and everyone kept informed at all stages. Sam explains: 'It all takes a lot of time and one has to step very carefully. We mustn't forget that people live here and we are disrupting their lives. But the cooperation in Lacock was amazing and everyone joined in the carnival atmosphere for the week's filming.'

THE PRODUCTION TEAM

While casting and location hunting are under way, a number of other critical roles are being performed by the rest of the production team. Budgets and schedules must be prepared, supporting artists booked, transport and hotel accommodation organized. Members of the Production Team describe their jobs:

ASSOCIATE PRODUCER: Julie Scott

The associate producer works to the producer and is responsible for the management of the production from pre-production through to delivery of materials for transmission.

I was lucky with *Pride and Prejudice* – there was a full set of scripts for me to take home and break down immediately, and I was then able to talk to Sue about her aspirations in terms of the production. Sometimes scripts aren't ready until a much later stage. I was given certain parameters in terms of the budget; we both had a gut feeling about what the production needed, which was roughly £1 million per episode, and it was really then a matter of looking at what the requirements of the production were. With a period production, design is the key element and it governs the shape of the shooting schedule.

One parameter I was set by the budget was that we could have twenty weeks' filming. So we then started to have a look at the shooting schedule to see how we could fit it in. We wanted to work on the basis of a five-day shooting week, because the demands of a period production mean very long days. We were aiming for $10\frac{1}{2}$-hour shooting days during the actual filming but, in terms of costume and make-up, actors and design, this meant that some cast and crew would work 15-hour days, and sometimes longer, in order for us to achieve $10\frac{1}{2}$ hours' actual filming time each day.

First of all I talked to Sue about the calibre of casting; she obviously wanted a very strong cast, which costs money. Add to that the fact that we were going to have a narrative repeat in the same week as transmission (which means it will first be seen on BBC-1 and, later the same week, be repeated on BBC-2). For this the cast are paid extra. Add to *that* the co-production cost of transmission in the United States. If we know there will be a transmission there, then the costs of this (actors' buy-outs, music and so on) will be paid up-front in the budget in return for co-production money. In this case, the money came from the Arts and Entertainment Network in New York, who will show *Pride and Prejudice* in three double episodes.

Then I go through the script again, identifying the estimated number of supporting artists. These are the people you see in the background of busy shots like street scenes or ballroom scenes. The production designer gave me an assessment of the type of locations and

Lucy Davis and Christopher Benjamin having lunch.

Lizzy at the Netherfield ball. Eighty supporting artists were used in this scene.

sets required and what would need to be built, so I could then do the estimates. I was also able to talk to the costume and make-up designers about their budgets because they need to know the scale of the cast and the number of supporting artists before they can do a cash budget for the costumes and the wigs, as well as looking at the staffing levels needed to sustain a production of this size. If, for example, there are sixty supporting artists as well as the main cast required for a scene, then it would be impossible to get everyone dressed and made-up in time without extra staff for that day.

In terms of the camera department, I estimated the kind of equipment and scale of lighting required. Filming in large period houses inevitably means large lighting rigs; so then I started talking to lighting companies about estimates for the cost of lighting.

There are inevitably changes, even in the pre-production stages. For instance, once Jane Gibson, the choreographer, joined and discussed the dancing requirements with Simon and Sue, she advised that it would be more efficient if the other dancers alongside our main actors in the ballroom sequences were trained dancers and not supporting artists – and dancers, having very special skills, cost more than extras. We agreed to use professional dancers, but then had to discuss with the director where he was prepared to make cost cuts in other areas to compensate for the additional expense.

I have to book the caterers – a vital area to get right! Good food, acceptable to the wide range of diets and appetites you'll inevitably find among a film crew, is a real bonus. Bad food each day will wear down even the most cheerful and resilient group when people are working so hard and the days are so long.

All of this takes time and several budgets are worked out before the producer and I are ready to submit our final budget for approval. Once this is approved, it's our responsibility to keep the production within these limits.

'Being roped in as an extra is not in the job description of production manager but, as I'm an Equity member, I was happy to oblige' (Paul Brodrick).

PRODUCTION MANAGER: Paul Brodrick

When I first sat down to schedule the filming for *Pride and Prejudice* I already knew from the associate producer that the overall budget allowed twenty weeks to complete filming, that it should take place between June and October and that we were aiming to film five days each week. Each of these facts helped to provide the framework for the schedule, even before taking the scripts themselves into account.

A basic rule of thumb for scheduling this kind of period drama is to assume that four to five pages of script (or three to four minutes of screen time) will take one day to film. In theory it would take about 100 days to shoot all six episodes, but this does not take into account the relative difficulty of each scene. For example, a scene in the Bennet household involving two or three characters sitting and talking to each other should be much quicker and easier to film than a scene with a large number of horses and carriages and extras on Meryton High Street. For the latter scenes I decided that we would, in fact, need a few extra days and turned several of the weeks into six-day filming periods.

The next decision was in what order to film the scenes. Rather than move the whole production unit backwards and forwards over the country in order to film in story order, it made obvious sense to group together scenes which take place in the same geographical location, even if this meant going from, say, a scene in Episode Five directly to one in Episode Two.

Even within the same location it made further sense to group together scenes according to which room they happened in, or in which part of the garden, or whether they were day or night scenes. Windows have to be tented over with black material for night scenes and this takes time, so it's best to shoot the night scenes one after the other. Of course, it makes it harder for the actors playing the scenes out of order, but it saves a huge amount of time and money if you don't have to keep moving people and equipment.

Of particular importance to *Pride and Prejudice* was the significance of the seasons as they reflected the ups and downs of the relationships between the characters. It was therefore important to try to film scenes at the right time of year whenever possible. This meant that we started at Lady Catherine's house, Rosings, and Mr Collins's parsonage in springtime. We then went on to Pemberley and Longbourn for the summer, before filming a number of interiors in the Ealing Film Studios in London. By this time it was October and we could return to Netherfield, Meryton and Longbourn to film scenes set in autumn and winter.

The availability of individual actors also affected the schedule. Only Jennifer Ehle would be working with us throughout the whole schedule – the others came and went according to the scenes they were in. Sometimes they had already been committed elsewhere before we booked them for our production, which meant that we had to schedule their scenes to fit in with their other commitments.

Another potential problem was the nature of the locations we had chosen. For example, some of the large historic country houses we were using were owned by bodies like the National Trust, so our timetable had to fit in with their requirements. This usually meant working inside the houses only on days when they were closed to the public or, in the case of Lacock Abbey and the village nearby, avoiding the summer season altogether and filming there in October, in order to cause as little disruption as possible to their tourist trade.

Having taken all these factors into account, I produced the filming schedule, which was treated almost like a Bible by the film crew, as it allowed everybody to plan their life ahead for the following five months.

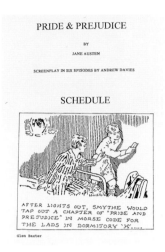

Glen Baxter provides the cover for the shooting schedule, which becomes the Bible that rules everyone's life for the next five months.

SCRIPT EDITOR: Susie Conklin

The script editor's role is to work alongside the producer and writer on the development of the scripts, and to act as a liaison between the writer and the rest of the team through the various stages of production. The most intensive period of work is the development stage, when the scripts are being written. Sue, Andrew and I would discuss the opening and closing of each episode, essential scenes and less essential scenes, what might need inventing and so on.

Luckily, Andrew and I had worked together before on *Middlemarch*, so we knew each other well, which is always an advantage. I remember getting a bit worried when Episode Four was late, especially as Andrew is always so punctual about delivery. So I rang him and asked gently when we might see the script, and he replied, 'Oh, I've got on such a roll I went on to write Five and Six as well. I'll have all three ready by the end of the week!' And he did.

At this stage I do rough timings of each episode and then make notes for the second drafts, as do Sue and Andrew. We then get together and talk through our ideas. This stage of rewriting is always hugely enjoyable because the framework has been laid down and now it's a case of enhancing what's already there. And one of the great pleasures of working with Andrew on adaptations is that he never allows his enjoyment of the prose to cloud his intention to make the screenplay as visual and pacy as possible. I think he has an excellent sense of rhythm and writes very lean first drafts, which provide a solid backbone to the story and a strong narrative drive.

Inevitably, there was a bit of haggling about what should go in – we all had favoured bits of dialogue, but the key is never to overload a scene or give a character great chunks of dialogue. It may read well on the page, but it's sure to make an audience glaze over when watching it. We finished this final process over the course of a month and had the six scripts marked up and ready for the director and production team by December 1993.

In the pre-production stage the script becomes a blueprint which every creative area uses, but the writer can't be available to answer all the queries that come up throughout the long production process. So the script editor acts as an interpreter of the script, responding to a number of queries as they arise – 'Can we move this scene from the dining room to the drawing room? Can we cut the carriage arriving and start with them entering the hall? Can you write a few lines to cover the long walk down the corridor? Can you make this a day scene rather than a night scene?' – and so on. The results of the location hunting and the scheduling always have an effect on the script, and inevitably a bit of rewriting and trimming is necessary. All these revisions are done in time for the read-through. The script should then be as final as possible for filming.

CONTINUITY SUPERVISOR: Sue Clegg

The continuity supervisor, or script supervisor as I'm often called, is a second pair of eyes and ears for the director. I'm there in the rehearsals and filming, taking notes of any action or dialogue changes and the camera moves. On the set the director will give an idea of the shots he wants, so I make a note of each one – a close-up here or a panning shot there. I make notes for the film editor, listing which 'takes' the director wants to use and why; this helps the editor to see quickly what we've shot.

The first thing I do in pre-production is to read the scripts three or four times so that I am really familiar with them. Then I break down the scripts into day order. Sometimes it's straightforward – when the action goes from a 'day' scene to a 'night' scene then that is obviously the end of one day. But there are times when a night scene doesn't separate two different days. It's important for wardrobe to know if someone should be wearing the same costume. I then do a breakdown for each scene. I list the characters and any props that might be required – Mary's prayer book or spectacles, for example; anything that needs to be remembered. I only had about three weeks to break the six scripts down before we started filming. This was quite daunting at first but I had enough time in the end – just!

Sue Clegg making continuity notes.

RESEARCHER: Clare Elliott

When Jane Austen wrote *Pride and Prejudice* she assumed that her readers were as familiar with the England that she was writing about as she was. Everyone knew that dinner was at 5 o'clock and that Mrs Bennet would have had a housekeeper – they did not need the novelist to tell them. However, 1813 is now worlds away, and society is organized rather differently.

As trainee script editor in the pre-production period, I was asked to pronounce on wildly disparate questions and I became an instant expert on the Life and Times of 1813. Did they have busy lizzies in gardens then? How many servants would the Bennets have had? What would a wedding look like? How was the alphabet game played? Did men bow when they came into a room? At first, I had no idea at all.

I tackled the servant question first. The production team needed to know exactly who did what, so that in the background of scenes there would be the correct servants opening doors, serving food, riding on carriages and populating the houses. I discovered an excellent book at the London Library published in 1825: *The Complete Servant*, written by Samuel and Sarah Adams, whose own credentials were 'Fifty Years Service in Different Families'. Written for prospective servants, it outlined what tasks were performed by everyone in the household. There seems to have been an army supporting each house, and they all worked incredibly long hours. I felt sorriest for the undercook, who was up at

5 a.m. to start a day full of scouring and washing up and wouldn't finish until 11 p.m. With the help of this book I worked out that the Bennets would probably have had eleven servants, and was able to give them all job descriptions, from housekeeper to undergroom.

I found that there were a number of experts who were extremely helpful. Mrs Mavis Batey, the president of the Garden History Society, kindly filled me in on what plants were popular and available in this period. Obviously, the owners of the houses where we filmed could not dig up their gardens to root out plants introduced only in the twentieth century, but at least the worst anomalies could be avoided. Chris Nicholson at the National Trust told me about the carriages and the number of postilions and footmen who would ride on them, and how the system of post-chaises worked across the country. Julian Litton at the Victoria and Albert Museum was able to give me the precise measurements for the decoration of an altar for the wedding scene. He shuddered when I asked whether silver candlesticks would have been used – that would obviously have been a disastrous error.

Simon was keen that the Bennet girls should be active in their scenes rather than just doing their embroidery, so I was asked to find out the kinds of games, apart from the ubiquitous cards, that were played at the time. Spillikins turned out to be popular – it was similar to 'pick-a-stick', played with bone spills shaped like saws and hooks. The alphabet game was an early form of Scrabble, and the grandly named Bilbocatch, perhaps more familar as 'cup and ball', was widespread. One game that sounded great fun was the 'bullet pudding', where a pudding was laid on a pile of flour which was then cut into by each player. The player who lets the bullet fall from the top of the pile must pick it up with his teeth, thus covering himself with flour. This was a great favourite of Jane Austen's young niece, Fanny Austen Knight.

One of my most enjoyable pieces of research was finding out about ballroom etiquette, for which I visited the library at Cecil Sharpe House. I had been asked to find out about a number of points, such as whether guests carried dance cards and whether they were given a full meal, sitting down. The library had a collection of women's pocket books from the early nineteenth century – delightful leather-bound diaries containing useful information such as hackney-carriage fares across London and sovereign heads of Europe. Among these I found a ballroom guide, which explained exactly how a hostess should hold a ball – how many musicians should play, what food should be served, with which ladies a gentlemen is duty-bound to dance and so on. The writer offered the helpful advice that candles should be provided with 'bobeches', to prevent wax falling on the guests. I am sure many a dancer was indebted to him.

There were a number of difficult questions. To find out what bee-keepers wore at the time, I tracked down a charming beekeeping

One of the popular games of the period, a variation of quoits played with sticks.

historian, Carl Showler (the answer is a smock and black veiling). Whether Darcy would have used a cheque or a banker's draft to pay off Wickham proved tricky, until the British Museum came to my rescue. The exact date at which quills were abandoned in favour of metal pens was initially puzzling (the metal pen was introduced around 1830). However, these were challenges and they were satisfying to solve.

Forty supporting actors were used to supplement the main actors on the wedding day.

ASSISTANT DIRECTORS: Pip Short, Amanda Neal, Melanie Panario, Simon Bird, Anne-Marie Crawford, Sarah White

There is a first assistant director (AD), a second AD and two third ADs. During pre-production, they are responsible for casting all the supporting artists. With the director, they go through the scripts and note how many extras are needed in each scene and what they should look like. For example, in Meryton High Street, the director wanted to see a variety of townsfolk in the background.

As filming takes place in different parts of the country, the supporting artists will be cast from local people. It is too expensive to bring

David Bamber as Mr Collins in his bee-keeping smock and hat with black veiling.

supporting artists from London. But this means that Melanie Panario had to trawl through large books of photographs sent from agencies around the country. It would have been very easy just to order thirty extras and leave it to the agents to supply them, but Simon was clear that he wanted the faces to look right for the period. Once cast, all the physical details and photos are sent on to costume and make-up so they can make their preparations.

The assistant directors will organize the read-through and attend rehearsals. During filming they will be responsible for organizing the call times for the actors, for transporting them to and from the location and for offering emotional support when needed.

ASSISTANT PRODUCTION ACCOUNTANT:
Elaine Dawson

As the APA my main responsibility is to maintain the financial records for the production. Before filming I assist the associate producer in preparing the budgets. The final budget is a fairly brief document but it represents many hours of detailed planning.

When filming begins I am based on location and return to London for only one or two days a week. On location I operate the bank account,

which involves preparing payments and monitoring fees and invoices for location transport and catering. I am also responsible for withdrawing cash from the bank and distributing expenses and other cash payments to the unit. This is the area of the job which the crew consider the most important and they always greet me on a Monday with hot-off-the-press expense forms, big smiles, a promise of a drink in the bar that night and the nickname of 'Moneybags'!

PRODUCTION COORDINATOR: Janet Radenkovic

The coordinator should act as the focal point of contact between the production team and the cast and crew. It's my job to book all the hotel rooms we will need during filming (and re-book them when the schedule changes!), to organize car hire, licences for child actors, medicals, insurance. I distribute cast and crew lists, script rewrites, schedules, movement orders, and make sure that the rushes are collected immediately by courier and delivered to the processing labs. On the social side, I am the only one who has the information about everyone's birth dates – so I organize the birthday cakes!

PRODUCTION SECRETARY: Julia Weston

The production secretary joins the team in pre-production, setting up an effective office system, liaising with agents and actors during the casting period, distributing scripts and contact lists.

The whole team departs to location, leaving you to man the fort – with endless urgent calls needing immediate response and a production team which is uncontactable on mobiles! From time to time you are 'let out' to assist on location – ferrying artists, costumes and breakfasts to and fro, manning doors to ensure all artists are kitted with rain-hats when going outdoors, assisting location managers at 5 a.m. and standing in bushes to cue actors on horses.

Filming continues in unpredictable fashion for about five months, so a flexible approach to all matters is recommended, particularly in connection with the demands of press and publicity. Then the majority of crew abandons ship and the core personnel return for post-production. Just when a steady, though busy, routine seems to be established, the producer is commissioned to write a book about the programme and the days become longer than ever. The whole process, from beginning to end, takes well over a year. It's frustrating yet rewarding, exhausting yet relaxed and, although there are times when you wonder – it's all hugely enjoyable.

chapter 3

PRODUCTION DESIGN

DESIGN: Gerry Scott

Laying the backbone

I met Sue and read the scripts before Christmas 1993, but I started work proper in January, which gave me five months' preparation. There were twenty-four locations to find, some of them grand houses, and eight studio sets to design and build. January was spent planning, discussing with Sue and Simon what they hoped to achieve, budgeting with the associate producer and hunting for locations with Sam. In February the Art Department joined.

Our main job is to lay the backbone of the production, so we have to consider everyone else's areas of work at the same time. It's no use finding a location that I think looks perfect if the director of photography can't light it, the film crew can't fit in it, we can't afford to hire it or we can't make sound recordings because it sits next to a motorway. Accommodating all these things obviously narrows down our options.

The nature of the job is to serve the text and the performances. There's an enormous amount of hard labour involved, but the irony is, if a location or set has worked well, then the final result on the screen shouldn't really be noticed; it should appear so natural that the audience won't even think it has been designed.

Historical accuracy

Every author is portraying a specific world, and it's our job to recreate that world and make it accessible to an audience. Though I like to be as historically accurate as possible, I'm not prepared to be a slave to it. It's important to understand the way people lived in 1813, but we are not making an academic study of the period; it's much more important to grasp the spirit of the time. In any case, even if we had all the time and money in the world, we could never be completely accurate because an awful lot of the things we'd need no longer exist, except perhaps in museums. So we get as much as we can and the rest we make up; we take something that has the flavour of the period – a pattern that is close, a colour that feels right – and we use it in a judicious way so it doesn't look out of place.

Gerry Scott.

Studio set for Lucas Lodge and fabrics to be used.

Wallpapers.

Coles Traditional Collection
- The Cadora 06/232

Coles Traditional Collection
- The Valliere Minor 06/211

Hamilton Weston Translations
Empire Stripe 701 (Red & Cream)
← drapes
← sofas

UNDERLINING THE SOCIAL LEVELS

A lot of the novel is about class and money, so an important part of our job is to underline the different social levels. As soon as a character is introduced their income is often mentioned. For example, we know immediately that Bingley has £4,000 or £5,000 a year; that Darcy has £10,000 and a great estate in Derbyshire; that Lady Catherine's new windows cost £800.

There are many areas where we can emphasize these differences for the audience. Obviously, we chose our main houses with this in mind, but we also graded a number of other items to underscore differences in wealth. The food that is seen on screen, for example, reflects the income levels of the different households. And, though every house had a piano, we graded them to ensure that the finest instrument was at Pemberley (the one Darcy bought for Georgiana) and the cheapest at Longbourn.

We also graded the carriages from the grand to the utilitarian in order to reflect the differences in social standing. On the whole, the richer families tended to have the smarter carriages, with four horses instead of two. For example, we had a stunning team of four chestnuts to pull Darcy's carriage. The whole image says, 'This is expensive-sports-car league,' whereas with Lady Catherine we felt she really had to have a big Daimler of a carriage.

Darcy would have had a collection of horses, but what sort of a horse an actor has, and how he sits on it, is really important. Fortunately,

Colin rides well, but it's still possible for someone to look ridiculous if he is on a horse of the wrong size. So each horse was especially selected for each rider; the classiest horse for the classiest character.

LOCATION OR STUDIO

Our aim was to film as much as possible on location because we wanted to use the English landscape as a player in the film. It makes a great difference if you can see real exteriors outside the windows of the rooms; it gives a true sense of the geography of the places. Some rooms you know you will never find; and if you are going to be shooting on a particular set for several days, it may make economic sense to build it in the studio. If there are several very short scenes, needing only small sets, sometimes you can build these almost in a row in a studio and shoot them one after the other very quickly. This avoids moving the whole unit around the country and so saves money.

SET DESIGN

I love designing studio sets. It's exciting to create something that never existed before. I go through the scripts and take out all the scenes that relate to each set and then draw little sketches of how every shot might look. Because the end product is the shot, I design shots first, not sets. Scale is very important; you have to know how figures will look in relation to each other in order to determine the size of the room and plan where the light should come from.

The next thing I do is to plot all the moves. I know that the director and actors will do this themselves, but it's vital that I work through each scene in this detail so I know that everything required by the script is possible. I have to know that the furniture can fit and that the positioning of it will work for every scene. After that comes the placing of the doors and windows and, finally, the walls.

Lady Catherine de Bourgh's carriage.

Back shot: a fisherman's hut, Ramsgate.

Lambton Inn: interior finished set.

ABOVE LEFT: Original room at Lacock Abbey – the model for the coaching inn.
ABOVE CENTRE: Set being built in the studio (top). Finished set (below) with windows to match originals (right).
ABOVE RIGHT: Windows at Lacock Abbey.

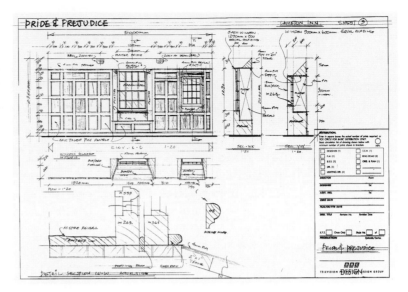

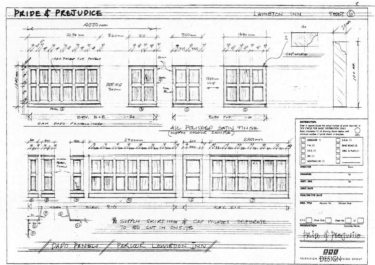

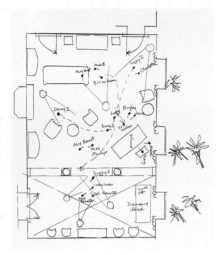

The Lambton Inn: working drawings for the set and designer's own shot plan.

If a scene is very short and simple to shoot, it is possible to build a set with only three walls. This can save money, but it imposes real limitations on the director. So, in the main, complete rooms with four walls are built. Sometimes they are designed so that sections of the walls can be moved out, to allow more room for the camera team to work. Likewise ceilings can be lowered in parts of the room, if the camera is pointing upwards, to prevent the studio from being seen.

It always surprises people how much detail goes into the working drawings for the sets; more than into some architect's drawings that I've seen. Art director Mark Kebby is responsible for this work, and he produced 180 drawings and seven models for *Pride and Prejudice*. Construction manager Barry Moll then takes these to a number of different workshops to be made. Mark and Barry have to ensure that everything is made exactly to specification, on budget and in time. Every joint, every moulding, every piece of timber is detailed; nothing is left to chance. Then I take over with the wallpaper and the paint colours.

DESIGNING THE MERYTON ASSEMBLY ROOMS

Getting the flavour right seemed to be most important. I based the design on the assembly rooms I had seen in Stamford, which are some of the earliest in the country. They have a rural feel to them – they are trying to be smart, but they can't match Bath. The scale of the assembly rooms varied from town to town; the ones built later are larger, so for our date we were looking for something of a medium size.

We had already found our Meryton High Street in Lacock, so that's where the rooms had to be found. There was only one building of a reasonable size, which we might believe formed the assembly rooms, and this was the Red Lion pub. Unfortunately, it didn't have one large room suitable for our use, so we decided to use its exterior only and to build the interior in the studio.

In doing so, there were many things to consider. We talked to choreographer Jane Gibson about the number of dancers and how much room they would need. Simon wanted the townsfolk to be able to sit at supper tables at one end and for there to be seating around the edges for spectators. We knew the room would be long and narrow, and we placed it as if it were going from the back to the front of the building. But it was obvious from the exterior that the room had a low ceiling, so we decided to imagine that it hadn't been purpose-built for assembly rooms but rather had started as an inn, the first and second floors of which had been knocked together, giving it a double height and three sets of windows at the front. This meant that the scale felt right for the numbers involved and that the interior and exterior looked like the same location.

TRANSFORMING LONGBOURN

The Bennets' house, Longbourn, was our main location. We had eight weeks' filming there and we needed several rooms, the principal one being the drawing room, where so many scenes take place. The script

Two of the small three-sided sets: Wickham's rooms in Newcastle and London.

Studio floors: one wood, one painted lino.

ABOVE: Assembly room set under construction (top) and being dressed (below).

RIGHT: Mark Kebby's sketch of the assembly room.

The Red Lion pub in Lacock, which became the Meryton assembly rooms.

also required a dining room, a hall, a study for Mr Bennet, bedrooms for the girls and Mrs Bennet, a staircase and landings.

To transform the house, Mark and Barry moved there three weeks before filming with a team of two carpenters and four painters. Sam settled the owner, Mrs Horn, in another wing and then organized the removal of her furniture and central heating. It was a very old-fashioned system with large pipes and radiators, so there was no way in which we could disguise it. Then all the electric fittings, ceiling lights, switches, sockets, wires and so on were removed and the carpets taken up.

Some structural work was also needed. We removed false ceiling panels in the dining room, blocked up the serving hatch to the kitchen, took out washbasins from the bedrooms, and built false walls and fireplaces to hide fitted wardrobes. Once all the rooms were stripped bare and cleaned we started the decorating.

At the same time work was being done outside. The conservatory needed new doors, as the existing ones were obviously from the wrong period. We had to construct false fronts for all the stable doors. We needed an extra bit of roofing done, so we used a local roofing man, working in weathered stone. We always try to employ local craftsmen to work alongside the design team.

The gardens had to undergo some replanting. This can always be a tricky area to negotiate with an owner because people are so fond of their gardens. We can always repaint a room to make it look the same as before, but digging up plants is a trickier proposition.

We brought in Lynn Hoadley, a local gardening specialist who does a lot of film work. She took Mrs Horn round her garden and explained what needed to be replaced. Mrs Horn was very cooperative – out went her red busy lizzies and in came old-fashioned marguerites. There were a couple of things she felt strongly about moving, so we tried to avoid those when filming.

LONGBOURN DINING ROOM

Apply heavier picture rail to existing

New cornice

Remove false ceiling section & strip lights Remove hanging lights & switches.

Remove serving hatch doors inds etc & fill flush.

Clear front t/place chimney to be swept – Sam checking.

Apply timber beading inside stone mullions to loose green glass.

All furniture cleared

Floor to be covered

Fit poles to both windows + pelmet boards.

Remove t/ing plates – fit new d/furniture

Wallpaper dado to picture rail Coles Countryside Clavdon 12 – 109

Picture rail frieze, ceiling – string?

Paint dado Bisaut no 38 flat oil Skirting no 41 Drab " use Drab as light drag on stiles use Bisaut mixed with old white no 4 as light drag on panels.

Paint windows old white no 4 Age lightly Door to match hall.

WEATHER COVER

Andrew Davies had set a great many Longbourn scenes in the gardens and surrounding countryside, which was a risk because bad weather can make filming impossible.

It was decided that we should have an extra room, always at the ready, to be used if it rained. So we turned a small, square store room behind the dining room into a 'still room' – a place where Jane and Lizzy might go to hang flowers to dry or make rose water and where they might escape for a private conversation. Clare Elliott found all the recipes for cosmetics that young ladies might have made, and we tried to reproduce the props.

The danger was that a room with lavender drying and bowls of rose petals on the table would look a bit 'Laura Ashley'. With period design it is difficult, now that so many things have been appropriated by advertising agencies, not to make sets look over-glossy or false. It's a shame because the room would have looked like that, but now there's a danger that people will say, 'Couldn't they have thought of anything better?'

COLOURS

There is a palette of colours that was very popular at that time, but we simplified it somewhat to make it more accessible to us. The truth is that almost every colour was available to people in the early nineteenth

The dining room at Luckington Court with designer's notes listing work to be done to convert it into Longbourn.

Jane in the still room.

Wallpaper and paint samples.

century; it's just that certain colours were more fashionable. They preferred soft colours to vibrant ones: bluey-greens, different greys, a lot of dark greens. Derek Honeybun, our painter, had to be able to reproduce with paint almost any surface, including brick, stone and marble, and he had to be able to 'age' it convincingly. He observes how things age naturally and can recreate the effect brilliantly.

Overall, I'm more interested in using colour to convey information about character, mood or atmosphere than in using it simply for the purposes of historical accuracy. For example, the green we used for the assembly room is the kind of institutional colour that you see now in a lot of hospitals. We wanted the room to have a utilitarian look by comparison with the Netherfield ballroom, with its gold paper and sumptuous features.

Historically, the interiors of the houses would have been quite pale, with lots of soft whites, creams and lemons. This was a problem because the muslin dresses were pale too, so, if we were not careful, we knew the dresses would 'disappear' against the walls, giving the effect of floating hands and faces. We decided to keep the main drawing room at Longbourn pale and simple to show that the Bennets are not a pretentious family, but I checked both fabrics and flesh against the wall colour to make sure they worked.

I reserved the really rich, strong colours for places where we needed to make an enormous impact. Rosings was a deep jade-green with gold. I thought that if anybody was going to dare to have a good powerful colour, it would be Lady Catherine. I gave Lucas Lodge regal overtones with reds and golds, which accentuate the family's social aspirations and echo Sir William's constant references to the Court of St James. By contrast, Pemberley had to be in exquisite taste. Though the grandest house, I wanted it to have a sense of natural elegance. Darcy's family has been secure in its place at the top of the social hierarchy for many generations, so there is no need to impress. The rooms were already painted in very soft colours – pale pink, oyster and cream – which were perfect.

SOFT FURNISHINGS

Finding soft furnishings for a period production is a nightmare because so little of the originals has survived, and what has is usually beyond our budget. It's also difficult to find items such as crockery in sufficient quantity, so you have to buy contemporary equivalents. The skill lies in judging how much liberty you can take. For example, if I were given the choice of a moth-eaten but original carpet for the Rosings drawing room or an immaculate carpet that was incorrect for the period, I would choose the latter because it says the right things about Lady Catherine's character.

We couldn't afford to have fabrics for the curtains and drapes printed and it's very rare to find matching sets of the correct style and colour,

Storerooms in prop house.

so Marge Pratt, our set dresser, bought fabrics that were as near in design to that period as possible and then had the drapes made.

PROPS

Finding furniture is less of a problem. There are a number of prop-hire companies that specialize in different areas: period furniture, contemporary furniture, paintings, silver or lighting. It's difficult if other period films are shooting at the same time because their stock is depleted. Marj and Sara Richardson, who did the prop buying, had to furnish all the rooms not only with drapes and carpets but also with pictures, door furniture, other contemporary furniture, ornaments, fire grates and so on, and everything had to be hand-selected. In one warehouse they might find a table for Rosings and in another some chairs they hope will match it. This means that no one ever sees the set dressing all together until it arrives on the set, so that can be an anxious time.

Every item is unwrapped and checked against the paperwork when it arrives on location and when it is packed to go back. As props are paid for on a daily rate, it's vital to return everything as quickly as possible. It's like moving house every four days!

Drapes for Mrs Phillips's house.

ACTION PROPS

These are items that belong to particular characters. With the Bennet girls, for example, we tried to give each of them a set of things to do that might help to establish their characters. Jane Austen says that the girls were never taught to draw or be involved in the cooking. But we wanted to avoid lots of scenes in which everyone just sits and talks.

We thought that Jane, being the steadiest of the girls, is the only one who might do something really useful, so we gave her linen shirts and petticoats to mend. Because she is patient, she also has some of the intricate white embroidery work that was popular at the time. We gave Lizzy letters and books. Mary practises the piano and reads solemn sermons. Lydia and Kitty have all sorts of things – bits of bonnets, ribbons, feathers and glue for paper cutting. We felt they would often generate an enormous amount of mess and confusion and then simply abandon whatever they were making.

Having established all this, it was easier for John Collins, the art director responsible for continuity, to suggest what the girls might be doing during each scene.

Fabrics and soft furnishings.

FOOD IN THE FILM

Much of the social life of the period was organized around eating and drinking. Giving and going to dinner parties was an important ritual, and, at the very least, all visitors would be offered tea. In the filming we wanted to use food as an indication of the wealth and social standing of the various families. Mrs Bennet is proud that she keeps a good table and serves soup that is 'fifty times better than the Lucases'', but she is still anxious about inviting Bingley and Darcy to an impromptu family dinner. When they do come two days later, the menu includes partridges and a huge haunch of venison 'roasted to a turn'. When Elizabeth pays a morning call on Miss Darcy at Pemberley she is offered 'beautiful pyramids of grapes, nectarines and peaches', which shows that there must be extensive hot-houses and a large team of gardeners.

'The period food looked stunning, but by the third day it needed as much make-up as some of the actors. I'm glad I only had to serve it!' (Neville Phillips)

Dinner scenes present great problems for filming. If a scene has to be shot again and again, the actors have to eat the same meal many times over, and always at the same places in the script; otherwise there will be continuity errors when the film is cut together.

Every time the shot is redone, the whole of the table has to be dressed afresh by Ron Sutcliffe and Mickey Booys, the stand-by props team, so that it looks exactly as it did before: wine glasses filled to the same level, bread rolls unbroken, cheese uncut and so on. The continuity supervisor will remind the actors what they were doing during the shots – when they

Roast capon on a bed
of forcemeat

Crayfish

Lobster

Game pies

Roasted quails

Haunches of cured pork

Baked fishes

Bantam eggs with herbs

Vegetables and
salads

Exotic fruits

Sweet meat pies

The Netherfield supper party.

'In the first dinner scene, I was placed in front of what looked like a large undercooked sheep. Being vegetarian, I found it a bit disturbing. From then on, I was tactfully placed in front of the decorative fruits.' (Lucy Briers)

lifted their spoons or cut their carrots. In the kitchen the film chef may be reheating the potatoes so the steam will rise as the lid is lifted. It was decided that wherever possible we would see the beginning or end of a meal, as soup or custard are easier to eat and replace than lamb cutlets. This doesn't mean that the tables look impoverished; at that time it was accepted that many dishes, from different courses, would be laid on the table at the same time. Everything had to look as if it had been made with equipment that was available in 1813. For instance, baking a loaf of bread on a griddle stone in front of a fire creates imperfections that won't be seen in modern cooking. The fruit and vegetables would have been organic and not uniform in size.

For the Netherfield ball supper scene, we asked chef Colin Capon to provide a sumptuous feast for forty to contrast with the simple dishes at the assembly-room dance. On screen, we will see events that happen over a period of half an hour, but we knew they would take three days to film. Obviously the food can't age. Any food actually eaten by the forty actors would be replaced for each shot. But because the centrepiece displays were so elaborate, they had to remain untouched and reappear each day looking as fresh as when they started, even after many hours under the hot film lights. At the end of each filming day everyone's plate or glass would be photographed with a Polaroid camera, so that it could be recreated the following day. Everything was wrapped in cling film and refrigerated. The next morning all the dishes were re-garnished and sprayed with a scented herb oil. This was partly to make them look fresh and partly to disguise the smell that became very noticeable by the third day!

Dinner at Longbourn.

'The Bennets do a lot of eating in the film, so Ron, the stand-by props man, asked me what I liked to eat. I told him gooseberry fool was my favourite pudding and he kindly provided it for me. It was so delicious that during the first two takes of the scene I gorged myself. At the other end of the table Alison Steadman cannily toyed with a couple of grapes. It took two days to shoot this and I shall never be able to eat gooseberry fool again!' (Ben Whitrow).

VISUAL EFFECTS: Graham Brown and Mark Haddenham

For *Pride and Prejudice* the visual effects team provided a range of effects from candles and gas fires through to changing weather conditions, including rain, snow and frost.

Candles required the most attention to detail, as many of the locations had chandeliers and other light fittings incorporating modern features. Most of the time it was impossible, and sometimes forbidden, to remove these, so we had metal tubes manufactured, in a variety of sizes, to cover all manner of light fittings so that they would appear to be candles. A recess was built in at the top to allow us to light a stub of candle, and a drip tray was added to the bottom. The whole thing was painted in heat-resistant paint of approximately the right colour, and then dipped in genuine beeswax to make a perfect match with the candles of the period. During a day's filming, these 'candles' would need constant monitoring, and the stubs in the top would often need to be replaced ten or more times a day.

We were also involved in simulating flambeaux and Argand lamps, which were the other methods of lighting used during the period. The latter was a predecessor of

the modern paraffin lamp and burned an oil that is very similar to modern cooking oil.

Traditionally, snow has been made using either fire-fighting foam or, even more harmful to the environment, salt. Both of these options would have been out of the question at most of the locations, so the alternative we chose was paper. To get the snow effect, one needs reasonably coarse fragments of paper, but for the frost, which we used in the final wedding sequence, one needs a very fine, almost dust-like, grade of paper. The whole location is sprayed with a fine mist of water where the frost is required, and the paper dust is blown on top of this. The water then holds it in position. Clearing the area after filming is not so bad as it might sound, as the whole location can simply be hosed down, and the paper disintegrates in the soil without doing any damage.

From winter to summer in one step: our snow effects cover only the filming area.

chapter 4

COSTUME, MAKE-UP AND HAIR DESIGN

Dinah Collin, the costume designer, and Caroline Noble, the make-up and hair designer, had worked together before on other films, and this was a bonus, as they were familiar with each other's working methods. They kept closely in touch during the pre-production period, often exchanging research material, which was important, as their two design areas overlapped. For instance, they needed to know that the hats and headdresses that Dinah provided would work with the wigs that Caroline was having made. During this research time, both would meet with the director and producer to discuss their ideas, and agreement would be reached on the direction to follow. Simon Langton explains what he was looking for: 'There are few better-documented eras than the classical/romantic age of Jane Austen. What struck me most of all was the obvious sense of freedom afforded by the light, soft materials. I wanted pale colours or creamy whites for the girls, to reflect both their zest and their innocence. This meant we could keep the darker, richer colours and exotic fabrics for characters like the Bingley sisters or Lady Catherine de Bourgh.'

THE COSTUMES: Dinah Collin

I was contracted about eight or nine weeks before filming began, but I actually got to work unofficially the moment I knew I had the job. I started going to museums and collecting pictures straight away; I don't think I could have done it in eight weeks.

With a period project you can generally go to see whichever costumier has the best available stock. Financially, that is the most practical thing. But there wasn't any stock for me to use – the rails of clothes from the 1850s and 1860s went on forever, but the early 1800s rail was empty, which was terribly frightening. This meant that I was going to have to make most of the costumes, which is not only more expensive but also entails such a lot of effort and meant that I'd have to find all the fabric.

RIGHT: Lydia, Lizzy and Jane in simple frocks in contrast to those of the Bingley sisters.

Miss Bingley and Mrs Hurst were 'very fine ladies ... but proud and conceited' and were 'in the habit of spending more than they ought' (Jane Austen).

EARLY RESEARCH

I phoned various museums and worked out a plan of action. It is a very laborious process, gaining access to collections – you have to write letters and arrange appointments because they have very limited time for viewings. I visited many excellent collections in Bath, Brighton, Manchester and Worthing. A woman named Alison Carter in Winchester was terribly helpful, as was the London Museum. Unfortunately, the V&A was closed at the time, but I had a very interesting chat with Avril Hart, their expert on men's clothes. She told me that they had just been given a coat made out of a fabric they had never seen before. It's called partridge – a sort of fleck with a stiff cotton weave. When I went to Cosprop, the costumier I used, I found they had been making a 1780s coat out of a fabric called India, which

Miss Bingley: designer's sketch with notes; finished costume and make-up.

was very similar. In the end we made one of Mr Bennet's long coats along those lines because it had exactly the right look.

I found some original clothes from this period, but they were often very, very fragile. Until the 1970s we used them extensively, but now these outfits are just too delicate. A lot of them have been put into what are called 'viewing rooms', which is useful for research because if you haven't got that as a basis from which to draw, then you're lost. Museums often have boxes of things that the curator hasn't had time to catalogue. Margaret Wicks, for example, who has been in the business for years, has a house just full of clothes. She brought me a little swan's-down nap and a tippet of exactly the right date. Having taken hundreds of photographs of clothes, it was great to find real things that I could actually use.

FABRICS

In 1813, in a family like the Bennets, everything would have been hand-made from patterns passed between families. Simon had described clearly the look he wanted; it had to appear fresh and light. I knew I wasn't going to be able to find the fabrics in John Lewis or Indian fabric shops. Then someone suggested I contact Amy Caswell, who had just completed a textile and print course at the School

Mrs Bennet with Mr Bennet, who is wearing the Banyan coat (top), modelled from this source drawing (above).

of Art, Design and Textiles in Bradford. She was very interested in helping, and the principal of the college, herself a Jane Austen fan, suggested we should use the college's printing facilities, which were excellent. In practical terms, though, this proved a little difficult because of the distance between Cosprop in north London, where the costumes would be made, and the college in Bradford. I became very familiar with the M1 motorway during my many lightning trips.

It is really difficult to dream up prints – you can't just copy them because if you get something that goes slightly out, the whole thing can fall apart. And we didn't want to make them too simple, which would have been a shame for characters like Mrs Bennet, for whom we wanted more feathery prints. So we went through absolute torture before they came out properly. The timetable was tight because I needed the fabrics in time to have the frocks ready for the fittings. I remember one of Mrs Bennet's frocks just wasn't working. In the end we dipped the material in pale dye, and it turned out very well. There is a point where you have to say, 'That's good enough!' and move on.

Amy created patterns from a variety of sources – for example, a wonderful shop in Bradford called Rainbow Textiles, which has an amazing collection of fabrics. We found lovely cotton saris with borders and decided to make a frock for Kitty from one of those patterns, which we printed and then dipped in pale-blue dye.

The muslin frock was a very important part of a woman's wardrobe during this period. While women would often wear the printed 'washing frocks', as they were called, these were not considered appropriate for the evenings or for visiting. Then the muslin frock was worn with a petticoat of a different colour underneath. I remember panicking slightly about how we were going to make the frocks, since not even Rainbow Textiles had any muslin prints. Amy came up with the wonderful idea that we could print designs directly on to muslin. She photocopied designs from several books, and we selected appropriate ones for each character; she then transferred them to a screen and printed them. The only problem was that we couldn't press them with a hot iron or they'd dissolve. But the overall look was well worth the difficulties.

MAKING THE COSTUMES

The great advantage of Cosprop, our costumier, is that you can draw on a tremendous amount of expertise all in one place, as they employ thirty-five highly skilled people. What they offer is unique – the other costumiers don't even attempt it. It's a very collaborative service and you can drop in and consult them on any bit of the process. They not only have a large stock that they hire out but they also make costumes all the time to add to it.

All the costumes they made for *Pride and Prejudice* will ultimately go into stock on a 'new to hire' basis. This means that instead of paying an initial lump sum when you hire a costume for the first week and then an additional sum for every week you need it thereafter, you pay a lump sum and that costume is yours for as long as you need it. All the things we have made will go into what we call 'embargo' until the programme is transmitted, which means they can't be used on another production before *Pride and Prejudice* is broadcast.

A NATURAL LOOK

One thing everyone agreed on was that all the clothes should look as natural for each character as possible. I was really anxious that the costumes shouldn't look at all fey. The key is to make the clothes like real clothes from a wardrobe rather than a set of costumes worn by actors. This is always a prime intention, but with a period piece one must be extra vigilant. I try to ensure that the actors feel comfortable in what they are wearing and not stiff and ill at ease. I work out a plot for each character – essentially the central things for their wardrobe – and then discuss with each actor how they'd like to wear the clothes. It's hard to

Some of the fabrics used for making costumes.

Mr Collins reassures Lizzy: 'Do not make yourself uneasy, my dear cousin, about your apparel. Lady Catherine will not think the worse of you for being simply dressed.'

Elizabeth in curry-coloured coat on her visit to Pemberley.

find time for that process, but it is terribly important. Changes can be made during filming, but it means you have a framework from which to work. And as I am not on set all the time, it allows my team to say, 'This is what you and Dinah agreed. Are you still happy with it?'

ELIZABETH BENNET

For Elizabeth I wanted to create a wardrobe that complemented the direct and practical aspects of her character. I chose colours that had an earthiness to them – a lot of browns, for example; I particularly liked her in a curry colour. I think the straw bonnet, the one that has a scrunchy look, really suits her character too. I had seen one on display at Jane Austen's house in Chawton and had something similar made. Overall I wanted a nice, straightforward look that was pretty but not fussy. And since Elizabeth is a very active girl, it was quite important that she had clothes that allowed her to move very easily and naturally.

MR BENNET

I found a picture for Mr Bennet that I particularly liked. It had a sense of relaxed complacency about it, which seemed appropriate. He's not interested in going out and about in society, so he wears a lot of velvets to be comfortable at home. We gave him spectacles and the banyan, a garment rather like a long dressing gown worn at home for warmth and comfort. In the days before central heating it would have been particularly useful.

MR DARCY

Colin Firth had a genuine interest in getting the wardrobe for Darcy right, which was a tremendous help. He has a very strong and virile quality to him, so the key thing was to make sure this wasn't diminished by the clothes, which can look rather sissy, especially the evening outfits.

We went through a laborious process, looking at various colours on him. He had a blue coat and a green one, and some in country colours, but we decided to leave the warmest tones for Bingley. Colin said he wanted to be saturnine, but didn't want to wear black, so I tended to go for dark greens and greys. Later on – maybe half-way through filming – he told me, 'I think I would now like a black coat.' One of the advantages of filming

DARCY
Colin Firth

over such a long period is that it allows actors to adapt their wardrobes as they become more comfortable with their parts, rather than my saying on the first day, 'This is all you've got.' I think the long, grey linen coat we made for him during filming was an important addition. Even though it is completely accurate for the period, it looks like something you could buy today, and this gives it a kind of contemporary relevance. After all, everything we're doing is an interpretation in the end – we aren't making a museum piece. We wanted to ensure that the clothes would look attractive to a modern audience.

THE BINGLEYS

Mr Bingley is such an instantly likeable and friendly character, I gave him warm colours and textures, like tweeds. He is less of an enigma than Darcy and needs to be a contrast to him. A gentleman like him would have had a great many coats, though probably all rather similar. I think you have to indicate wealth in the houses of the characters rather than in their clothes. We made an exception, though, with the Bingley sisters; we felt we could point out differences in wealth and class by contrasting their wardrobes with the pretty simplicity of the Bennet girls'. The Bingley sisters wear the equivalent of Gucci.

Darcy's source sheet: 'I try to find an image that gives a visual key to the character ... I then start to put other features with it and a fuller picture begins to form,' says Dinah Collin.

'I never in my life saw any thing more elegant than their dresses,' says Mrs Bennet.

'I think this cartoon, which appears in all the big costume books about the period, was the key to Lydia. It has such a jaunty feel to it.'

Adrian Lukis as Wickham.

I used a lot of shot silks from India, quite a lot of lace and much brighter and stronger colours – pinks and lime-greens, for example. Evening head-dresses were more elaborate and reflected the medieval influence fashionable during this period. Apart from wanting to look like Grecian columns, women aimed to look exotic, so they used rich colours with lots of wonderful feathers. We really wanted something that would stop the conversation in the village assembly rooms when they walked in.

HAIR AND MAKE-UP DESIGN: Caroline Noble
Early research

I went straight to the Victoria and Albert Museum; their reference library is the best and they have fantastic facilities for photographing material. I spent a week in there photographing hundreds of plates from books of the period at no cost at all. That's what's so wonderful about

Uniforms and liveries brought from Rome.

BARBARA LEIGH-HUNT (on costume)
'We're very lucky to have been working in the most wonderful locations on this production – that can be such an important dimension. There was a lovely touch, for example, picked up by Dinah, our costume designer, from a scene set in the dining room of Lady Catherine's house. There were these huge paintings of birds on the wall, some live and others after they had been slaughtered, in various attitudes of death. Then in the later scene where I confront Elizabeth and forbid her engagement to Darcy, there in my hat is a small dead bird. It's a delightful witticism, I think, as well as a visual comment on the predatory nature of Lady Catherine's world.'

the V&A; they allow you to do it as long as you're researching and are a member.

I looked at paintings of the period and bought an excellent book called *Regency Portraits*. This was a major source for the work that followed. As I was going through all the pictures, I started to think about the characters. Then I sorted the photographs into groups for each character, to make reference sheets to show Simon and Sue. Nothing is firmly fixed, of course, because once an actor is cast, the 'look' I'm thinking of may not work for him or her. But I am building up images all the time.

ABOVE: Mrs Hurst and the hairstyle inspired by this source picture from the Victoria and Albert Museum.

Screen tests

During this research period the casting was under way and screen tests were needed. I was sent details and photographs of the actors to be tested and prepared wigs or facial hair for them. Naturally, it's understood that all these will come out of the stock store, so it's unlikely that anything will fit perfectly. But it can help an actor to get into character and gives the director and producer a good idea of how the actor could look as that character. For instance, they might have auditioned an actress with long, flowing locks. But women's hairstyles in 1813 did not disguise the jaw-line. All the hair was lifted and pinned into a small shape, so the face was revealed. It's very important to see how actors will look on screen.

I also look at people's skin and their colouring. For example, Jennifer Ehle is quite fair, so we needed to see what she would look like darker, as Elizabeth is a brunette in the book. Fortunately she has dark eyebrows, and when we put her in a dark wig everyone thought she looked good. Simon thought the wig we gave her was too dark, so we had a slightly lighter one made for her.

The make-up team

In an ideal world, I probably would have had four assistants, but the production could only afford three. An assistant will always make up the same character because, however good someone's

LEFT: Make-up artists at work in their caravan.

BELOW: Ashley puts the finishing touches to Susannah.

notes and photographs are, the effect is never the same when done by someone else.

I give a general brief, but then I think it's really important for my assistants to be allowed as much individual creativity as possible, because otherwise it's just painting by numbers. The characters are discussed in detail and a central 'look' is found. Then we get the actors' input, which is important. There can be problems when actors have a very fixed idea of what they should look like and aren't prepared to consider anything else. Luckily, that didn't happen on

Colin Firth as Darcy.

had left before filming. When it was long enough we dyed it and his eyebrows and lashes. His eyes are dark, so his adopted colouring certainly looked natural.

Jennifer Ehle

Because her hair is fair and was the wrong length we knew right away that we would have to wig her. We thought we'd have at least two wigs, so one could be prepared while the other was used, but in fact we ended up with three. As she was going to be wearing a wig for five months, she decided that she wanted her own hair cut really short to make it more comfortable. But it made our job a lot more difficult because we didn't have any of her own hair to use to cover the nape of her neck where the wigs fitted. The front of the wigs would be relatively easy because they were knotted on to very fine lace, rather like the lace a ballet tutu is made of, but because of the shape of the head wigs don't fit in quite the same way at the back. I felt sorry for Philippa, who was Jennifer's make-up artist, because there were a lot of nape shots in which the camera was shooting right up behind her ear. Philippa and I drew some sharp intakes of breath at various stages, but Rob Southam, the focus puller, who is married to a make-up artist, would always call us when he knew we needed to adjust things before a shot.

Contrasting the Bennet sisters

There wasn't a huge amount of variety in hairstyles during that period, so I had to work hard to make distinctions between the Bennet girls. Dinah Collin very much wanted to keep Lizzy's look simple, so I went along with that – beautiful and unadorned. By contrast, I wanted Jane to look classically Greek, a style that was popular at that time and is terribly elegant. I wanted to give her the most beautiful and ornate hairstyle of the Bennet girls'. Susannah Harker's hair was her own, though we did make it a tiny bit lighter to contrast with Jennifer's.

Mary, of course, is meant to be ugly and there's a reference to bad skin, so we did put her through a little spot phase! Lucy Briers was very game. She told us that her ears naturally stick out a bit, so we chose a hairstyle that would make them visible all the time. I was very cruel with the front of her hair: to make her look very plain we used quite a bit of grease on the roots so it looked unwashed.

As for Lydia, very early on I said that I'd really like her to be lopsided – sort of imbalanced, messy and tomboyish. I had found some lovely illustrations of this lopsided look. So Dinah and I worked on that. Julia Sawalha has this wonderful curly, slightly frizzy hair, which looks very right for the period, so she was really very easy. Kitty is a shadow of Lydia, and not as lopsided, though she wasn't as neat or precise as Jane. Both she and Lydia are very young anyway and consequently would have been given less time for the maids to do their hair.

'Dinah and I discovered that we both wanted to base Lady Catherine on a portrait we had seen of Queen Caroline.'

'Mr Bennet was so odd a mixture of quick parts, sarcastic humour, reserve and caprice' (Jane Austen).

Benjamin Whitrow as Mr Bennet.

Lydia (Julia Sawalha) and Kitty (Polly Maberly).

'Our life has few distinctions, Mrs Bennet, but I feel I may safely boast that here stand two of the silliest girls in England' (Mr Bennet in Andrew Davies's adaptation).

Lucy Robinson (Mrs Hurst) plays the piano on set.

'I had been given this piano music about a month before filming. Being new to it all, I thought I might really have to play. I have never practised so hard in my life! So when it came to the actual filming, and it was a muted piano, and I had an earpiece with Carl Davis playing so I could mime, I didn't know whether to be hugely relieved or sadly disappointed' (Emilia Fox).

How did you start?

I always begin by rereading the novel, to immerse myself in the world of the book and of the characters. With something like this, you are working with a very rich text – it's like working with a Bible. You can't go wrong if you stick to your Bible; you have such fertile inspiration for the music. At this stage I also make notes of any specific music references – whether, for example, any song titles are named, or dance tunes or musical instruments mentioned. In fact, these references were thin on the ground in *Pride and Prejudice*, although the story is shot through with scenes involving music. Well, imagine it: a world with no television and no movies, a town with no theatre – what were all those young ladies to do? They were all expected to play and sing, of course, and to show off these accomplishments at balls, parties and home entertainments. It was all part of the mating game.

My first job was to select the music that the television audience would see being played or danced or sung by the characters on screen, and Andrew had written a great many of these scenes. This is called the 'source music', and it has to be authentic, in the way that locations and costumes are. Sue, Simon and I spent a lot of time making our choices. It was easy to imagine what they might be playing; the period was contemporary with Haydn and Beethoven, Mozart had just died and Schubert was just starting to write music.

The real fun, of course, lies in choosing music that adds to the dynamic of a scene or gives a little lift to the characters. For example, poor old Mary, who is the plainest of the sisters and doesn't have much going for her, grinds away at practising the piano but is really not very good. She's expected to churn it out, though, at small gatherings, when people want to roll back the carpet and dance. But when she insists on playing and singing at the Netherfield ball, it's a terrible embarrassment. For that we chose a Handel song, beautiful if played well but just enough beyond Mary's range, poor thing, for it to be appalling. And then, to underline Elizabeth's embarrassment, we chose a very flourished, showy piece for the much more accomplished Bingley sister to play, and it's performed very much as a put-down – the London set versus the Bennets, if you like.

What about choosing the dance music?

This was a very important element of the source music, and Jane Gibson, the choreographer, was involved in those sessions. She had already researched the dances she wanted to use and so was able to tell us, 'These are the steps, this is the number of couples and they need to go around this many times,' and so on, which was a tremendous help. So we worked through the various choices, with me at the piano and

The orchestra playing at the Netherfield ball.

Jane dancing all the movements around my studio and everybody chipping in: 'Nice dance but boring tune,' or 'This is a dialogue scene; we need something sustained for this one.' Jane had to make sure the tempo was right and would sometimes ask me to add bars to give time for couples to get to their places, or she would tell me, 'I need an ending for this one for the reverence' (that's the bow or curtsy). It took quite a time but was great fun.

What happened then?

I arranged all the source music, and there's so much that we spent six hours recording it. It's necessary to pre-record it because, even if we are using real musicians in the film, as we did for the two ball sequences, we can't let them actually play their instruments. We need to have complete control over the sound and you can't record dialogue against music, so the musicians or actors have to mime to the playback tape. To help them, they are given tiny earpieces, hidden by their hair, which are linked to the recorded music.

For the two balls we wanted a great contrast of sound. The Meryton assembly rooms needed a rougher, cruder sound, so we used a trio playing authentic instruments. The musicians we found were really village players who provided the music for barn dances. They had a style of

'I drove my fiancé mad by practising the dance tunes for up to two hours each day. Eventually, whenever he saw me move towards the piano, he'd rush out for a long walk' (Lucy Briers).

Carl conducts the orchestra at the
music-recording session.

Melvyn Tan plays Darcy's theme on
the fortepiano.

about very early on: the character of the sound. If we'd been doing a vast
Victorian novel, then I'd have had no qualms about going for a huge
symphony orchestra, but it wouldn't have been right for this. I wanted
the sense of a small town in 1813. The merit lay in containing the
sound. The model I started from was a marvellous Beethoven septet
that was written just about that period. It was enormously popular at the
time, and I thought that was the sound I wanted for the intimate scenes
in *Pride and Prejudice*. For the longer scenes, where the story is sweep-
ing along, I use a group of eighteen musicians. Early on we made what
I felt was a very exciting decision, which was to feature one of the out-
standing instruments from that period – the fortepiano. This was the
forerunner of today's piano and produces a unique and fascinating
sound, quite different from that of the modern instrument, and it was
just what I was after. And we were incredibly lucky to find both the right
instrument and the player for it – in fact, not just a player but a real star,
Melvyn Tan, who plays beautifully. He completely captures the essence
of that time.

How much practice time do the musicians have before recording?
I'm sure this will surprise people, but they have none at all. They turn
up at the recording studio and see the score for the first time. We made
an exception, though, for Melvyn and sent him his part a couple of days
ahead; we knew we were going to make a lot of demands on him, with
a very rapid rippling up and down the fortepiano keyboard, so we
decided to give him a sporting chance. The others had no preparation
time whatsoever. But this is the great characteristic of London's session
musicians; they were all hand-picked and this means you can move very
fast. We had nine three-hour recording sessions in which to do everything, but they have no fear. It's one read of the score and off we go!

In the sound gallery at the recording
session.

chapter 6

*D*ANCING

In Jane Austen's time dancing was an integral part of social life. Given her own love of dancing and the crucial role it played in courtship, it is no surprise that she set many key scenes in the book at dances or balls. This provided the production with an exciting opportunity – here was the chance to bring this vital part of the story vividly to life. The challenge was to find the appropriate dances and then teach them quickly to a large cast, many of whom had never danced before. For this daunting task the team sought the considerable experience of Jane Gibson, who has not only an in-depth knowledge of historical dance but, as a well-known teacher of movement at drama schools, also the experience of working with actors.

'*Pride and Prejudice* was a fantastic job for me because it called for exactly those things which interest me, that is to say the social dimension of dance; how dance is both a reflection of a society and a clue to the way people think and feel. As we know, it is a very important element in *Pride and Prejudice*. Significant things happen during the dances. So it was good to find that the director and all the production team were enthusiastic and agreed that it is an important aspect of the story. The first thing I did was reread the book and make a note of all the references to dance. I knew a lot of the dances from the period already, but I started to do quite a lot of additional research. The end of the eighteenth century is a very interesting time, as it's moving into this tremendous period of change.'

THE HISTORY OF ENGLISH COUNTRY DANCE

'The so-called English Country Dances are England's great contribution to Western European dance. In France there was the Baroque, which centred on Versailles. Baroque dance is wonderful – the nobles danced superb minuets and sarabands. They were introduced to England but didn't take off in the same way. Because Versailles was the epicentre of French society, everyone across France copied what went on there. In England we went a different route, very much to do with Englishmen in their wonderful houses on their country estates. Out of that came their fondness for what is called the English Country Dance.

Jane Gibson (back, right) and members of the cast in the rehearsal room.

Filming the dancing on the Meryton assembly rooms set.

BELOW: Filming the assembly rooms.

BOTTOM: Julia Sawalha (Lydia) and Polly Maberly (Kitty) learn the dances.

importance of the dance to wooing and courting. In a dance girls were able to do what they weren't able to do anywhere else, which was to be with a man unchaperoned. This is why they talked to each other as they danced. They had more privacy in a dance than they would have anywhere else. A man might ask the woman of his choice for two dances, as Bingley does with Jane at the Meryton assembly. That meant they could spend a lot of time together because, if the set was long, the dances could go on for some time.'

DANCE REHEARSALS

Some fifteen separate dances had to be chosen, choreographed and rehearsed before filming could begin. Simon recalls how they were put together: 'Jane Gibson had this wonderful book from the period called *The Apted Book of Country Dancing*, which has all these Country Dances with instructions on how to do them. They have wonderful names like 'The Shrewsbury Lasses', 'A Trip to Highgate' or 'Mr Beveridge's Maggot'. So we went to composer Carl Davis's studio and worked our way through them.'

The two most important gatherings in the film are the assembly at Meryton, which is the village-hall affair, and the elegant private ball at Netherfield, and dances were chosen to contrast the two events as much as possible. There are also many smaller party scenes in which the younger girls suddenly decide to roll back the carpet and dance. This, in effect, means that Lydia and Kitty are seen dancing every single dance during filming, whether it is at the assembly rooms or at Mrs Phillips's Christmas party. Julia Sawalha and Polly Maberly had to learn all fifteen dances over a three-day period. They spent practically twenty-four hours dancing.

THE MERYTON DANCE AND THE NETHERFIELD BALL

'Although people would have danced the same dances at Meryton as at Netherfield, some would have been much more popular at the assembly than others,' says Jane Gibson. 'For example, at Meryton they want to enjoy themselves. They're from a different class. The occasion is all about the community – the butcher, the baker, the candlestick maker – getting together to enjoy themselves. They are less concerned with elegance and might kick their legs up a bit. So I chose faster dances in jig or reel rhythm. But, if you look closely, you'll see that the dance forms are the same; the difference is in the style.'

At the Netherfield ball Darcy and Elizabeth dance together for the first time – an electric moment that needed just the right music and movement to complement the mood. For Simon it was one of the most challenging aspects of the filming: 'The scene was five and a half pages long, with Elizabeth and Darcy having to dance and talk at the same time, which is the sort of thing a director dreads. I wasn't sure how to do it at all, but I thought if the dance was right in the first place, then something would evolve out of it. I loved the music immediately, but the moment I saw "Mr Beveridge's Maggot" danced collectively I knew it was perfect.'

Jane Gibson, who knew the dance well, felt the same: '"Mr Beveridge's Maggot" is a beautiful dance with a fantastic spatial pattern. It is satisfying to dance and pleasing to watch because there is such a sense of harmony about it.

'I used to think it was called a "maggot" because the movement of the couples up and down the room was like a maggot moving through putrefying matter. But then I found out that a "maggot" was a "fancy", and there are many dances called maggots. Mr Beveridge would have been the dancing master who devised the dance, so it was really "Mr Beveridge's fancy".'

Andrew Davies: 'At the Netherfield ball there's a conversation between Darcy and Elizabeth that's almost like a fencing match caught in dance. It echoes a tango or a *pasa doble*. There's a lot of stamping feet, they come together and they part, and some turns they make are like the turns of a matador. You get a sense of combat as well as dancing.'

BELOW: The Netherfield ball.

Lighting platforms built to protect flowerbeds.

protected from lamps and heavy boots. The solution was to build low scaffolding platforms that could be speedily removed and laid over the flowerbeds without harming the plants.

THE READ-THROUGH

About two weeks before filming everyone involved in the project is invited to the read-through of the scripts in the BBC rehearsal rooms. In the case of *Pride and Prejudice* this meant seventy people gathered together for the first time. In fact, it was the only time some actors were to see each other if they were involved in different scenes. With so many people, we decided to organize a seating plan, so we could make sure that the right groups of actors were together for their scenes and to give Simon a sporting chance of being able to introduce everyone by name.

Lucy Briers was grateful for this: 'On my first job, when I'd just left drama school, I went to the read-through. I didn't know what the form was, so I just grabbed a chair and sat down, and then found, to my great embarrassment, that I was between the leading actor and the producer.'

As Simon Langton says: 'It's a nerve-racking time. Everyone feels that they are on show for the first time, and we were very aware that we had about five hours of reading to get through – a daunting task. We were worried that the energy might disappear during the day. Some people say: "Oh, it's only a read-through. It doesn't matter how you read it." But I remember hearing about the read-through of *Othello* when everyone turned up at rehearsal in sweaters and gym shoes, smoking cigarettes and sitting down feeling a bit tired. Suddenly Olivier came out with this extraordinary performance and everyone woke up and thought, "This is the read-through!" Well, at ours Alison Steadman had the same effect. She took off like a bolting chariot with amazing energy, force and pitch – it was wonderful. And you saw people wake up and then decide to join in, which made all the difference.'

REHEARSALS

We had a week of rehearsals which, compared with theatre, is not very much. But sometimes with filming there is no rehearsal at all. Simon Langton found it essential. 'Most of the time was spent discussing the scripts. The rehearsal period is really a chance for the actors to do what there is not time for on set, which is to try things out, take risks, get things off their chests and get to know each other and relax into their parts. There are some very complicated relationships in *Pride and Prejudice* – and, don't forget, we were to film scenes out of order, so, for example, the first proposal scene was filmed before the characters had actually met in the story. It's hard enough for the actors to do this, but without some rehearsal it would have been impossible.'

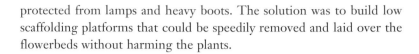

Julia Sawalha and Adrian Lukis in the rehearsal room.

Another essential was for the actors and dancers to learn the dances, to practise (or, in some cases, start to learn) horse riding, to brush up their fencing, to take piano lessons and singing-to-tape sessions. In this way, all the skills needed would be ready ahead of the actual filming.

HEALTH AND SAFETY

Anything that involves a risk to cast or crew, such as riding a horse, fencing, swimming or using lighted candles, has to be itemized on a BBC safety form, with details of the precautions to be taken to minimize the risks. There may be safety boats and trained divers ready in the water for a swimming scene or an episode where two little boys fish by the edge of the lake. The water will have already been tested in the lab. Trained stunt doubles may be used if anything is considered too dangerous for an actor to do.

The people on set responsible for first aid have refresher courses, and the first assistant director, the producer and the director sit exams about safety on set, as in law they are ultimately responsible for this.

Finally, the leading actors, producer and director have insurance medicals to determine whether they are fit enough to cope with the months of filming ahead.

Swimming and riding on horses or in carriages can pose safety risks.

Simon's storyboard.

TOP: Waiting to be called on set.

ABOVE: Cast and crew have to work closely together, both inside (left) … and out (right).

ABOVE LEFT AND RIGHT: Filming in all weathers.

Darcy's second proposal.

the proposal it was vital that the weather was as romantic as possible. To compound our difficulties, Barbara Leigh-Hunt, who played Lady Catherine, was performing in Los Angeles and could not be back until our final week. We had intended to shoot the proposal scene at the beginning of that week but, as each day dawned, the weather was dull. We gambled on the weather improving later in the week and hastily rescheduled. This meant that two of the biggest scenes in the film were to be shot on the last Thursday and Friday of the schedule. It was a tremendous risk, and there was great anxiety in case the weather deteriorated. In fact, we were blessed with two gloriously bright, if cold, autumn days and just managed to finish both scenes before we lost the light.

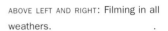

TOP: Lady Catherine's big scene.
ABOVE: Sometimes there's no room for the leading lady.

AROUND THE CAMERA

First Assistant Director

During filming there is a small group of people who work as a unit around the camera. It is essential that they all understand the aims of the director and are on the same wave-length. They have to work closely together, sometimes literally, as they may be squashed into a small room, with camera equipment, lights, furniture and, of course, the actors.

At the centre is the first assistant director (1st AD), who is there to interpret the director's wishes. Time is precious, and it is the 1st AD's job to ensure that everyone is in the right place with the right props or equipment at the right time – and to achieve this while keeping everyone in harmony, so tact and sensitivity are as essential as efficiency.

John Kenway checks the shot.

Tim Wylton and Joanna David as Mr and Mrs Gardiner.

Anthony Calf as Colonel Fitzwilliam.

LIGHTING

The logic, when lighting for any scene, is to decide on the source of the light and from where it is coming. For a scene in a room during the day, you might decide there would be sunlight through the windows and place large film lights outside to simulate this. In a modern house there could be a central ceiling light or lamps (called 'practicals') to switch on. These would be supplemented by film lamps, but, essentially, it would look as if the room were being lit by these practicals. In a kitchen at night, the light from an open fridge, for example, could be used to light an actor's face. But for a drama set in country districts in 1813 the options diminish. There would have been no street lighting; rooms would have been lit by candles, and this posed problems for John Kenway: 'It's difficult to achieve the effect of a room lit only by candles and still be able to make out what's happening. I suspect that, even with the big chandeliers of the grander houses, it would still have been quite dark beyond their direct glow, and in smaller houses, because of the expense, candles would have been used sparingly. We have to strike a balance between what would be truthful and what seems truthful. If it's too dark, it can become a real strain on the eye, and the audience becomes disorientated and anxious. I try to give the light the right effect by making it soft and warm and by making it appear to come from the practical source. If you have a glorious room with a hundred actors in costume and make-up, and I lit it so you couldn't see them, I think no one would be happy, even if the lighting were authentic.

'Outside scenes at night are a cameraman's quandary. What are you supposed to use as a light source if it's night and there aren't any lights? It was helpful to know that balls or dinners were organized around the few days near to the full moon, so carriages could find their way down the lanes. So we always put up a moon of some sort and made it blue, which gave our general light. Then we tried to see what practicals we might introduce. In the courtyards of grand houses, like Pemberley and Netherfield, there would be metal brackets to hold the flambeaux, or flaming torches, and there would be young men to run in front of the coaches as they travelled, also carrying flambeaux. For the night scene outside the assembly rooms, we placed film lamps inside several of the houses in Lacock to simulate candle-light, which spilled out into the road to supplement the light from the assembly-room windows. We lit flambeaux outside the door and had lots of runners with flaming torches. These, plus our "moon", meant that we could see all the way down the street as the carriages arrived and could get a good look at the rich Netherfield party as they climbed out. It's my guess that directors of photography worry a great deal about the logic of lighting, but if the audience knows it's night and can see what's going on, they're not at all worried by the rest of it.'

JENNIFER EHLE AND ELIZABETH BENNET

I was so excited when we first began filming. I knew I would only have five days off during the entire five months of shooting, as Elizabeth is in nearly every scene, but I didn't feel daunted by that at all. I learned the first month's worth of dialogue before we began. This made me feel secure and meant that I had time to get to know everyone rather than having to rush back to my hotel room every night to learn new lines.

It took nearly two hours every day to get costumed and made-up, so my call times were always very early, between 5.30 and 6 a.m. Because time away from location became so precious, I got quicker and quicker at getting out of costume and make-up at the end of each day. I would often take the pins out of my hair as I sat in the bath.

I thought I was the luckiest person in the world to spend an entire summer being Elizabeth Bennet. What a fantastic thing to do! But after ten weeks of filming, I felt exhausted. People would say encouragingly, 'It's all right; we're halfway there,' but suddenly I found it all terrifying. Elizabeth is a wonderful character, but it can make you go a bit loopy being someone else every day for a long period, especially if you are physically so different. Fortunately, at that point, we had a five-day rehearsal period in London, so the days were shorter and I could live at home. I just slept and slept whenever I could, and I built up the strength to face the next ten weeks. I learned to pace myself and rest when possible. I would sometimes fall asleep between set-ups, while the lighting was being changed. Unbelievably, I once even managed to nod off, sitting up, between the first and second takes of a shot!

The last scene I had to shoot was the one with Lady Catherine de Bourgh. When it ended and Simon called, 'Cut!' I was in a complete state of shock. I couldn't believe it was all over. It had not been like acting in a play in the theatre for five months, because there you have a life of your own during the day. This had been five months away from everything normal – rather like being on a ship. It was good to get back to my own life, but I was sad too that it was finished. My summer as Elizabeth Bennet had been wonderful.

DIARY OF A FILMING DAY

FRIDAY, 14 OCTOBER 1994

Overnight

The previous day's filming is developed and the sound rushes are transferred.

7.30 a.m.

Sam (location manager) phones RAF base and Bristol airport for weather check for our area.

Alan in Ranks Lab looks at previous day's rushes (picture only) at high speed to check if the exposure is correct, if there are scratches on the negative and if it's in focus. He then sends developed rushes on a van to the cutting room.

The first carriage arrives on location.

8.00 a.m.

The catering manager goes to the market to buy fresh supplies for 110 people. The first horses start their journey to the location.

8.30 a.m.

Editor and assistant look at yesterday's rushes without sound. They realize that in the long Steadicam shot of Lizzy and Wickham film lamps can clearly be seen in the windows along the street. They check all the material to see if they can edit the sequence to avoid seeing these. They can't. This is a big problem.

Art Dept is re-laying part of ground cover on the village street.

Item about our filming is broadcast on local radio.

9.00 a.m.

Editor phones film unit and tells them that part of sequence will have to be reshot. This means remounting this scene in addition to the scheduled day's filming. The Steadicam operator left yesterday for another job, so we can't reshoot the entire sequence. Editor suggests linking shot. We need to see the material to know exactly what is to be shot. Assistant editor transfers rushes to a VHS cassette and sends it on courier bike to Wiltshire.

Paul (production manager) starts to change the schedule to include new shot. We need to call back three actors who have been released. Roger Barclay is in London, and Adrian Lukis is about to leave Malmesbury for Cornwall. The coordinator phones Roger Barclay in London and asks him to go to Paddington Station immediately. He is due to rehearse at his drama school. Coordinator promises to ring his drama school to excuse him from rehearsals.

Catering team is peeling potatoes in preparation for lunch.

Wayne and his transport team are cleaning out costume, make-up and actors' rest-room caravans, toilets and mobile office.

9.30 a.m.

Paul contacts all departments with new schedule for the day. All call times are adjusted. The 2nd AD calls the actors and organizes transport.

In the cutting room, the editing assistant links the sound and picture of yesterday's material. All the shots are logged.

Jennifer Ehle and Julia Sawalha are collected from hotel by 3rd ADs.

Roger Barclay leaves London by train.

Rest of horses start journey to location.

Art Department dresses shop front.

10.00 a.m.

Sam asks pub landlady if we can borrow her sitting room (which has TV and video machine) to view cassette when it arrives.

Simon discusses the scene with Susannah and Jennifer.

Adrian Lukis changes his plan, and coordinator rebooks his travel for later in the day.

3rd ADs collect Susannah Harker, Polly Maberly, Lucy Briers and David Bark-Jones from the hotel.

Coordinator rings Roger Barclay's drama school to explain that he's been called for reshoot.

Team of extra costume and make-up assistants arrive; they will work on the fifty-two supporting artists.

Adrian Lukis collected from hotel.

First spectators arrive.

Second item is broadcast on a local radio station.

10.30 a.m.
Jennifer Ehle and Julia Sawalha are called for make-up.

The first of the fifty-two supporting artists arrive for make-up and costume.

Stand-by painters are touching up the shop fronts.

Sam phones for weather update.

First of local reporters and photographers arrive for a story about the filming.

The editor is watching yesterday's rushes with sound.

The assistants are logging each shot.

11.00 a.m.
Director arrives on set and walks alone around the location to decide how to shoot scenes.

Continuity checks all locations against the script.

Our unit of supporting-artist 'soldiers' arrives. They are put into costume and make-up.

Editor starts cutting together the previous day's rushes.

Transport leaves to collect Roger Barclay from Chippenham station.

Third item on local radio.

Regional TV news team arrives to film an item for the teatime local programme.

Adrian Lukis to make-up.

11.30 a.m.
Director, director of photography, 1st AD and continuity walk the set to discuss all the scenes. DOP then instructs the gaffer, who starts to rig the lamps.

Susannah Harker, Polly Maberly and Roger Barclay to make-up.

Julia Sawalha, Lucy Briers and David Bark-Jones to costume.

The 'soldiers' are sent to practise their drill.

John Collins and stand-by props team check action props for the day.

Sue discovers a new director in the shape of Colin Firth.

12.00 p.m.
VHS cassette arrives. Director, producer, designer, DOP, camera operators, locations manager, continuity, 1st AD and 2ADs all crush into sitting room of landlady of local pub to view on her VHS recorder. Discuss how to remount shot. Production manager then visits each department to spread information.

Director talks to actors. Art Department checks all in order for this extra shot. DOP talks to gaffer.

Lucy Briers and David Bark-Jones to make-up.

Adrian Lukis and Roger Barclay to costume.

First lunches served.

Colin Firth, David Bamber, Crispin Bonham-Carter are collected from hotel.

Full rushes report from editor. Associate producer passes on report to producer, director and DOP.

Mark (art director) and Barry (construction manager) record an interview for local radio.

Sue Birtwistle does interview for local paper.

12.30 p.m.
Second service of lunch.

The unit stills photographer arrives. He will photograph the scenes and the unit at work from now until the end of filming.

Sue and Gerry do live interview for local radio.

The first spectators of the day arrive. By the end of the day about 300 people will come to watch. The police erect barriers for crowd control. Extra location managers arrive to help.

1.00 p.m.
'Biteback' team arrives. Between now and 4 p.m. they film the filming. Carriages, men and horses on set: 1 green cart, 1 grey horse, 1 carthorse, 2 animal handlers.

Cherry-picker crane and scissor-lift arrive on location.

Jennifer Ehle to costume.

BBC press officer arrives with the two winners of the Penguin *Middlemarch* essay competition. Their prize is a location visit to *Pride and Prejudice*. They have lunch. Peter discusses the day's interviews with the actors and production team. He (with Paul Brodrick and Julia Weston) will coordinate all the press, local photographers and filming teams.

1.30 p.m.

Jennifer Ehle, Julia Sawalha, Polly Maberly, Adrian Lukis, Roger Barclay and David Bark-Jones on set to rehearse.

1st AD and team organize all the supporting artists into their places.

Colin Firth and Crispin Bonham-Carter to make-up.

David Bamber to costume.

More spectators arrive. They are asked not to take flash photographs while we are shooting.

Filming starts on rescheduled scene.

Coordinator phones for weather check.

Assistant production accountant is preparing travel expenses for the supporting artists.

2.00 p.m.

BBC Education Unit arrives to film the filming for a school programme.

David Bamber to make-up.

Susannah Harker, Crispin Bonham-Carter and Colin Firth to costume.

Pick-up shot is finished.

Stills photographer has five minutes to do set-up photos of Julia Sawalha and Adrian Lukis.

Roger Barclay and David Bark-Jones are released. They get out of costume and make-up. Transport arranged to hotel and Chippenham station.

Unit sets up for next shot..

Adrian Lukis interviewed by BBC Education Unit and is then released for the weekend.

Caterers wash up after lunch.

Wayne and team clean dining buses, ready for next meal.

2.30 p.m.

Jennifer Ehle, Julia Sawalha and Polly Maberly change costume and join Colin Firth, Susannah Harker, Lucy Briers, David Bamber, Crispin Bonham-Carter on set to rehearse.

Horses for Darcy and Bingley on set.

'Biteback' film interview with Sue Birtwistle, watched by entire fifth form of a local school, who take notes.

Local radio interviews Dinah Collin, Sam Breckman, Julia Sawalha.

Scene 2/12 is filmed.

Caterers start to prepare tea.

3.00 p.m.

Anna Chancellor to make-up.

BBC Education film crew films the unit base and the filming.

A hat needed for night shoot arrives by Red Star at Chippenham. Unit car sent to collect it.

Sue reads winning *Middlemarch* essays, talks to the two winners and introduces them to the actors and crew.

Scene 2/12 is completed.

'Biteback' interviews Dinah Collin.

Special effects check flambeaux for night shoot.

3.30 p.m.
Vic Young blacks out windows.

Electricians rig lights in cottage windows in preparation for night shoot.

Film unit moves to location on bridge just outside village.

Jennifer Ehle, Susannah Harker, Lucy Briers, Julia Sawalha, Polly Maberly and David Bamber rehearse scene 2/11.

Police stop traffic.

Another report on local radio.

Scene 2/11 is filmed.

4.00 p.m.
Some of supporting artists change costume and make-up for evening filming.

Tea is served to unit as they work.

Sam requests weather update.

Paul prepares call sheet for next filming day, after consultation with make-up and costume departments and 1st AD.

4.30 p.m.
Lucy Robinson to make-up.

Rupert Vansittart to costume.

Scene 2/11 is finished. Unit moves back to base.

Unit photographer shoots interior set-ups of actors.

5.00 p.m.
Anna Chancellor and Lucy Robinson to costume.

Cherry-picker, scissor-lift moved into place on set.

First suppers for 110 served.

Professor Marilyn Butler arrives to film an interview with Colin Firth – a room in the pub is borrowed for this.

Call sheets are printed out.

Sue Clegg types up continuity notes of filming so far.

Rushes already shot are packaged and labelled.

The following artists are taken out of costume and released: Jennifer Ehle, David Bamber, Susannah Harker, Julia Sawalha, Polly Maberly, Lucy Briers.

5.30 p.m.

Carriages on stand-by: Bennet carriages, Bingley carriages, large gig, red gig.

Animals on set: Bennet horses x 2, Bingley horses x 4, 1 x varnished horse, 1 x red-gig horse; 4 animal handlers on set.

Third sitting for supper continues.

Special effects prepare all torches.

Main lamps for night shoot are rigged.

Rostrum for camera positions erected.

Item on local TV and radio programmes.

6.00 p.m.

Lights rigged inside Red Lion for our exterior assembly-room shot.

Last suppers served.

Final costume and make-up checks.

Horse trough filled with water for later stunt.

David Bamber drives to London.

Adrian Lukis and Crispin Bonham-Carter are driven to Chippenham station.

Susannah Harker, Lucy Briers, Polly Maberly and Julia Sawalha return to hotel.

6.30 p.m.

Colin Firth, Anna Chancellor, Lucy Robinson, Rupert Vansittart, Crispin Bonham-Carter on to set to rehearse scene 1/17.

On set two dogs, two mongrels and thirty-five supporting artists.

Peter Mares and Penguin winners leave for London.

More spectators arrive.

7.00 p.m.

Rehearsals of carriage arriving continue.

In between set-ups Colin Firth continues his filmed interview.

Caterers wash up after supper.

Transport team clean dining buses.

7.30 p.m.

Filming on scene 1/14 starts.

More spectators arrive.

8.00 p.m.

The BBC Education film unit leaves.

9.00 p.m.

It is now very cold. Hot chocolate and snacks served as the unit works. The night shoot continues with scene 1/17.

9.30 p.m.

One of supporting artists is allergic to horses and has a very bad asthma attack. Paul Brodrick administers first aid and she is sent for medical treatment.

10.00 p.m.

Filming continues until 11.30 p.m., still watched by crowds of spectators.

Sam delivers flowers to each house on the main street to thank them for their cooperation.

11.30 p.m.

Filming finishes.

Actors get out of costume and make-up.

Hot snacks and drinks are served as people work.

Horses are loaded into boxes for return jouneys.

Carriages start journey home.

The lights are derigged. The rostrum is taken apart.

Camera equipment is checked and packed.

The rushes are packaged and collected by courier to go to labs.

Call sheets are handed out for the next filming day.

Anything fragile is moved by Art Department, small props are packed, false doors are removed from cottages.

Dogs return to kennels.

Preparation for large trucks to clear road cover next morning.

12.00 midnight

Caterers do final washing up, and all the day's rubbish is packaged and driven to the tip.

Make-up and costume pack up and store everything for next filming day.

Wayne and team lock all vehicles in preparation for large unit move the following morning back to main location.

Night security takes over.

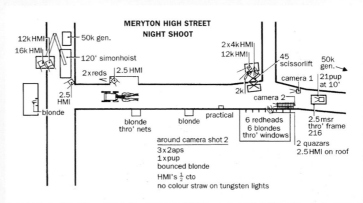

John Kenway's camera plan for a night shoot.

SOCIAL LIFE

Naturally, working such long hours over a period of five months can be exhausting, but it mustn't be forgotten that everyone had chosen to do the work and that, compared with some jobs, it can be great fun. Strong friendships are formed when such a gregarious group is away from home and working together so closely, and it's essential to find time to relax. Ron Sutcliffe became the social secretary. He set up a weekly raffle and organized quiz nights, many barbecues and *boules* competitions. David Bamber, Adrian Lukis and Colin Firth all brought their guitars and practised late into many a night (but never quite reached performance standard). Several birthdays were celebrated with large cakes. We even had one engagement announced, and three babies were born (not, I hasten to add, to the same couple – the shoot wasn't that long!).

Alison Steadman:

One evening Ron organized a *boules* competition. Because some people were very skilled, he drew names out of a hat to select partners. I was paired with Mark, the special effects assistant, who had arrived on location only that week and was still rather shy. I'd never played before, so I wasn't very good, but I was very enthusiastic. There were so many people playing that it became very late, and some started to get anxious because everyone had a very early call the next morning. But I was so thrilled to get through to the next round that I was determined

not to give up and kept trying to encourage Mark to be more enthusiastic. I saw him the next morning in the breakfast queue, but this time, of course, I was in full Mrs Bennet wig and costume. I didn't realize that he hadn't connected me with the character he'd seen on set each day, and I said cheerily, 'Well, wasn't it fun last night playing *boules*?' I was completely taken aback when he said, 'Oh, I had this terrible partner called Alison. I kept trying to lose so I could go home, but she insisted that we must go on and on.
I was so tired this morning. I'm certainly going to avoid her in future.'

Colin Firth and Julia Sawalha celebrate their birthdays on the set.

LEFT: Colin, Crispin and Jennifer at the summer barbecue.

RIGHT: Mel, Wayne and baby Olivia.

THE GLAMOUR OF FILMING

'The hairnets were the worst bit for the men. Suddenly a swank of nineteenth-century Romantics was turned into a Grump of Nora Battys' (Paul Moriarty)

chapter 9

A CONVERSATION WITH COLIN FIRTH

How did you first become involved?

I was sent all six scripts at a point when I was finding script reading very difficult. Everything seemed unreadable, and so the last thing I thought I needed was six episodes of BBC costume drama, against which I had a prejudice. I was casting my mind back to the 1970s, when it was the last thing in the world I watched on television. I remembered it as stiff – stiff acting, stiff adaptations.

Had you ever read any Jane Austen before?

No, not a page. Nineteenth-century literature didn't seem very sexy to me. I had this prejudice that it would probably be girls' stuff. I had always been rather attracted to the tormented European novels, partly as a reaction against what you're served up at school. So, when *Pride and Prejudice* was offered, I just thought, without even having read it, 'Oh, that old war horse,' and I unwrapped the huge envelope with great trepidation. The other anxiety is devoting so much time to something; I think a lot of actors flinch at making such a long commitment. So there were lots of reasons why I didn't want to open the first page, but I think I was only about five pages in when I was hooked. It was remarkable. I didn't want to go out until it was finished. I don't think any script has fired me up quite as much, just in the most basic, romantic-story terms. You *have* to read on to know what happens next. You fall in love with the characters instantly, and Jane Austen is an amazing tease; she has a capacity to frustrate you in a very positive way. She'll place a series of possibilities in front of you and then divert you. Also, I hadn't realized how funny *Pride and Prejudice* is, how witty and light and how far from 'homework' it is to read.

And when I first went to meet Sue Birtwistle I hadn't had time to read the end of Episode Six. I didn't know anything about Jane Austen, and I didn't know that she ended the story happily. Sue actually spoiled it for me because she let slip that Darcy and Elizabeth get married. And

OPPOSITE: 'He is a most disagreeable man; so high and so conceited' (Mrs Bennet on Darcy).

I was rather surprised because, not knowing the story at all, I could easily imagine that something was going to go wrong; it is a very charged situation. You can read that book about three or four times and still wonder each time whether it's going to work out.

So why did you hesitate?

I knew that I had to listen to the voice inside me which said, 'You enjoyed this. It's the only script you've been able to read for a long time.' I had to take that seriously. But then the other thing was that I didn't feel I was right for Darcy. I didn't feel I would be able to make him what he should be. He seemed too big a figure somehow.

I had never realized that Darcy was such a famous figure in literature. I mean, I didn't know the book and had never heard anyone really talk about it. But then, when I mentioned it, everyone would tell me how they were devoted to this book, how at school they had been in love with Darcy, and my brother said, 'Darcy? Isn't he supposed to be sexy?' So I heard these things and started to think, 'Oh, God, Olivier was fantastic and no one else could ever play the part.'

Darcy watches Elizabeth: 'Darcy had never been so bewitched by any woman as he was by her' (Jane Austen).

But the doubt came from more than that. Darcy's rather fascinating – he's terribly exciting on the page – but at first I didn't think he was written from an inner perspective at all. Jane Austen writes from the women's point of view – in this book, specifically from Elizabeth's point of view. Darcy is created to be an enigma through much of the story, until near the end, where you get his perspective. I just didn't feel it was personal to me at all. I did not know how to make it specific to me as an actor. It's just impossible to play an image because that's an external thing. So I began to think that it was impossible; that I would let everyone down and frustrate myself because I wouldn't be able to do enough to turn Colin into Darcy.

And yet the paradox is that you can't do very much when playing that part anyway; he doesn't ever do very much, and that felt like a trap. I reasoned: 'To make myself different enough to play Darcy, I will have to do an awful lot. But doing anything is the last thing that is right for playing Darcy. The only way for it to work is to be Darcy already.' I looked in the mirror and I didn't see Darcy. I know one can be brave and try to stretch oneself, but one also has to be sensible about what is realistic. I didn't feel capable of it, so I thought it best to say 'no'.

What made you change your mind?

Sue's conviction that I was right for it was so strong that I just had to re-consider. And in reading it again, the script started to weave its spell on me; it insidiously sucked me in – it's so seductive and intoxicating. I didn't realize that was happening, but once you start to develop an involvement with something like this, it gets under your skin, and it stops being such a matter of choice. I agonized and imagined myself doing it, and then tested the notion of not doing it, and it occurred to me that I would feel rather bereaved if I turned it down. I realized that I had begun to appropriate the character and I now owned it. The thought of anyone else doing it made me feel rather jealous.

What was the read-through like? Crispin Bonham-Carter remembers being so nervous he went straight to the gents and found you groaning in there.

I knew I had been caught by somebody! It was utterly terrifying and nerve-racking because not only is it a tremendously large number of people to take the plunge with suddenly, and to read it with, but the stakes are very high too. It's a huge shoot. We're all going to be on this for five months, and you're worried that you're being judged. It felt a bit like a great audition for everybody. The other thing that I realized at that read-through was that I really wouldn't relish playing Darcy on the radio. The physical dimension is essential. He's basically a taciturn person, and what he doesn't say is much more important than what he does a lot of the time. In film, of course, we can cut to his face and see him even when he's not speaking. But you can't do that on the radio or at the read-through; you can't say, 'Everybody, wait a minute because I'm going to do this, and it's going to be – nothing.' And I was surrounded by all these fantastic characters making everyone laugh, and I was thinking, 'Well, I was dull, wasn't I?'

Not a soul came up to me. I knew one or two people and talked to them, but I would say out of a cast of over fifty people, very few seemed willing to talk to me. I think because I was playing Darcy I had to work quite hard to convince people that I would be friendly during filming.

Andrew Davies says that he wanted to convey that there is more to Darcy than we at first think. How did you try to communicate this?

You really can't walk into a room and start acting your socks off, and doing all sorts of ambitious things, because Darcy wouldn't do that. But *not* doing anything is one of the most difficult things about acting. I remember thinking before I started that I was going to have to get together a very lively, dynamic, varied performance and then not act it. For example, in that first assembly-room scene I have to go in and be hurt, angry, intimidated, annoyed, irritated, amused, horrified, appalled, and keep all these reactions within this very narrow framework of being

Lizzy: 'Your defect is a propensity to hate everybody.' Darcy: 'And yours is wilfully to misunderstand them.'

'Bingley was sure of being liked wherever he appeared, Darcy was continually giving offence' (Jane Austen).

inscrutable because nobody ever knows quite what Darcy's thinking. I've played some far more physically energetic parts, but I don't think that I've ever been as physically exhausted at the end of a take as I have with Darcy.

I remember this particularly from the scene where Elizabeth and I have the argument at Netherfield: Darcy's emotional and doesn't want her to know it, he hates her because he fancies her, he hates her for being cleverer than he is during this particular conversation, and he's got the Bingleys as an audience. So there are a million things going on inside him, yet he has to keep himself together and not show that he is in the slightest bit ruffled; he mustn't reveal his turmoil. So he sits there, as still and calm as his emotions can possibly allow. Technically, you just try to assume all that and then play against it.

What was the most difficult part of the process?

The thing I disliked most about the filming was the inevitable fact that Darcy is absent from a lot of it and therefore I was going to have big breaks to deal with. I felt that a wonderful momentum started up in the first month, and the film seemed to be stretching out in front of us to infinity, and everything was possible – and suddenly I was banished for five weeks. It was awful. I had the odd day to do in the middle of that period, and I came down to location, and all these other people were there, whom I didn't know at all, doing another film that seemed to be about a family of girls. I felt just a bit of an outsider really – and, of course, that's what Darcy is in that part of the story. I remember saying, 'I want to come down, even if I'm not filming, so I can keep the part turning over.'

And then when you start filming again there's the fear that whatever magic spell you wove on yourself isn't going to happen again this time. These things are so amorphous. Then two weeks would go by and I was sent off again. It did interfere tremendously, I think, with my sense of being part of it. I found keeping the momentum going very difficult, right to the end. It's a huge cast, and there are all sorts of people I never really connected with simply because I never worked with them, and my character had absolutely no relationship with theirs. The filming schedule sets you slightly apart.

Did Andrew's scripts help you to understand Darcy's character?

Yes, I think they were a wonderful way into Jane Austen because he doesn't have that absurd, academic reverence that people sometimes have for a great work of literature. He treated it like a vastly enjoyable story. Had I started with the novel, I might not have become involved.

I think Andrew's earthiness, and the fact that he sometimes made things a lot more specific than Jane Austen does, were very helpful. He offers very strong suggestions as to what Darcy is thinking when he's looking, poker-faced, at the people in a crowd scene, and that helps Darcy to become more than simply an image.

What's interesting when you're doing a part like this is if you can find fluidity from moment to moment. When something is somehow not truthful, it jars because you've got to try to force your imagination to think up justifications for what you're doing. I never had to do that with Darcy – or very rarely – and it suddenly hit me that Jane Austen really did have an instinctive grasp of Darcy's inner self, even though she didn't have the arrogance to write it. But she writes the outer man so logically that the inside 'plays'.

Darcy: 'I have been meditating on the very great pleasure which a pair of fine eyes in the face of a pretty woman can bestow.'

Can you think of a specific example?
I remember thinking that it makes sense when Darcy slights Elizabeth at the Meryton assembly. I agree to go to a party with my friend Bingley. He encourages me: 'Come on, it'll be a great party with lots of women.' I arrive. I'm terribly shy – terribly uneasy in social situations anyway. This is not a place I'd normally go to, and I don't know how to talk to these people. So I protect myself behind a veneer of snobbishness and rejection. Bingley immediately engages with the most attractive woman in the room, and that makes me feel even less secure. He comes bounding over with a big, enthusiastic smile and tells me I should be dancing. I say, 'You've got the best-looking girl in the room,' and he replies, 'Well, never mind – what about the less attractive sister?' and this exacerbates the position I've put myself in. Then I say, 'She's okay, but not good enough for me,' but what I'm really saying is: 'Look, I'm supposed to be better than you, so don't give me the plain sister. I'm not even going to consider her.' By keeping this in mind when filming, I found that the scene actually played itself.

At the end of the story Darcy tells Lizzy that he doesn't know when he first fell in love with her. But you would have needed to plot his journey more specifically.
Yes, it's very interesting to watch out for the triggers that lead to Darcy's falling in love. Of course, love often starts with something trivial that attracts your attention. In Darcy's case, very little had ever attracted his attention. So I think the first trigger is the moment when Elizabeth rejects him so impertinently – when she overhears him saying, 'She's tolerable, I suppose, but not handsome enough to tempt *me*.' When she walks past and gives him a cheeky look, Andrew was very helpful here

Darcy visits Elizabeth at Hunsford Parsonage: 'He seemed astonished on finding her alone … and when her inquiries after Rosings were made, seemed in danger of sinking into total silence.'

in writing: 'Darcy was used to looking at other people like that, but was not used to being looked at like that himself.' So at that moment, I think, he notices her simply out of bewilderment and curiosity; he becomes intrigued by her, which, I suspect, is the first time he has ever been intrigued by a woman, and he has to know a little bit more about her. It strikes me that you can be on a fatal course from a moment like that whether you know it or not.

Darcy starts to show his interest in Elizabeth during the Lucases' party, when he asks her to dance and she refuses. What did you feel was happening to him at this stage?

Up to this point I don't think Darcy has ever really looked at a woman – I mean looked with real eyes, with real interest – though he's admired women in a casual way. The truth is that he's very bored. He's one of the richest men in England, and until now that's always been enough to make him attractive to women. I remember reading a very helpful saying: 'A man who is eligible needs to entertain no one.' For me, that was a great key to understanding Darcy – I thought that if he were charming as well, life could be intolerable for him. So out of both shyness and a lack of necessity he remains aloof. Then Elizabeth comes along and actually gives him a chance to respond, and it's probably the first opportunity he's ever had in his life to be the pursuer rather than the pursued: it's irresistible. That's when he first notices her eyes. What starts off as intriguing becomes profoundly erotic for him.

And she finally does agree to dance with him at the Netherfield ball...

Yes. I think the sequence where they dance together is wonderful because it lays out the whole of their relationship at that point perfectly. We see an honesty and playfulness in Elizabeth, while there's something slightly comical about Darcy trying to maintain his formal manner while holding up his end of the repartee. She'll say something that stings him, and he has an entire eight-step circle to do before he is permitted to respond.

Jane Austen offers some clues here as to Darcy's resolution to hold back and cure himself of this 'madness' he's just contracted, but he's in over his head before he realizes what has happened. To begin with, it was a bit of sport. And then suddenly he's feeling vulnerable and resents it bitterly. Several times he decides that he is going to pull himself together, and this is when his behaviour becomes rather confusing and paradoxical – he's pursuing and rejecting Elizabeth at the same time.

'Mr Darcy took her so much by surprise in his application for her hand that, without knowing what she did, she accepted him.'

He's certain he won't dance with her, and then he asks her to dance; he waits in places where he knows he'll find her walking and then doesn't speak to her; he shows up at Hunsford Parsonage and then acts as if she had called on him.

You had to film Darcy's first proposal scene in the second week of filming. How did that affect you?

It seemed a catastrophe at first. Everybody knows how important the scene is. For scheduling reasons we had to film a lot of Darcy's later scenes first – where he appears a much nicer person – and then do this scene with him at breaking point. Because it's so inappropriate to do it early and it's so nerve-racking, we gave it a tremendous amount of attention and got a degree of adrenalin working up to it, so that perhaps it's invested with something that it would never have had if we had done it later, when everyone had settled in. It was a case of jumping in at the deep end, and Simon Langton handled it brilliantly.

How did you approach this scene?

I asked myself some extremely basic questions about what it was I wanted to do in the scene. I asked, 'What's my character trying to get?' and then, 'How will he overcome any obstacles that are in the way?' In this case, the main question was: 'How is Elizabeth going to make it difficult for me, and how am I going to make it difficult for myself?' If you address problems like these, you come up with ways and means that help to make the approach clear.

I felt, for instance, that when Darcy goes into that room and says those shocking things – 'I'm too good for you, but will you marry me anyway?' – if I played it as if I knew I were being shocking and arrogant, it would never work. I realized that I had to make it the most reasonable thing in the world to say, but I wondered, 'How do I do that? How do I turn that extraordinary speech about her family connections being utterly disastrous into something reasonable?' And I thought, 'Okay, let's think ourselves into the time for a moment, into 1813,' and from Jane Austen's perspective this business about appropriate and inappropriate marriages made an awful lot of sense. It might be a disaster to cross class barriers; it could lead to all sorts of misery and unhappiness; the social fabric of the time was threatened by it, and so on.

He is also arrogant enough to think he has bestowed an enormous gift on her. Every woman he has ever met would say 'yes' to a proposal from him. It would be insane for Lizzy to say 'no', not because he assumes she finds him attractive – I don't think that's the reason – but because it's the most practical offer that even someone considerably her social superior could ever hope to receive. I think he assumes, as everybody would at that time, that it would be a Cinderella ending for her.

And so Darcy is coming in with a very imprudent proposal, as he

'I believe we must have some conversation, Mr Darcy. A very little will do,' says Lizzy.

Lizzy refuses Darcy's proposal:'Mr Darcy, who was leaning against the mantelpiece with his eyes fixed on her face, seemed to catch her words with no less resentment than surprise ... he was struggling for the appearance of composure' (Jane Austen).

'He needs to show her in about three minutes flat that he is prepared to be apologetic and tender and amenable and unsnobbish' (Colin Firth on Darcy's meeting with Elizabeth at Pemberley).

Meryton society decided that Darcy was 'the proudest, most disagreeable man in the world, and everybody hoped he would never come there again'.

sees it. He's saying to her, 'I'm going to put to you a proposal that may make me seem rash, irresponsible and even, possibly, juvenile, but I don't want you to believe I'm those things. I have thought through every detail of this; I know that my family will be angry, that people will frown on us and that our social positions are very different. So don't think that I haven't dealt with these issues – don't imagine that I'm just some reckless schoolboy. Nevertheless, having thought it all through, I find that my love for you is so overwhelming that these objections are rendered insignificant.' And, from that point of view, it's a terribly romantic proposal. I was a bit hurt when we filmed it, and everybody thought I was saying something terrible: I had got myself so far into the notion that he had come in with a really charming thing to say. Of course, when you watch it, you don't see it from his point of view. You see a self-important man entering and expressing these pompous sentiments as if they were the most natural reactions in the world and then having the gall to be astonished by Elizabeth's rejection – and I think that's right. But I couldn't have played that astonishment without approaching it the way I did.

He doesn't see her again until he unexpectedly runs into her at Pemberley. What's he trying to do at this stage?
Jane Austen is rather vague in her description of Darcy during this period, and I found myself foraging for clues about how he is supposed to come across. There are contradictions. People often ask whether Darcy changes in the course of the story or whether we find out what he is really like. I think it is a mixture of the two. His housekeeper talks affectionately of him and reveals that he has always looked after his sister and taken care of his household in a very kindly way. He hasn't suddenly turned into a good man; I think that he has always been a good man underneath that stiff exterior.

I realized that when he runs into Elizabeth at Pemberley he needs to prove a great deal to her in a short space of time. He needs to show her in about three minutes flat that he is prepared to be apologetic and tender and amenable and unsnobbish. He's just got to get a foot in the door and prove that he has tried to change those aspects of his nature that alienated her before. He wants her to love him: but how do you make somebody love you in just a few minutes? And how do you do that while still being true to Darcy's character?

Does Lizzy's rejection effect any real changes in Darcy, then?
Oh, yes. You cannot think that Darcy is simply going to return to the way he was. The fact that he writes her a letter explaining himself and

disclosing some very personal information – which is ostensibly a tremendously out-of-character thing to do – suggests this. I think he suffers enormously as a result of her rejection because he loves her. I think he endures torment because a lifetime's behaviour, even his very character, has been thrown into relief by her words.

His real crime, I think, is silliness. I know that's a terribly undignified way to look at him, but I believe his failing is foolish, superficial, social snobbery, and that's the bitter lesson he has to learn. And I think in that sense he does change. He actually says in the book that his father instilled in him good values but also taught him to think meanly of the world outside his own social circle. He is rather afraid of anything outside his immediate experience and is quite convinced that he will encounter nothing but barbarianism. People do make assumptions about other areas of civilization, and that's precisely what Darcy does. It's ignorance.

He learns his lesson when he falls in love with one of those barbarians and realizes that she's at least his equal, if not his superior, in terms of wit, intellectual agility and sense of personal dignity. He is so profoundly challenged by her that his old prejudices cannot be upheld. I still think he'll always have something of the old view – he'll always be disgusted by ridiculous, boring people who talk too much. I don't think he'll ever learn to adore Mrs Bennet or develop an enormous admiration for Sir William Lucas.

And, of course, he hasn't quite learned to laugh at himself. He's learned to criticize himself, which is probably the first step, but he doesn't yet know how to find himself ridiculous and enjoy it. With Lizzy as a partner, however, married life will be a matter of survival, and it's plain that he's going to learn *that* lesson before too long.

Elizabeth accepts Darcy's second proposal: 'The happiness which this reply produced was such as he had probably never felt before; and he expressed himself on the occasion as sensibly and as warmly as a man violently in love can be supposed to do' (Jane Austen).

Lizzy: 'It is settled between us already that we are to be the happiest couple in the world.'

$\mathcal{P}$OST-PRODUCTION

With the filming completed, work is over for most of the film unit. They will need anything from a few days in order to reinstate locations or return props to a few weeks to complete the paperwork but, essentially, when filming finishes, so does most of the team.

The cutting room then becomes the centre of the production and editor Peter Coulson and his team have to turn the 1,385 filmed takes into the six edited episodes that will be seen on the television screen.

The schedule has already been worked out, starting from when Peter joined together the first film at the beginning of the shoot and ending with the delivery of the final product, but as Fee McTavish, post-production associate producer, comments: 'Nothing in this schedule is set in concrete except the delivery dates. With six episodes, there are many ways this process can be organized, and things shift constantly. We decided to do the rough cuts of all six episodes first and then concentrate on the first three, completing all of the processes of sound effects, music recordings, negative cutting, picture grading, opening titles and closing credits and delivering to our co-producer in America. We would then repeat the procedure with the last three episodes. All of this had to be done within the budget and by the agreed delivery date.'

PETER COULSON DESCRIBES THE PROCESS OF EDITING

Occasionally when asked what I do, I say, 'Well, in a sense it's not unlike editing a newspaper because I take the material and paste it in a different order to give it a certain sense, or pace, or style.'

I met Simon to discuss the style of the film: what I found most interesting was the fresh approach, so unlike the usual 'Victorian' style of doing it. We talked about the overall structure and what we felt was the main thrust of the story. The marvellous thing about Andrew's scripts is that he gives you a real insight into what each scene is about and who's at the centre of it. This is important because the most difficult thing about editing is knowing when to cut to a particular character. A series of shots can be cut in an infinite number of ways. They can be cut together very simply, whereby you always cut to the person who's speaking, but that doesn't always allow you to see other characters' reactions or reveal secondary action. We

Peter Coulson in the cutting room.

Peter and Julius sort and view the rushes.

discussed the fact that we mustn't just chase the direct story, because the motor of the plot is the relationship of Darcy and Lizzy, and that we wanted to keep it pacy to offset the amount of dialogue.

EDITING DURING FILMING

From the shoot, the first material we get is picture and sound from the film unit. We view this material in the morning and synch up the picture and the sound, using the clapper board as our signal, so that you get simultaneous picture and sound, which are called 'synch rushes'. We send a video copy to Sue and Simon and we look at the original. We select what we feel are the good performances, and from the continuity notes we get comments from Simon about the shots, like 'Don't use that mid-shot, it never worked' or 'Her close-up is wonderful.'

A matter of lighting or a certain performance might have changed the way the scene was played from the way it was written or the way the director envisaged it, so we try to make a merit of that. In *Pride and Prejudice* it was always a case of looking for the best performance and this might change the way the scene was structured.

For example, there is a panning shot of Lizzy at the beginning of the scene in which she tries to urge Mr Bennet to prevent Lydia from going to Brighton. There is also a shot of Mr Bennet, who's speaking as Lizzy walks to and fro. There were two takes – one where she went in and out of frame slowly because of the way she was playing her off-screen performance and another where she was striding very fast across it. Ben Whitrow reacted wonderfully to her pacing, so it seemed right to start the scene with that take before moving back to see both of them in a wide shot.

THE NETHERFIELD BALL

There was a huge error in one shot of Lizzy during the dance: a hair had been trapped in front of the lens of the camera and was sticking down into the picture, which meant that a lot of it was unusable. So we had to rely on the Steadicam shot more than we wanted to. There were only three shots available: the Steadicam shot, which moves in among the dancers, a close-up of Darcy and a close up of Lizzy from the static cameras. To cut together a sequence like that is very complicated, and it took the best part of a week. It isn't the amount of the material that determines how long the editing takes – another quite lengthy scene could perhaps be cut in half a day – it's the complexity of the shots.

With the ball and the Meryton assembly, we were dealing with playback to music, which is hell for them on location and hell for us in the cutting room, but the end result of such scenes can be marvellous when the dialogue, action and music combine to give a wonderful driving force through the scene.

THE STAGES OF EDITING

In addition to performance, I look for pace and rhythm and try to keep my mind focused on the story that each scene is telling. I also have to keep an eye on the structure of the whole film because if you lose sight of that, it won't make sense. This is not easy with six hours of film.

There are four stages in putting the pictures together. The first is the 'assembly', which is the trial run of what's been shot. Then we go to a 'rough cut', which gives us a much better sense of the time and the shape of each of the six episodes. At this stage, the filming is finished and Simon joins us. We go through each episode in detail, tidying it up, and arrive at the 'director's cut', which is then shown to Sue. Because we rotated the editing of the six episodes, we managed to build in more thinking time. Simon and Sue could work together on one episode without delaying things in the cutting room. In this way, we reached a 'fine cut', which was then viewed by the executive producer and the writer.

There is still time to make changes, if necessary, but soon after this stage, it's all torn from our hands and taken over by the sound department, the composer and the labs.

THE TECHNICAL PROCESS

Film used to be cut with old scissors and joined with cement in a very laborious, factory-like manner, but these days we use a simple joiner, which cuts and tapes the film and the sound together. Using a white wax pencil, we make marks all over the film to indicate which parts of shots we will use. We then cut those shots out and literally stick them together. That's our basic equipment. In addition, we have a machine called a Steenbeck, which we use to view this film and the cut sequences, and we have a synchronizer for working on the more complicated editing.

Because of the requirements of television and the way pictures are scanned in this country, the film was shot at twenty-five frames per second. There are three film sizes used in film and television. The traditional one for cinema is 35-mm film, which is very high-quality. In television, it was once usual to shoot on 16-mm but, by carefully opening up the gate of ordinary 16-mm film, more picture or negative area is made available so that you can achieve nearly the same quality as you can on 35-mm at a fraction of the cost. This film is called 'Super 16', and it gives a much nicer image for the eye than the usual square television one. That's what we used on *Pride and Prejudice*.

The picture is shot on to negative in the

The editing process.

The material is logged and stored.

Pride and Prejudice
Post Production Recording Notes

NOTES FOR ANDREW DAVIES

Following meeting at Anvil, 12-12-94

EPISODE ONE
P.6   Additional dialogue for Mrs Bennet, to cover cut into hall
P.11   Additional chatter for Mrs Bennet and the girls outside the house to
          cover Mr Bennet crossing the hall
P.31   Additional line for Bingley as he takes his leave of Mrs Bennet and
          girls - "Pray, excuse me" or similar
P.33   Chatter to cover shots of Mrs Bennet "holding court"

EPISODE TWO
P.19   Another line for Kitty about the bonnet in the shop window
P.24   Additional line for Collins before his first speech
P.26 on   Additional b/g dialogue for Collins at the card table
P.46   Possibly need f/g speech for Mrs Hurst to cover Miss Bingley's
          greeting Jane

EPISODE THREE
P.8   Need to add "my brother" or similar to "Charles"

EPISODE FOUR
P.6   Additional dialogue between Collins, Charlotte and Lady Catherine to
          show that supper is going on
P.44   Extra dialogue required for Charlotte

EPISODE FIVE
P.20   Background whispering between Darcy and Georgiana
P.38   Extend Jane's V/O to cover gap after "I cannot think so ill of him".
          (Also - extend it all the way through to cover Elizabeth's lines?)

EPISODE SIX
P.12   Rewrite Mrs Bennet's 1st oov speech

Post-synch dialogue from Andrew Davies.

camera. For viewing, we make a positive reproduction of that negative image and that is what we physically cut and join. When the editing is completed, our cutting copy goes off to people called 'neg cutters', who, using a synchronizer, cut the original negative exactly the way we have cut our copy. Then it goes to the laboratories, where a grader takes the negative and puts it under an analyser to adjust the colour for the vagaries of lighting and shooting conditions. This is then printed and taken to the machine called the 'telecine', which projects the image into an electronic medium; this will make the copy that is actually transmitted on television.

The only problems with this production came from the sheer scale of it. There were reels and reels of rushes – somewhere in the region of 1,500 different images, varying in length from a few seconds to a few minutes.

TEAM WORK

Given the large volume of work involved in the editing process, the assistant film editors played a crucial role in ensuring the smooth running of the cutting room. First assistant film editor Julius Gladwell explains how it worked. 'I'm responsible for liaising with the laboratory and sound-transfer house, synching up the daily rushes, marking the film for dissolves and fades, video transferring, making opticals, ordering reprints of damaged film and supervising the second assistant's duties.

'To speed up the editing process, I assembled some of the scenes, and made numerous picture and sound changes. The sequences are arranged in many different ways and, after discussions with the editor, director and producer, I take notes and make alterations. Some shots needed a helping hand: for example, one of the location owners had mowed a part of the lawn so it had modern stripes on it. I had to disguise this with an instant hedge, which we produced optically. In the wedding scene there was a stained-glass window behind the vicar that was clearly Victorian; it had to be toned down to disguise its origin.'

Second assistant Clare Brown provides additional back-up. 'I perform the tasks that the first assistant doesn't want to do and the editor wouldn't dream of doing. Every day the cutting room is deluged with thousands of feet of film and sound. I number, log and store away every piece of it, so that, months later, when the editor's shouting, 'Get that close-up of Georgiana in Ramsgate,' I should be able to find it quickly among the other 1,500 shots.

'If we're due to screen an episode in the preview theatre for the production team, then I'll check all the joins in the film to make sure the film won't snap in the middle and cover up bad scratches with a felt-tip pen. This is when my job becomes slightly bizarre. How many people do you know who spend their day scribbling over Colin Firth's face with a Pentel?'

SOUND DIALOGUE

Once all the film is cut together, the sound team takes over. Mike Feinberg is the dialogue editor, and it is his job to 'smooth out' the dialogue that was recorded on location. 'We have to make sure that the audience is not distracted by dramatic changes in sound level. We must create the illusion of smooth or continuous dialogue. There may have been takes in which extraneous noise makes the dialogue unacceptable. Perhaps over part of the shot we can hear a plane or motorway noise. Normally if this happened, one

Jennifer Ehle post-synching some lines.

would immediately reshoot the scene, but sometimes there is no time or the director considers the performance better in the first take even though there are sound problems. If the track can be cleaned up, the original recording will be used. If this is impossible, some of the dialogue may have to be re-recorded (or "post-synched"). This is done in a studio, and the actors have the difficult job of matching the words to the movement of their own lips, which they can see on a large screen. At these sessions we also record crowd noises and other sound effects we might still need.'

EFFECTS

John Downer is the sound editor. 'I have to add ambience and atmosphere to the original dialogue in order to create a fuller, richer texture of sound. For example, when Jane rides to Netherfield in the rain, I can lay the sound of thunder to add an extra dimension. All these effects, which include teacups clinking on saucers and fires crackling, have to be recorded on a separate track, which is called the "footsteps track", so when the film is sold to other countries, they can dub on the dialogue in their own language, without losing all the sound effects.'

DUBBING

The final member of the sound team is Rupert Scrivener, who is the dubbing mixer. Mike and John will present him with twenty-four separate tracks each of dialogue and of effects. He has to combine all of these, plus the recorded music, on the final sound track that will be

The telecine suite where the film is transferred on to tape for television transmission.

heard on television. 'I do this digitally on a computer. This means that no sound quality is lost as it goes through the processes, and you can't hear the "joins" as you used to. Music also sounds better; with big orchestral pieces there was always the problem of sound flutter. Any long, sustained note, like a church bell, would "wobble" a bit as it played. I balance all the dialogue and effects tracks and layer them to give them a good stereo effect. The music is the last to be added and the final track should then appear seamless.'

One of the many storyboards suggested for the opening titles.

Simon and Sue choosing the lettering for the opening titles.

OPENING TITLES: Liz Friedman and John Salisbury

The title sequence has to contain at least the name of the programme and, usually, the names of leading actors, writer, director and producer. For one-off films, this information can be placed over the beginning of the story but, with a series or serial, a specially made sequence is designed that can go at the front of each episode. It should set the mood without attempting to tell the whole story. The brief here was to do something lively and bright to match the adaptation, while still recognizing that it is a period piece. It was decided to go for an almost abstract treatment of some of the costumes used in the programme. These were mounted on moving dummies and filmed in close-up at different exposures by a 35-mm camera moving in another direction. This gives a stylized but vivacious image to complement the music. The most difficult part is relating the credits to the visual images.

PUBLICITY

By May 1995 all six episodes were completed and ready for transmission. At this stage the process of planning screenings for the press and the promotion of the programme began in earnest.

PICTURE PUBLICITY: Patricia Taylor

I'm responsible for making sure that the BBC has an excellent set of photographs with which to publicize drama series and serials. I read the scripts, decide with the producer which are the key scenes and arrange to photograph these during filming. This allows us to take a variety of photographs that reflect the atmosphere of the drama. But we also need the posed shots. Actors hate doing these, and I recognize that it's inconvenient for them to be interrupted in the middle of a busy filming day. But it's important because we need to tell people when it's being broadcast – and the best way to do that is to have a number of magazine front covers on the newsagents' shelves in the week of transmission.

With *Pride and Prejudice* we were fortunate because Sue put aside one special day in the schedule for photography, which is unusual. This meant that artists were there solely to have their photographs taken and weren't being pulled away by the 1st AD because they were needed to shoot a scene. We had lots of photographers from a wide variety of newspapers and magazines. We allowed them to release only one photograph in the next day's papers – a shot of Darcy and Elizabeth. The rest of the pictures we asked them to keep until transmission.

PRESS OFFICER: Peter Mares

My job is to get the best publicity in the right papers and magazines at the right time and to keep out the stories that we may not want printed. If a story appears that is factually incorrect, then I will try to squash it before it becomes accepted as the truth.

This project was rather unusual in that there had already been a lot of press coverage of it before it even started filming. So Sue and I had a meeting to plan a strategy. She gave me all the cuttings, and, as she'd predicted, the phone started ringing very early on: the first questions were always about 'the nude Darcy scene'. Journalists can be quite lazy. They sometimes don't bother to check facts; they simply regurgitate what they've read in the cuttings file, even when it's not true.

At this stage we were trying to minimize the publicity, because it was far too early and people would start to wonder if they were ever going to see *Pride and Prejudice*. But it is important to have material ready for the few weeks leading up to transmission. It's possible for actors to be interviewed at that time, but one can't guarantee that they will be available. So we arrange some interviews with actors during filming, and these take advantage of the 'colour' of a visit to location.

Of course, it's difficult to orchestrate these interviews during filming, and some actors find it very difficult to split their concentration in this way. But we do need to have the material to build interest in the programme immediately before transmission. If we want coverage in the monthly magazines, then we have to plan that perhaps five months ahead. At the beginning of autumn a short excerpt from the film will be shown at the BBC Drama Launch. This is the first time anyone not involved in the production will have seen some of the material. A brochure with photographs and copy will also be sent to all journalists. Nearer to transmission time I will organize preview screenings for the press. Sometimes we decide to screen all of the programme for a mixed audience of what are called 'opinion formers'. As there has already been so much reaction to this version of *Pride and Prejudice*, before a frame has been seen by anyone, it may be useful to have a serious debate in the press about it when the 'How Dare They . . . ?' letters are printed.

The press photo-shoot day.

APPENDIX

CAST

Mr Darcy	**Colin Firth**
Elizabeth Bennet	**Jennifer Ehle**
Mr Bennet	**Benjamin Whitrow**
Mrs Bennet	**Alison Steadman**
Jane Bennet	**Susannah Harker**
Lydia Bennet	**Julia Sawalha**
Mary Bennet	**Lucy Briers**
Kitty Bennet	**Polly Maberly**
Mr Bingley	**Crispin Bonham-Carter**
Miss Bingley	**Anna Chancellor**
Mrs Louisa Hurst	**Lucy Robinson**
Mr Hurst	**Rupert Vansittart**
Lady Catherine de Bourgh	**Barbara Leigh-Hunt**
Miss Anne de Bourgh	**Nadia Chambers**
Mr Collins	**David Bamber**
Wickham	**Adrian Lukis**
Sir William Lucas	**Christopher Benjamin**
Lady Lucas	**Norma Streader**
Charlotte Lucas	**Lucy Scott**
Maria Lucas	**Lucy Davis**
Georgiana Darcy	**Emilia Fox**
Fitzwilliam	**Anthony Calf**
Mr Gardiner	**Tim Wylton**
Mrs Gardiner	**Joanna David**
Alice Gardiner	**Natasha Isaacs**
Kate Gardiner	**Marie-Louise Flamank**
William Gardiner	**Julian Erleigh**
Robert Gardiner	**Jacob Casselden**
Mrs Phillips	**Lynn Farleigh**
Denny	**David Bark-Jones**
Colonel Forster	**Paul Moriarty**
Mrs Forster	**Victoria Hamilton**
Sanderson	**Christopher Staines**
Chamberlayne	**Tom Ward**
Mrs Reynolds	**Bridget Turner**
Sarah/maid	**Kate O'Malley**
Hill	**Marlene Sidaway**
Carter	**Roger Barclay**
Mary King	**Alexandra Howerd**
Mrs Jenkinson	**Harriet Eastcott**
Hannah/serving girl	**Sarah Legg**
Hodge	**Roy Holder**
Fossett	**Neville Phillips**
Priest	**Sam Beazley**
Maggie/maid	**Annabel Taylor**
Baines	**Peter Needham**
Fortepiano played by	**Melvyn Tan**

CREW CREDITS

Screenplay:	**Andrew Davies**
Music by:	**Carl Davis**
Casting:	**Fothergill and Lunn**
Choreography:	**Jane Gibson**
Assistant Choreographer:	**Jack Murphy**
First Assistant Directors:	**Pip Short**
	Amanda Neal
Production Manager:	**Paul Brodrick**
Location Managers:	**Sam Breckman**
	Clive Arnold
Continuity:	**Sue Clegg**
Production Coordinator:	**Janet Radenkovic**
Post-production P.A.:	**Sue Card**
Second Assistant Directors:	**Melanie Panario**
	Simon Bird
Third Assistant Directors:	**Sarah White**
	Anne-Marie Crawford
Contracts Executive:	**Maggie Anson**
Assistant Production Accountant:	**Elaine Dawson**
Production Secretary:	**Julia Weston**
Art Directors:	**Mark Kebby**
	John Collins
Set Dresser:	**Marjorie Pratt**
Properties:	**Sara Richardson**
Stand-by Props:	**Ron Sutcliffe**
	Mike Booys
Period Chef:	**Colin Capon**
Prop Master:	**Bob Elton**
Painters:	**Patrick Black**
	Dennis Ring

PREVIOUS PAGE: Filming the Christmas wedding.

Stand-by Carpenter:	**Joe Willmott**	Music Dubbing Mixer:	**Chris Dibble**
Stand-by Painter:	**Derek Honeybun**	Dubbing Editors:	**Mike Feinberg**
Construction Manager:	**Barry Moll**		**John Downer**
Production Operative Supervisor:	**Vic Young**	Dubbing Mixer:	**Rupert Scrivener**
Visual Effects Designer:	**Graham Brown**	Camera Operator:	**Roger Pearce**
Visual Effects Assistant:	**Mark Haddenham**	Hair and Make-up Designer:	**Caroline Noble**
Graphic Design:	**Liz Friedman**	Costume Designer:	**Dinah Collin**
	John Salisbury	Associate Producer:	**Julie Scott**
Costume Design Assistants:	**Kate Stewart**	(Post-production)	**Fiona McTavish**
	Yves Barre	Script Editor:	**Susie Conklin**
Wardrobe Master:	**Michael Purcell**	Film Editor:	**Peter Coulson**
Wardrobe Mistress:	**Donna Nicholls**	Production Designer:	**Gerry Scott**
Make-up Assistants:	**Philippa Hall**	Photography:	**John Kenway**
	Ashley Johnson	Executive Producer:	**Michael Wearing**
	Jenny Eades	Produced by:	**Sue Birtwistle**
	Di Wickens	Directed by:	**Simon Langton**
Focus Puller:	**Rob Southam**	Developed for television in association with	
Clapper/Loader:	**Adam Coles**	**Chestermead Ltd**	
Grip:	**Brendan Judge**		
Lighting Gaffer:	**Liam McGill**	A BBC/A & E Network Co-Production © BBC MCMXCV	
Best Boy:	**Phil Brookes**		
Electricians:	**Jimmy Bradshaw**		
	Joe Judge		
Transport Captain:	**Wayne Thompson**		
Sound Recordist:	**Brian Marshall**		
Boom Operator:	**Keith Pamplin**		
First Assistant Film Editor:	**Julius Gladwell**		
Second Assistant Film Editor:	**Clare Brown**		
Steadicam Operator:	**Alf Tramontin**		

Susie Conklin, Sue Birtwistle and Gerry Scott

Elizabeth's spirits soon rising to playfulness again, she wanted Mr Darcy to account for his having ever fallen in love with her. 'How could you begin?' she said.

'I cannot fix on the hour, or the spot, or the look, or the words, which laid the foundation. It is too long ago. I was in the middle before I knew that I had begun' (Jane Austen).

ABOUT THE AUTHORS

Sue Birtwistle started work as an actress with the Belgrade Theatre in Education Company in Coventry, before becoming Director of the Royal Lyceum Theatre in Education Company in Edinburgh. She was the founder director of the Nottingham Playhouse Roundabout Company. She served as a member of the Arts Council Drama Panel and toured many plays in Europe. She has written two plays for children. Her television credits as producer include the award-winning *Hotel du Lac* and Tony Harrison's 'v.'. She has also produced *Scoop, Dutch Girls, Or Shall We Die?, Educating Marmalade* (BAFTA nomination), *Ball-Trap on the Côte Sauvage, Oi for England*, the pilot programme of *Anna Lee*, the highly acclaimed *Pride and Prejudice* and *Emma*.

Sue Birtwistle lives in London with her husband, Richard Eyre, and has one daughter.

Susie Conklin grew up in the American south-west and studied English literature at Columbia University and Scottish and Irish literature at Aberdeen University. She worked as a publications editor in New York and as a freelance writer and sub-editor in London before joining BBC Television as a production trainee in 1989. After working on a variety of arts, education and documentary programmes, she moved to the drama department, where she script-edited *Middlemarch, Between the Lines* and *Pride and Prejudice*, and oversaw the 1995/96 season of films for Screen Two. She is currently a drama script associate at Granada Television.

The Making of Jane Austen's Emma is also published by Penguin.

ACKNOWLEDGEMENTS

The publishers would like to thank the following for providing photographs and for permission to reproduce copyright material. While every effort has been made to trace and acknowledge all copyright holders, we would like to apologize should there have been any errors or omissions.

The Hampshire County Council Museums Service
Mrs Hurst Dancing ('The Lord of the Manor and his family . . .')
The Museum of Costume, Bath
Museum of London
The National Art Library, Victoria & Albert Museum
Pictures copyright © Neville Ollerenshaw, 1981
Radio Times

Picture on the front of the filming schedule reproduced by kind permission of Glen Baxter copyright © 1995
The Guardian cartoon by kind permission of David Austin copyright © 1990

STILLS PHOTOGRAPHERS

Sven Arnstein
Christopher Baines
Joss Barrett
Michael Birt
Matthew Ford
Robert Hill
Fatimah Namdar
Jenny Potter
Catherine Shakespeare Lane
Stuart Wood
George Wright

The authors would like to thank the cast and crew for their co-operation in the writing of this book and the following for allowing their personal photographs to be used:

Colin Capon
Mark Kebby
Caroline Noble
Julia Sawalha
Lucy Davis
Polly Maberly
Gerry Scott
Lucy Scott

They would also like to thank warmly:

Ray Marsten and Valerie Yule of Ray Marsten Wig Studio and Jill Kelby and Jane McDonach of CosProp for allowing them to photograph them at work

Angela Horn of Luckington Court

Peter Mares for reading the material at an early stage and giving advice

Patricia Taylor for her help with the production photographs

Lucy Eyre

Peter Nurse for his watercolour of Rosings

Particular thanks are due to Pat Silburn and Julia Weston for all their support, hard work and encouragement and to Julie Martin, who designed the layout of the book.

The authors are especially indebted to Gerry Scott for her design advice, illustrations, and unstinting work on all the visual material and for sharing many late nights and early mornings so cheerfully.

CLA GRIL  ✗ UES TING

CLASSIC BARBECUES
GRILLS & OUTDOOR EATING

100 of the best barbecue and grill recipes
from around the world

From tempting appetizers to fabulous
ideas for fish, shellfish and meat, all shown
step by step in 350 sizzling photographs

Consultant Editor: Jan Cutler

This edition is published by Southwater, an imprint of Anness Publishing Ltd, Hermes House, 88–89 Blackfriars Road, London SE1 8HA
tel: 020 7401 2077; fax 020 7633 9499
www.southwaterbooks.com; www.annesspublishing.com

If you like the images in this book and would like to investigate using them for publishing, promotions or advertising, please visit our website www.practicalpictures.com for more information.

UK agent: The Manning Partnership Ltd; tel. 01225 478444; fax 01225 478440; sales@manning-partnership.co.uk
UK distributor: Grantham Book Services Ltd; tel. 01476 541080; fax 01476 541061; orders@gbs.tbs-ltd.co.uk
North American agent/distributor: National Book Network; tel. 301 459 3366; fax 301 429 5746; www.nbnbooks.com
Australian agent/distributor: Pan Macmillan Australia; tel. 1300 135 113; fax 1300 135 103; customer.service@macmillan.com.au
New Zealand agent/distributor: David Bateman Ltd; tel. (09) 415 7664; fax (09) 415 8892

Publisher: Joanna Lorenz
Editorial Director: Helen Sudell
Project Editor: Catherine Stuart
Recipe text: Linda Tubby and Jan Cutler
Design: Adelle Morris and Diane Pullen
Production Controller: Don Campaniello

ETHICAL TRADING POLICY
Because of our ongoing ecological investment programme, you, as our customer, can have the pleasure and reassurance of knowing that a tree is being cultivated on your behalf to naturally replace the materials used to make the book you are holding. For further information about this scheme, go to www.annesspublishing.com/trees

A CIP catalogue record for this book is available from the British Library.
Previously published as part of a larger volume, *180 Barbecues*, by Linda Tubby with contributions by Jan Cutler.

Main front cover image shows Vegetables in Coconut and Ginger Paste, p103.

NOTES

- Bracketed terms are for American readers.

- For all recipes, quantities are given in both metric and imperial measures and, where appropriate, in standard cups and spoons. Follow one set of measures, but not a mixture, because they are not interchangeable.

- Standard spoon and cup measures are level. 1 tsp = 5ml, 1 tbsp = 15ml, 1 cup = 250ml/8fl oz.

- Australian standard tablespoons are 20ml. Australian readers should use 3 tsp in place of 1 tbsp for measuring small quantities of gelatine, flour, salt, etc.

- The nutritional analysis given for each recipe is calculated per portion (i.e. serving or item), unless otherwise stated. If the recipe gives a range, such as Serves 4–6, then the nutritional analysis will be for the smaller portion size, i.e. 6 servings. Measurements for sodium do not include salt added to taste.

- Medium (US large) eggs are used unless otherwise stated.

CONTENTS

CLASSIC BARBECUE COOKING

Cooking *al fresco* has become so popular that, in many countries, the summer now plays host to a "barbecue season", with party invitations coming thick and fast. But while often associated with larger gatherings, a barbecue can be a delightfully spontaneous affair, with delicious food prepared and cooked quickly. In hotter climates, daily cooking takes place outdoors partly for practical reasons, as the heat makes it unbearable to cook inside. Yet the barbecue is a worldwide phenomenon, and this is perhaps because cooking takes on a completely different appeal when transferred outside. It becomes social, and that's probably the most important aspect of the barbecue today: sitting together and chatting, surrounded by the aroma of food cooking over open coals.

In countries where good weather prevails for much of the year, some families invest in prefabricated units that enable them to create a mini-kitchen outside until the weather turns cooler. For the less frequent cook, however, a little equipment can go a long way. The griddle, for example, is the perfect companion for a barbecue – it is ideal for quick-cooking all kinds of sumptuous light bites while the coals are red-hot. Larger dishes can then be cooked when the heat is less fierce.

Above: Sometimes the method of cooking contributes to the spectacle, as with this raffia-tied mackerel.

PLANNING A PARTY

If you are catering for larger numbers, there are certain things you should consider. How many people are attending, and will there be children? Light bites lend themselves well to all appetites, and an original yet broadly appealing selection of quick-to-cook nibbles could include Hot Avocado Halves, Butterfly Prawns, and Chilli and Herb Polenta. Kids will love savoury treats such as Ham Pizzettas with Mango or Grilled Chicken Balls.

There are likely to be at least a couple of vegetarians within a large group, so, in addition to perennial meaty favourites such as Home-made Burgers with Relish or Mixed Grill Skewers, be sure to include some substantial vegetarian mains on the menu. Tented foil packages offer an extremely useful way of cooking stuffed vegetables, as they preserve texture and juiciness while preventing the filling from spilling out! The vegetarian dishes in this book are likely to have broad appeal: Onions Stuffed with Goat's Cheese is a great example of how many textures – crispy, chewy, mouth-wateringly melting – can be combined within a simple package.

Have some popular party condiments on hand, too – for what is a barbecue without a Classic Pasta Salad or a home-made Blue Cheese Dip? Baked breads are excellent for soaking up juices, and they can either be prepared ahead or cooked on the barbecue itself. Saffron Bread Skewers – a flavoursome version of the campside favourite, damper – can be cooked on a heated rack in just five minutes. They look great spiked with rosemary stalks, too. Finally, round off the occasion with a sweet finale: Calvados-flamed Bananas are dramatic as well as delicious, while refreshing drinks such as Apple-spiced Beer are the perfect antidote to rich barbecue flavours.

TRY SOMETHING NEW

Admittedly, a large outdoor gathering might not be the best time to experiment, so while you have some warm, bright evenings at your disposal, try a little on-the-spot grilling for a partner, for family members, or for an impromtpu gathering of friends. Once you learn how versatile the barbecue can be, you can try out a world of different techniques. The key to success is not purely in the cooking, either. Many fish and meat dishes

Below: Butterfly Prawns served with a mild spicy dip make a perfect appetizer.

benefit from being marinated ahead of time, as this is essential for tenderizing texture and ensuring fullness of flavour. There are all kinds of tips on which marinades to use in the pages that follow, as well as ideas for dry rubs, glazes and butters.

You can then try your hand at all the different ways of cooking, from simple vegetable skewers such as Mushrooms with Garlic and Chilli Sauce to super-fast seared dishes such as Grilled Foie Gras. Fish can be easily cooked as whole fillets, though there are some colourful ways to package seafood – try, for example, the spectacular Giant Prawns Wrapped in Lime Leaves. When it comes to poultry and meat, you are spoilt for choice on approach – from popular drummers and kebabs to spicy coatings, spatchcocked treats and even spit-roasted joints. Although it requires a couple of hours to marinate, once mounted on a spit Barbecue Roast Beef takes less than thirty minutes to cook – and is delicious mopped with a rich, dark beer. Should this begin to sound a little indulgent, you can stay healthy and trim throughout the summer simply by replacing oily marinades with low-fat ones, by misting with oil, and by using lean meat or fish in your recipes.

Below: Summer Vegetable Kebabs are just one of the non-meat treats here.

SUCCESSFUL GRILLING

Barbecuing techniques have changed over the years and modern barbecues, too, have made cooking more efficient. The kettle barbecue, for example, has a lid and this helps to create an even temperature for cooking small items of

Above: Who can resist the exquisite allure of Tandoori Drumsticks?

food as well as whole joints. Use this book to help you choose the right barbecue for your requirements, and to understand the basics of setting up and cooking. Because barbecues come in all sizes and to suit all pockets, you can cook outside even if you have a fairly small space, as long as you are careful not to site the barbecue unsafely, such as under a garage door or a carport or within 3m/10ft of the house.

If you don't want to wait until summer to cook the delicious recipes in this book, remember that a number can be cooked indoors during cooler weather, under a grill (broiler), in the oven, or over the hob. However, it can't be denied that they will be extra special when cooked and eaten outside. As the juices of barbecued food drip on to the coals and form aromatic smoke, stimulating the appetite, there is just one universal rule when catering for a barbecue – cook plenty!

CHOOSING YOUR BARBECUE

Barbecuing food gives it a delicious smoky taste, but it is not the charcoal that flavours the food. When the food cooks, melted fat is released and drips on to the heat source. This then gives off smoke, which permeates the food. If you marinate the food first in herbs, or in spice-and-oil combinations, they will contribute to the taste, as will aromatic wood chips or herbs strewn over the charcoals or used in a smoking box in a gas barbecue. So, whether you choose a charcoal or a gas barbecue, you will still achieve fantastic flavours.

The main thing to consider when choosing your barbecue is how often you intend to use it. If you enjoy regular family meals *al fresco* or party barbecues in the garden, a larger one might be the best for you. If, however, you like to act spontaneously and light up a barbecue on the beach or in the countryside you will need something portable – and this smaller kind of barbecue would also be perfect if you plan to use a barbecue at home only occasionally. Remember that the larger barbecues will need to be stored somewhere dry when not in use, so you will most likely need a shed or a corner of the garage to tuck them away into.

CHARCOAL BARBECUES

Among the plethora of barbecues you will find in any showroom are the three basic types of charcoal barbecue. In the first category is the original small and compact Japanese hibachi, which is basically a firebox on short legs with a tray in the base to hold the coals. There are several rungs for the grill rack so that the height can be adjusted over the heat source. On some models, the lid opens to create a windshield at the back; and when closed the unit is easily transported.

Above: You can use an old grill rack to improvise a beach-style barbecue.

Also in this category are small disposable barbecues that contain their own coals set beneath a grill rack. The heat cannot be controlled so you must keep the food moving all the time, and it's best to choose food that cooks quickly for these easily portable all-in-one barbecues that are used just once.

The second category is the brazier type, which normally has an open firebox on a stand with a windshield at the back. The pedestal barbecue, made from stainless steel, comes into this category. It comprises a pillar that is packed with newspaper beneath a rounded bowl containing the coals and grill rack. When the paper is lit the coals soon ignite. Although pedestal barbecues look stylish, beware that the pillar gets very hot indeed and needs to be positioned on a stable and level flameproof surface.

The pot-bellied or barrel type of barbecue also comes into this second category. It is made from cast iron and has air vents to speed up the

Left: The Japanese-style hibachi barbecue is small, inexpensive and ideal for impromptu meals at home, or when planning an outing in the country.

burning process. The coals will be ready to use in 30 minutes. The grill rack can be adjusted to several heights.

The third category of barbecue is the kettle barbecue, which is made from steel and is usually round. It has a lid that can be lifted off and there are air vents in the firebox and the lid. Kettle barbecues come in a range of sizes and the smaller ones are portable. Because this has a lid it is probably the most efficient barbecue, as it enables you to cook either directly over the coals or indirectly (when the coals are pushed to either side of a drip tray) so that larger cuts of meat, such as whole chickens, can be cooked. With the lid on, the food cooks evenly in the all-round heat and this is beneficial for indirect and direct cooking.

GAS AND ELECTRIC BARBECUES

If you are not keen on the hands-on, getting-mucky-with-the-coals type of barbecuing, a gas or electric one will probably be a wise choice, as they are easy to use and efficient. You will still achieve the authentic barbecue aroma and taste with a gas barbecue because

Above: Brazier barbecues are popular with those seeking portable, fold-away barbecues, and their tall legs make them very accessible to the cook.

the juices from the food will drop on to the ceramic rocks, hot lava rocks, or vitreous enamelled steel bars, and once connected up to the gas bottle it is lit by the flick of a switch. You will find small portable ones as well as table-height versions that are easily moved around on their trolley units.

The heat from an electric barbecue comes from heated elements beneath the grill rack. Electric barbecues are probably the easiest to use and heat up almost immediately. The lack of smoke means that they are the only kind of barbecue viable for use inside. Quick and clean, they are, however, usually smaller than gas grills. If you decide on one, you will probably need to use an extension lead for cooking outside.

EQUIPMENT

For ease of cooking and safety, always use long-handled tools. Here are some of the most useful items of equipment.

Brushes

As well as using a long-handled basting brush, you can make herb brushes by tying together twigs of thyme, bay, rosemary or sage to give flavour to foods when basting. Soak them in oil for a few hours beforehand to flavour the oil.

Dishes

Use shallow, non-corrosive dishes and bowls for marinating that are large enough to hold the food in a single layer (do not use metal).

Drip trays

When cooking by indirect heat, place a metal drip tray beneath the food to catch the juices. You can use disposable foil trays or make your own from heavy-duty foil.

Foil

Heavy-duty foil is useful for making a lid if your barbecue does not have one. Use regular foil for wrapping food in parcels for cooking. Tented parcels can be used to gently steam many meat, fish and vegetable dishes – and are particularly useful for holding fragile foods, such as those with a filling.

Above: Make tented foil parcels to cook delicate foods such as stuffed vegetables.

Fork

Use a long-handled fork for lifting large pieces of meat from the barbecue.

Gloves or mitts

For the best protection choose oven gloves or mitts with a long sleeve.

Griddle

A cast-iron ridged griddle makes cooking small items of food on the barbecue easier. As it needs high heat, it is best to use it when the coals are first alight (or you can increase the heat if using a gas or electric barbecue).

Grills

Hinged wire grills are available to hold burgers, fish and small items. They come in a range of shapes and make turning easy and keep foods intact that might otherwise easily disintegrate.

Skewers

Keep a range of skewers in different thicknesses and lengths. Choose flat

Below: A large spatula made of wood or metal will help when turning hot foods.

Above: Metal skewers can be used to hold food in place during cooking.

metal skewers, as they will stop food from spinning round as you turn them. Try cocktail sticks (toothpicks) and wooden and bamboo skewers as well, but always soak them in water for 30 minutes before use.

Spatula

A wide spatula or pizza server with a long handle will make turning flat foods, such as steaks, easier.

Tongs

Use one pair of tongs for the coals, another pair for handling raw food and another for cooked food.

Trays

Metal trays are ideal for carrying raw food to the barbecue; keep others handy to hold the cooked food.

Wire brush

Use a stiff wire brush to clean the grill rack after cooking. Scrub clean with lots of hot soapy water.

Below: Use long-handled tongs for arranging hot coals.

SETTING UP YOUR BARBECUE

Have everything ready to hand before you set up the barbecue, including anything you need in case of accidents – see the Safety Tips opposite.

GETTING STARTED

Whichever type of barbecue you are using, always ensure it is stable before lighting it. For a gas barbecue check that you have enough fuel in the gas bottle before lighting up and follow the manufacturer's instructions carefully. Once switched on, the barbecue will be ready to use within about 15 minutes. Ensure that an electric barbecue is safely connected away from any patches of water before switching it on.

Charcoal barbecues are a little more involved to get started; understanding the properties of different types of fuel will help to ensure success. Lumpwood charcoal and charcoal briquettes are the most frequently used types of fuel and are ideal for all uses; wood, however, is less easy to use.

Lumpwood charcoal is usually made from softwood and comes in lumps of varying sizes, although the larger sizes are best. It is easier to ignite than briquettes but tends to burn up faster.

Charcoal briquettes will burn for a long time with the minimum of smell and smoke, although they can take a

Below: If using a fire chimney to light a barbecue, fill it with newspaper first.

little while to ignite. Use charcoal from sustainable managed forests; this will carry the FSC (Forest Stewardship Council) logo.

Self-igniting charcoal is simply lumpwood or briquettes that have been treated with a flammable substance. Always wait until the ignition agent has burnt off before cooking, or the smell may taint the food.

Wood

Hardwoods such as oak, apple, olive and cherry are best for barbecues, as they burn slowly with a pleasant aroma – which should keep everyone in the vicinity happy too. Softwoods, however, burn too fast and give off sparks and smoke. Wood can be used as kindling or to add aroma while cooking, but as it requires more care than charcoal it is best to use for impromptu beach barbecues than garden parties.

Firelighters

Use only odourless barbecue firelighters and push two between the pieces of fuel. Use a long match to light them. If using firelighter fluid or gel, spray or squeeze on to the cold fuel, leave for a few minutes, then light with a long match, following the manufacturer's instructions carefully.

Below: Light the newspaper using a long match and it will soon ignite the charcoal.

Above: Always use a long match or taper to light a barbecue.

Aromatics

Woodchips or herbs can be added to the coals to give a pleasant aroma to the food. Scatter them straight on to the coals during cooking, or place them in the drip tray under the grill rack. Try hickory or oak chips (soaked for 30 minutes before use), which are easily available from barbecue stockists, or scatter twigs of juniper, rosemary, thyme, sage or fennel over the fire. They can also be added to a smoke box for use with a gas barbecue. Put the aromatics into the smoke box and position it to one side on the grill rack.

LIGHTING A CHARCOAL BARBECUE

1 Spread a layer of wood, charcoal or briquettes on the fire grate, about 5cm/2in deep. Pile the fuel into a small pyramid in the centre of the grate. Use newspaper or kindling beneath the pile, if you wish, or push two firelighter sticks into the centre of the pyramid. Alternatively, add barbecue firelighter liquid or gel over the fuel, according to the manufacturer's instructions, then leave for 1 minute.

2 Light with a long match or taper and leave until the coals are covered with a grey ash – this will take about 25 minutes. (While the coals glow red with a light dusting of white or grey ash, thin foods can be seared quickly, and it is ideal for cooking rare steaks, but most other foods require a grey ash.)

3 Use tongs to arrange the coals. For cooking by direct heat spread them evenly over the surface of the fire grate;

for indirect heat either push them all to one side or part them in the centre so that a drip tray will fit into the space.

4 Place the grill rack over the heated coals and leave for about 10 minutes to heat up before adding the food.

USING A FIRE CHIMNEY

A metal, tube-shaped fire chimney is an easy way to get the fire going. Place the chimney on the fire grate and fill with newspaper. Pile coals on to the paper. Light the paper with a long-handled match and leave it to ignite the coals. When the top coals are dusted with ash, lift off the fire chimney. The coals will then spread evenly over the fire grate.

CLEANING

Brush the grill rack with a wire brush after use while still hot – you can turn on a gas barbecue to reheat the rack if necessary. For charcoal barbecues brush the grill rack after use while the coals are still warm. Brush again thoroughly before use when heating up.

Make sure gas and electric barbecues are turned off at the gas tank or power switch. If your barbecue has a lid, close this and close the air vents. If on the beach, make sure that the coals are fully extinguished before leaving.

Below: You can check large joints of meat are cooked by gently piercing them.

STORAGE

You can buy plastic covers to protect charcoal and gas barbecues for short periods when they are not in use. However, note that these covers will provide limited protection if a barbecue is left outside for several months. When storing for winter, make sure that the equipment is thoroughly cleaned and dried before putting away in a dry utility space, such as an attic or cellar.

Controlling the heat

All you need to control the heat on a gas or electric barbecue is to turn the control knob to high, medium-high, medium or low heat – so nothing could be simpler. For charcoal barbecues, however, there are three basic ways to control the heat during cooking:

1 Raise the grill rack for slow cooking; or use the lowest level for searing foods.

2 Push the burning coals apart for a lower heat; or pile them closer together to increase the heat.

3 Open the air vents to make the fire hotter; or close them to lower the temperature.

Safety Tips
• Ensure the barbecue is firmly sited on a level surface before lighting it. Never move a lit barbecue. Position the barbecue away from trees and shrubs, and shelter from the wind.
• Read the manufacturer's instructions for your barbecue, as there are some types that use only one type of fuel.
• Never pour flammable liquid, such as firelighter fluid, on to the lit barbecue.
• Extinguish a flare-up by closing the lid and all vents and turning off a gas barbecue. Use a fire extinguisher or bucket of sand if it gets out of control. Do not use water.
• Keep children and pets away from the fire.
• Keep a first-aid kit handy. Hold burnt skin under cold water immediately.
• Always use long-handled tools and oven gloves or mitts.
• If using a frying pan or griddle over the barbecue, opt for one with a metal hand if possible. If the handle is plastic, it may melt upon prolonged contact with the heat, so wrap it in thick foil before using and reserve use for quick cooking only.
• Keep raw foods cold until ready to cook. A cool bag is useful if you are barbecuing away from home. Keep raw and cooked foods apart.
• Make sure meats are thoroughly cooked with no traces of pink in the juices. Test by piercing the thickest part of the flesh; the juices should run clear.
• Wash your hands after handling raw meats and before touching other foods. Use different utensils for raw and cook foods, and never return cooked food to a plate where raw has been.
• Trim excess fat from meat and avoid using too much oil in marinades as fatty foods can cause dangerous flare-ups.

BARBECUE TECHNIQUES

Preparing whole fish for grilling
Small whole fish are ideal for barbecuing, especially oily fish such as mackerel or trout. You can ask your fishmonger to prepare them but it is also very easy to do yourself. A hinged wire basket is ideal for barbecuing fish.

1 Cut off the fins and strip out the gills with scissors.

2 Hold the fish firmly at the tail end and use the back of a small knife blade to remove the scales, scraping towards the head end. Rinse under cold water.

3 Cut a long slit under the fish, from just under the tail to just behind the gills, to open up the belly. Use the knife to push out the entrails and discard them. Rinse the fish in cold water.

4 Rub the inside cavity of the fish with salt and rinse again; then dry with kitchen paper.

A successful impromptu barbecued meal can be put together at the last minute with very little planning. If you are cooking for a crowd or planning something special, however, think through your menu carefully and organize yourself so that everything will run smoothly when you begin cooking. It's worth getting to know some basic preparation techniques and cooking procedures before you start.

GETTING READY

For smooth barbecuing, have everything prepared in advance so that as soon as the coals reach the correct temperature cooking can begin. This means that all chopping, marinating, stuffing and skewering should be done beforehand. Plan your menu thoughtfully; for example, if you are using a griddle it's

Above: By learning a few simple techniques, you can use the barbecue to prepare all kinds of dishes.

best to take advantage of the fierce early heat for this, so perhaps your first course could be griddled. During preparation, remember to trim all excess fat away from meat as this can drip on to the coals, causing flare-ups.

Remember to take any foods out of the freezer in good time, but if you are using frozen seafood try to cook it when it has just thawed and before the juices start to flow.

HOW TO GRILL

The key to successful grilling is to give the food just enough time to allow the heat to penetrate fully to the centre without overcooking the outside. To

achieve that lovely caramelized and smoky taste, sear the food for just a short period first, then continue to cook over a lower heat.

Cooking in foil parcels

Delicate foods or foods that are best cooked slowly in their own steam can be cooked in foil parcels and either placed directly into the coals or on the grill rack. You can wrap all kinds of flavourings in the foil parcels, too.

1 Use heavy-duty foil and cut two equal pieces to make a double thickness large enough to wrap each fish or portion of food. Lightly brush the centre of the foil with melted butter or oil.

3 Make a double fold in the top of the foil so that fish will cook gently in its own steam.

2 Place the food in the centre of the foil and add any flavourings and seasonings. Pull up the edges of the foil on opposite sides, over the food.

4 Fold over the ends of the foil or twist them together, making sure the parcel is sealed completely, so that the juices cannot escape.

Be careful not leave a large piece of meat over a high heat for too long or all the juices will bubble up to the surface and a thick crust will form and blacken, but the insides will be cold; or if the food is cooked over a longer period it will become tough. Once it is seared and golden, move the food frequently between the cooler and hotter areas of the barbecue for the remainder of the cooking time. A kettle barbecue is useful here, as when you close the lid you will have an all-round heat.

Before serving, rest meat and fish away from the heat. They will continue to cook for a little while and meat needs to rest to allow the juices to settle.

Try to avoid turning food more often if the recipe tells you to turn only once. Also avoid the temptation to prod or cut meat while it is cooking to test if it is done, as this will allow the juices to escape. You can check for doneness by piercing cooked meat with a skewer – the juices should run clear if it is ready. Similarly, avoid pressing down with a spatula while food is cooking as this will also cause moisture to be lost.

COOKING FOOD WITH DIRECT AND INDIRECT HEAT

Although we usually associate barbecued food with individual portions of food such as steaks, burgers, small fish and chicken portions, larger cuts can also be cooked using a barbecue. Some barbecues have a spit attached, which is useful for cooking whole chickens and joints of meat directly over the coals at high heat; otherwise cook them over indirect heat. For charcoal, this is when the coals are moved either to one side of the fire grate or parted in the centre and a drip tray placed in the space. The meat is then positioned over the drip tray. You will need a lid or tented foil for this method. Most small portions of food will be cooked directly over the coals (direct heat). If you are cooking a large joint of food as well as smaller foods, move the coals to one side so that the joint can be positioned to one side and smaller foods can be cooked over the coals. Gas barbecues can be set to cook using indirect heat.

HOW LONG WILL FOOD TAKE TO COOK?

You might prefer beef or lamb to be slightly pink inside but poultry or pork must always be well done until all the juices run clear with no trace of pink. Most foods need to be turned only once but small items such as kebabs or sausages may need to be turned more frequently to ensure even cooking. Foods cooked in foil will take a little longer to cook.

If your barbecue allows you to adjust the height of the grill rack, this is the easiest way to adjust the heat of the coals during cooking. For a medium heat the grill rack should be about 10cm/4in from the coals. Raise the rack to obtain a lower heat or lower it for a higher heat. If you wish to sear food, such as steaks, over a very high heat,

Below: This ornamental barbecue has slats for grilling kebabs on skewers.

Above: Meat can be cooked on a spit over a high heat and brushed regularly to keep it moist.

move the rack to 4–5cm/1¹/2–2in from the coals and then finish cooking over a lower heat. If the barbecue has air vents you can also use these to control the heat.

The chart to the right gives you a rough guide to the lengths of time that different types of meat, poultry and fish take to cook.

HOW TO KNOW WHEN IT'S DONE

In addition to piercing the thickest part of the meat as advised, you can also test for doneness by pressing it with your finger:

• Rare meat will be soft to the touch.
• Medium meat will be springy.
• Well-cooked meat will be very firm to the touch.

For large joints of meat use a meat thermometer to check the temperature inside: chicken 85°C/185°F; beef 65°C/150°F; lamb 60°C/140°F; pork 75°C/170°F.

USING A GRIDDLE

A ridged, cast-iron griddle is a useful piece of equipment to use on a hot barbecue. It is important that it is searing hot and very dry when the food is first put on it. Test by splashing a few drops of water on to the surface; they should evaporate instantly. Oil the food rather than the pan and, to help reduce the amount of smoke, pat any excess marinade off with kitchen paper. You need only a very small amount of oil. A good time to use the griddle is while the coals glow red with a light dusting of white or grey ash; this is just before they are ready. Use this time to sear thin foods, remembering to lower the heat when they are done.

LOW-FAT BARBECUES

Although barbecuing is often associated with rich foods – meats in particular – there are many ways to cook healthy foods over hot coals. You just need to give a little thought to preparation, and to substitute one or two of the more indulgent ingredients in a dish.

BASIC TIMING GUIDE			
type of food	weight or thickness	heat	cooking time (total)
beef			
steaks	2.5cm/1in	hot	rare: 5 minutes; medium: 8 minutes; well done: 12 minutes
burgers	2cm/³/4in	hot	6–8 minutes
kebabs	2.5cm/1in	hot	5–8 minutes
joints, such as rump or sirloin	1.6kg/3¹/2lb	spit or indirect heat medium	2–3 hours
lamb			
leg steaks	2cm/³/4in	medium	10–15 minutes
chops	2.5cm/1in	medium	10–15 minutes
kebabs	2.5cm/1in	medium	6–15 minutes
butterflied leg	7.5cm/3in	low	rare: 40–45 minutes well done: 1 hour
rolled shoulder	1.6kg/3¹/2lb	spit or indirect heat medium	1¹/4–1¹/2 hours
pork			
chops	2.5cm/1in	medium	15–18 minutes
kebabs	2.5cm/1in	medium	12–15 minutes
spare ribs		medium	30–40 minutes
sausages	thick	medium	8–10 minutes
joints, such as shoulder or loin	1.6kg/3¹/2lb	spit or indirect heat medium	2–3 hours
chicken			
whole	1.6kg/3¹/2lb	spit or indirect heat medium	1–1¹/4 hours
quarters, leg or breast		medium	30–35 minutes
breast fillets, boneless		medium	10–15 minutes
drumsticks		medium	25–30 minutes
kebabs		medium	6–10 minutes
poussin, whole	450kg/1lb	spit or indirect heat medium	25–30 minutes
poussin, spatchcocked	450kg/1lb	medium	25–30 minutes
duck			
whole	2.25kg/5lb	spit or indirect heat high	1–1¹/2 hours
half		medium	35–45 minutes
breast fillets, boneless		medium	15–20 minutes
fish			
large, whole	2.25–4.5kg/5–10lb	low/medium	allow 10 minutes per 2.5cm/1in thickness
small, whole	500–900kg/1¹/4–2lb	hot/medium	12–20 minutes
sardines		hot/medium	4–6 minutes
fish steaks or fillets	2.5cm/1in	medium	6–10 minutes
kebabs	2.5cm/1in	medium	5–8 minutes
large prawns, in shell		medium	6–8 minutes
scallops/mussels, in shell		medium	until open
large prawns, shelled		medium	4–6 minutes
scallops/mussels, shelled or skewered		medium	5–8 minutes
half lobster		low/medium	15–20 minutes

Above: An upside-down wok will fit snugly over a small grill rack as a lid, and helps to seal in moisture.

Which foods?

Red meats such as lamb and beef are particularly high in saturated fats and should either be avoided or kept to a minimum if you are following a low-fat diet or want to reduce the unhealthy fats (saturated fats) in your diet. Chicken and turkey, however, are good low-fat meats, although it is best to remove the skin. This can be done after cooking, if you like.

When choosing fish, look out for white fish such as cod or monkfish for a low-fat diet (although oily fish contains the healthy omega-3 fatty acids so can be included in most healthy diets). Be creative with the vegetable dishes that you barbecue – adding marinated tofu to vegetable kebabs, for example.

Avoiding too much fat

Keep oil to a minimum and use olive oil in preference during marinating and cooking. You can always adjust a recipe to use the minimum amount of olive oil supplemented with citrus juices or fat-free yogurt mixed with spices. Baste the food with the marinade to keep it moist but do this sparingly so that you are not replacing oil that has already dripped away. Brush once just before you turn the food during cooking, and if the food becomes dry, squeeze on a little citrus juice. You can also buy oil misters, which can be useful for adding a fine haze of oil before cooking.

Barbecue fish in its skin to keep it moist; it is easy to skin once cooked.

Above: Stuffing meat and fish with citrus is a great way of adding flavour without fat.

Cook small vegetables, baked potatoes or fish in foil parcels to seal in the moisture and avoid using too much oil.

Use wine, (hard) cider, vinegar, lemon or lime juice to provide liquid in place of large amounts of oil. Avoid using large amounts of wine, however, as the alcohol may not burn off sufficiently from quickly cooked foods.

Adding flavour without fat

It's not necessary to use lots of fat to add flavour into your food. Try rubbing herbs, spices and crushed garlic into

skinless chicken before cooking, or pierce the skin and tuck herbs and garlic underneath to trap in their flavour during cooking. Remove the skin before eating. Try prepared mustard marinades to spread over skinless chicken breasts to trap in moisture and add piquancy. Use finely chopped shallots, onions or spring onions for a pronounced flavour in marinades.

Brighten up the taste buds by accompanying your barbecued food with a refreshing salsa or relish made from finely chopped fruit or vegetables, spring onions and chopped fresh herbs. These are also delicious tucked into pitta bread kebabs. Salads with light dressings and fat-free dips also taste great with barbecued food, and a pile of wholemeal rolls or pitta breads make a healthy, substantial accompaniment, and are, of course, useful for soaking up juices. Remember to choose low-fat yogurt, fromage frais or crème fraîche for your marinades or dips – they will taste just as delicious as their full-fat counterparts and are guilt-free!

Below: Use the timing guide opposite to cook lean cuts of meat according to your preference.

APPETIZERS

All of these recipes are perfect bitesize delicacies with the power

to whet the appetite. Some are designed to be dunked, like the

classic Potato Wedges with Basil and Lemon Dip, or Mini Chicken

Fillets served with a spicy-sour marmalade. Others can be nibbled

delicately from skewers, like the mouthwateringly aromatic

Mushrooms with Garlic and Chilli Sauce. Or try the exotic

Grilled Foie Gras served with caramelized pears.

WALNUT BREAD WITH MASHED AUBERGINE

THIS TURKISH DISH CONSISTS OF GRILLED MASHED AUBERGINE WITH CHEESE SERVED WITH OLIVES AND TOASTED BREAD. YOU CAN BUY MARINATED OLIVES INSTEAD OF MAKING YOUR OWN, BUT IT'S FUN TO DO IT YOURSELF, BY STEEPING THE OLIVES WITH VARIOUS FLAVOURINGS IN A GOOD QUALITY OIL.

3 While the mixture is still hot, add the finely grated cheese and lemon juice, and stir well to mix these ingredients in thoroughly. Add salt and pepper to taste. Drain most of the oil from the olives and mix it into the pulp. Cover the aubergine mixture and put in a cool place until needed.

4 Brush the bread slices sparingly with oil on one side and toast on the griddle or on an oiled grill rack over the barbecue. Keep an eye on the toast because it just needs to become crisp, not blacken, and the coals are hot at this stage.

5 Serve the toast with small bowls of the aubergine and cheese mixture and the marinated olives.

COOK'S TIPS
• This dish can also be cooked next to a slow-cooking main course. Get the main course food going, then cook the aubergines beside it directly on the grill rack.
• If you cannot obtain Kefalotiri or Kasseri cheese it can be substituted by finely grated Parmesan cheese.

SERVES EIGHT

INGREDIENTS
  3 aubergines (eggplants), about
    675g/1½lb total weight, cut
    widthways into 5mm/¼in slices
  60ml/4 tbsp finely grated Kefalotiri
    or Kasseri cheese
  juice of ½ lemon
  1 loaf walnut bread, sliced as thinly
    as possible
  extra virgin olive oil, for brushing
  salt and ground black pepper
For the marinated olives
  175g/6oz/1 cup olives of
    various colours
  fennel seeds or dried fennel seed
    heads and ground black pepper
  fresh hot chillies and rosemary sprigs
  lemon slices and fresh
    thyme branches
  120ml/4fl oz/½ cup extra virgin
    olive oil

1 To make the marinated olives, divide them among three bowls and add a different flavouring combination to each: try the fennel seeds and pepper with mixed olives, the chillies and rosemary with black olives, and the lemon and thyme with green olives. Divide the oil among the bowls and leave to stand for several hours.

2 Prepare the barbecue. Heat the griddle on the grill rack over hot coals. Brush the aubergine slices with some of the oil from the olives and griddle for 5 minutes, or until soft and branded with griddle marks on both sides. Tip the slices into a small bowl and mash to a rough pulp.

Energy 240kcal/1004kJ; Protein 7.5g; Carbohydrate 23.2g, of which sugars 2.5g; Fat 13.5g, of which saturates 3.1g; Cholesterol 7mg; Calcium 94mg; Fibre 5.2g; Sodium 823mg.

TOMATO AND MOZZARELLA SALAD

GRIDDLING THE TOMATOES ADDS A NEW DIMENSION TO THIS DELICIOUS DISH AND A SUPERB SWEETNESS TO THE TOMATOES. AVOID MAKING THE BASIL OIL TOO FAR IN ADVANCE SO THAT ITS FRESH FLAVOUR AND VIVID EMERALD-GREEN COLOUR WILL BE RETAINED.

SERVES FOUR

INGREDIENTS
6 large plum tomatoes
350g/12oz fresh mozzarella, cut into
    8–12 slices
fresh basil leaves, to garnish
For the basil oil
25 fresh basil leaves
60ml/4 tbsp extra virgin olive oil
1 garlic clove, crushed
For the salad
90g/3½oz salad leaves
50g/2oz/2 cups mixed herbs, such
    as coriander (cilantro), basil and
    rocket (arugula)
25g/1oz/3 tbsp pumpkin seeds
25g/1oz/3 tbsp sunflower seeds
For the salad dressing
60ml/4 tbsp extra virgin olive oil
15ml/1 tbsp balsamic vinegar
2.5ml/½ tsp Dijon mustard

1 To make the basil oil, place the basil leaves, olive oil and garlic in a blender and whizz until smooth. Transfer to a bowl and chill.

2 Start to prepare the salad. Put the salad leaves in a large bowl. Add the mixed herbs and toss lightly with your hands to mix. To make the salad dressing, combine the ingredients in a screw-top jar or bowl. Shake or mix with a small whisk or fork until combined. Set aside.

3 Cut the tomatoes in half lengthwise and remove the seeds. Prepare the barbecue. Heat a griddle on a grill rack over hot coals. Place the tomatoes skin-side down on the griddle and cook for 12–15 minutes or until the tomatoes are tender.

4 Meanwhile, toast the pumpkin and sunflower seeds in a dry frying pan on the grill rack for 2 minutes, or until golden, tossing frequently. Cool then sprinkle them over the salad. Stir the dressing then pour over the salad and toss to mix.

5 For each serving, place the tomato halves on top of 2 or 3 slices of mozzarella and drizzle over the basil oil. Season well. Garnish with basil leaves. Serve with the salad.

COOK'S TIP
Try to keep an eye on the toasting seeds even if griddling tomatoes at the same time – they will burn quickly if left.

Energy 528kcal/2189kJ; Protein 20.3g; Carbohydrate 8g, of which sugars 5.5g; Fat 46.3g, of which saturates 15.9g; Cholesterol 51mg; Calcium 351mg; Fibre 2.7g; Sodium 361mg.

HAM PIZZETTAS <u>WITH</u> MANGO

THESE INDIVIDUAL LITTLE PIZZAS ARE TOPPED WITH AN UNUSUAL BUT VERY SUCCESSFUL COMBINATION OF SMOKED HAM, BRIE AND JUICY CHUNKS OF FRESH MANGO.

2 Turn the dough out on to a floured surface and knead it for about 5 minutes, or until smooth.

3 Return the dough to the bowl and cover it with a damp cloth or oiled clear film (plastic wrap). Leave the dough to rise in a warm place for about 30 minutes, or until is doubled in size and springy to the touch.

4 Prepare the barbecue. Divide the dough into six and roll each piece into a ball. Flatten out with your hand and use your knuckles to press each piece of dough to a round of about 15cm/6in diameter, with a raised lip around the edge.

5 Halve, stone (pit) and peel the mango and cut it into small dice. Arrange with the ham on top of the pizzettas. Top with cheese and tomatoes and sprinkle with salt and ground black pepper.

6 Drizzle the remaining oil over the pizzettas. Place them on the oiled grill rack of a medium-hot barbecue and cook for 8 minutes, or until golden brown and crisp underneath.

SERVES SIX

INGREDIENTS
225g/8oz/2 cups strong white bread flour
10g/¼ oz sachet easy-blend (rapid-rise) dried yeast
150ml/¼ pint/⅔ cup warm water
60ml/4 tbsp olive oil
For the topping
1 ripe mango
150g/5oz smoked ham, sliced wafer-thin
150g/5oz Brie, diced
12 yellow cherry tomatoes, halved
salt and ground black pepper

1 In a large bowl, stir together the flour and yeast, with a pinch of salt. Make a well in the centre and stir in the water and 45ml/3 tbsp of the olive oil. Stir until thoroughly mixed.

Energy 326kcal/1369kJ; Protein 13.6g; Carbohydrate 34g, of which sugars 5.3g; Fat 15.5g, of which saturates 6g; Cholesterol 38mg; Calcium 124mg; Fibre 2.2g; Sodium 444mg.

POTATO WEDGES WITH BASIL AND LEMON DIP

BARBECUED POTATO WEDGES TASTE GREAT SERVED WITH THIS FRESH MAYONNAISE. THE POTATOES ARE PAR-BOILED IN ADVANCE AND NEED ONLY A FEW MINUTES GRILLING ON THE BARBECUE.

SERVES FOUR

INGREDIENTS
    4 large potatoes, peeled
    90ml/6 tbsp olive oil
    sea salt and ground black pepper
For the dip
    2 large egg yolks
    15ml/1 tbsp lemon juice
    150ml/¼ pint/⅔ cup olive oil
    150ml/¼ pint/⅔ cup sunflower oil
    handful of green basil leaves
    handful of dark opal (purple)
        basil leaves
    4 garlic cloves, crushed
    green and dark opal basil leaves and
        sea salt, to garnish

4 Tear both types of basil leaves into small pieces and stir into the mayonnaise with the crushed garlic and seasoning. Transfer to a serving dish, cover and chill until ready to serve, garnished with basil leaves and sea salt.

5 Slice the potatoes into wedges about 7.5cm/3in long and 2.5cm/1in thick. Place the wedges in boiling water and cook for 4–5 minutes (the potato should be just tender but still firm). Drain the potatoes and refresh under cold running water. Dry thoroughly then toss quickly in the olive oil to coat, and season with salt and pepper.

6 Prepare the barbecue. Position a lightly oiled grill rack over the hot coals. Place the potatoes on the grill rack over a medium-high heat and cook them for 3–4 minutes on each side, turning carefully with tongs, so that they are heated through, golden and tender. Serve with the dip.

1 Place the egg yolks and lemon juice in a food processor or blender and process them briefly together.

2 In a jug (pitcher), stir the two oils together. With the machine running, pour in the oil very slowly, a drop at a time.

3 Once half the oil has been added, the remainder can be incorporated more quickly. Continue processing the mixture as you add the oil to form a thick and creamy mayonnaise.

VARIATION
If you prefer, of course, you can serve these wedges with a rich barbecue sauce – such as the home-made recipe in the Accompaniments chapter.

COOK'S TIP
Dark opal basil has crinkled, deep-purple leaves with a hint of blackcurrants.

Energy 680kcal/2803kJ; Protein 3.4g; Carbohydrate 11.1g, of which sugars 0.9g; Fat 69.4g, of which saturates 9.8g; Cholesterol 101mg; Calcium 18mg; Fibre 1.1g; Sodium 11mg.

HOT AVOCADO HALVES

IF YOU MAKE THE BASIL OIL IN ADVANCE, OR BUY A READY PREPARED BASIL OIL, THIS IS AN ULTRA-SIMPLE DISH THAT CAN BE READY IN A FLASH. IT MAKES AN EYE-CATCHING FIRST COURSE AND IS AN EXCELLENT APPETITE TEASER TO SERVE WHILE THE REST OF THE FOOD IS BARBECUING.

SERVES SIX

INGREDIENTS
    3 ready-to-eat avocados, preferably
      Hass for flavour
    105ml/7 tbsp balsamic vinegar
For the basil oil
    40g/1½oz/1½ cups fresh basil
      leaves, stalks removed
    200ml/7fl oz/scant 1 cup olive oil

COOK'S TIPS
• When choosing Hass avocados, watch out for any with marked indentations in their bumpy skin – this indicates that the flesh underneath may be bruised.
• Remember, the griddle is ready to use when a few drops of water sprinkled on to the surface evaporate instantly.

1 To make the basil oil, place the leaves in a bowl and pour boiling water over. Leave for 30 seconds. Drain, refresh under cold water and drain again. Squeeze dry and pat with kitchen paper to remove as much moisture as possible.

2 Place in a food processor with the oil and process to a purée. Put into a bowl, cover and chill overnight.

3 Next day, line a sieve with muslin (cheesecloth), set it over a deep bowl and pour in the basil purée. Leave undisturbed for 1 hour, or until all the oil has filtered into the bowl. Discard the solids and pour into a bottle, then chill until ready to cook.

4 Prepare the barbecue. Cut each avocado in half and prize out the stone (pit). Brush with a little of the basil oil.

5 Heat the balsamic vinegar gently in a pan, on the stove or on the barbecue. When it starts to boil, simmer for 1 minute, or until it is just beginning to turn slightly syrupy.

6 Heat the griddle on the grill rack over hot coals. Lower the heat a little and place the avocado halves cut-side down on the griddle. Cook for 30–60 seconds until branded with grill marks. (Move the avocados around carefully with tongs to create a chequered effect.) Serve hot with the vinegar and extra oil drizzled over.

Energy 222kcal/916kJ; Protein 1g; Carbohydrate 1g, of which sugars 0.3g; Fat 23.8g, of which saturates 4.1g; Cholesterol 0mg; Calcium 6mg; Fibre 1.7g; Sodium 3mg.

CHILLI AND HERB POLENTA

POLENTA HAS BECOME AS WIDELY ACCEPTED AS MASHED POTATO AND CAN CONFIDENTLY BE CLASSED AS COMFORT FOOD. HERE IT IS FLAVOURED WITH PASILLA CHILLIES, WHICH HAVE A DRIED FRUIT AND SLIGHT LIQUORICE HINT TO THEM. SERVE IT WITH A TANGY SALSA CALLED PEBRE.

SERVES SIX TO TWELVE

INGREDIENTS
- 10ml/2 tsp crushed dried pasilla chilli flakes
- 1.3 litres/2¼ pints/5⅔ cups water
- 250g/9oz/2¼ cups quick-cook polenta
- 50g/2oz/¼ cup butter
- 75g/3oz Parmesan cheese, finely grated
- 30ml/2 tbsp chopped fresh dill
- 30ml/2 tbsp chopped fresh coriander (cilantro)
- 30ml/2 tbsp olive oil
- salt

For the *pebre*
- ½ pink onion, finely chopped
- 4 drained bottled sweet cherry peppers, finely chopped
- 1 fresh medium hot red chilli, seeded and finely chopped
- 1 small red (bell) pepper, quartered and seeded
- 10ml/2 tsp raspberry vinegar
- 30ml/2 tbsp olive oil
- 4 tomatoes, halved, cored, seeded and roughly chopped
- 45ml/3 tbsp chopped fresh coriander (cilantro)

1 Chop the chilli flakes finely. Put them in a pan with the water. Bring to the boil and add salt to taste. Pour the polenta into the water in a continuous stream, whisking all the time. Reduce the heat and continue to whisk for a few minutes. When the polenta is thick and bubbling like a volcano, whisk in the butter, Parmesan and herbs.

2 Pour into a greased 33 x 23cm/ 13 x 9in baking tray and leave to cool. Leave uncovered so that the surface firms up, and chill overnight.

3 About an hour before you plan to serve the meal, make the *pebre*. Place the onion, sweet cherry peppers and chilli in a mortar. Slice the skin from the red pepper quarters. Dice the flesh finely and add it to the mortar with the raspberry vinegar and olive oil.

4 Pound with a pestle for 1 minute, then tip into a serving dish. Stir in the tomatoes and coriander. Cover and chill.

5 Remove the polenta from the refrigerator and leave for about 30 minutes. Cut into 12 even triangles and brush the top with oil.

6 Prepare the barbecue. Heat a griddle on a grill rack over hot coals. Lower the heat to medium and grill the polenta triangles in batches, oiled-side down, for about 2 minutes, then turn through 180 degrees and cook for 1 minute more, to get a striking chequered effect. (Alternatively, you can sear them directly on the oiled grill rack.) Serve the polenta at once, with the chilled *pebre*.

Energy 181kcal/751kJ; Protein 5g; Carbohydrate 17.3g, of which sugars 2g; Fat 10g, of which saturates 4g; Cholesterol 15mg; Calcium 88mg; Fibre 1.2g; Sodium 98mg.

BUTTERFLY PRAWNS

THE SUCCESS OF THIS DISH STEMS FROM THE QUALITY OF THE PRAWNS, SO IT IS WORTH GETTING REALLY GOOD ONES, SUCH AS KING PRAWNS, WITH GREAT FLAVOUR AND TEXTURE. A FRUITY, SLIGHTLY SPICY DIP IS SUCH AN EASY BUT FABULOUS ACCOMPANIMENT.

4 Stir the chilli into the raspberry purée. When the dip is cool, cover and place in a cool place until needed.

5 Butterfly each prawn by making an incision down the curved back, just as you would when deveining. Use a piece of kitchen paper to wipe away the dark spinal vein.

6 Mix the oil with a little sea salt in a bowl. Add the prawns and toss to coat, then thread them on to the drained skewers, spearing them head first.

7 Position a lightly oiled grill rack over the coals to heat. Grill the prawns over high heat for about 5 minutes, depending on size, turning them over once. Serve hot, with the chilli and raspberry dip.

SERVES SIX

INGREDIENTS
  30 raw king prawns (jumbo shrimp), peeled, with heads removed but tails left on
  15ml/1 tbsp sunflower oil
  coarse sea salt
For the chilli and raspberry dip
  30ml/2 tbsp raspberry vinegar
  15ml/1 tbsp sugar
  115g/4oz/⅔ cup raspberries
  1 large fresh red chilli, seeded and finely chopped

1 Prepare the barbecue. Soak 30 wooden skewers in cold water for 30 minutes.

2 Make the dip by mixing the vinegar and sugar in a small pan. Heat gently until the sugar has dissolved, stirring, then add the raspberries.

3 When the raspberry juices start to flow, tip the mixture into a sieve set over a bowl. Push the raspberries through the sieve using the back of a ladle. Discard the seeds.

COOK'S TIP
These prawn dippers also taste delicious with a vibrant chilli and mango dip. Use one large, ripe mango in place of the raspberries and slice the flesh thinly.

Energy 44kcal/185kJ; Protein 5.6g; Carbohydrate 0.9g, of which sugars 0.9g; Fat 2.1g, of which saturates 0.3g; Cholesterol 59mg; Calcium 29mg; Fibre 0.5g; Sodium 58mg.

MUSHROOMS ᵂᴵᵀᴴ GARLIC ᴬᴺᴰ CHILLI SAUCE

When you are planning a barbecue for friends and family, it can be tricky finding something really special for the vegetarians in the party. These mushroom kebabs are ideal because they look, smell and taste wonderful.

SERVES FOUR

INGREDIENTS

   12 large field (portabello), chestnut
      or oyster mushrooms or a mixture,
      cut in half
   4 garlic cloves, coarsely
      chopped
   6 coriander (cilantro) roots,
      coarsely chopped
   15ml/1 tbsp granulated sugar
   30ml/2 tbsp light soy sauce
   ground black pepper
For the dipping sauce
   15ml/1 tbsp granulated sugar
   90ml/6 tbsp rice vinegar
   5ml/1 tsp salt
   1 garlic clove, crushed
   1 small fresh red chilli, seeded
      and finely chopped

1 If using wooden skewers, soak eight of them in cold water for at least 30 minutes to prevent them burning. Prepare the barbecue.

2 Make the dipping sauce by heating the sugar, rice vinegar and salt in a small pan, stirring occasionally until the sugar and salt have dissolved. Add the garlic and chilli, pour into a serving dish and keep warm.

3 Thread three mushroom halves on to each skewer. Lay the filled skewers side by side in a shallow dish.

4 In a mortar or spice grinder pound or blend the garlic and coriander roots. Scrape into a bowl and mix with the sugar, soy sauce and a little pepper.

5 Brush the soy sauce mixture over the mushrooms and leave to marinate for 15 minutes. Cook the mushrooms over medium heat for 5–6 minutes on each side. Serve with the dipping sauce.

Energy 63kcal/267kJ; Protein 4.2g; Carbohydrate 9.6g, of which sugars 9.1g; Fat 1.2g, of which saturates 0.2g; Cholesterol 0mg; Calcium 43mg; Fibre 2.8g; Sodium 1040mg.

MINI CHICKEN FILLETS

THE AJI AMARILLO IS A YELLOWY ORANGE PERUVIAN CHILLI, VERY FRUITY AND QUITE HOT, WHICH IS WHY IT IS A GOOD IDEA TO PREPARE THE MARMALADE THE DAY BEFORE SO THAT THE FLAVOURS CAN MELLOW AND BLEND. PERFECT SERVED WITH GARLICKY CHICKEN FILLETS.

SERVES FOUR

INGREDIENTS
    500g/1¼lb mini chicken breast
        fillets or skinless chicken breast
        fillets, each cut into 4 long strips
    2 garlic cloves, crushed to a paste
        with 2.5ml/½ tsp salt
    30ml/2 tbsp olive oil
    ground black pepper
For the aji amarillo marmalade
    50g/2oz dried aji
        amarillo chillies
    120ml/4fl oz/½ cup water
    20ml/4 tsp olive oil
    2 onions, finely chopped
    3 garlic cloves, crushed
    5ml/1 tsp ground cumin
    10ml/2 tsp Mexican oregano
    130g/4½oz/scant ¾ cup sugar
    200ml/7fl oz/scant 1 cup cider or
        white wine vinegar
    2 small orange (bell) peppers,
        quartered and seeded

1 To make the aji amarillo marmalade, heat a heavy frying pan, add the dried chillies and roast them by stirring them continuously over the heat for about 1½ minutes without letting them scorch.

2 Put them in a bowl with just enough almost-boiling water to cover. Use a saucer to keep them submerged and leave to rehydrate for about 2 hours, or longer if you prefer.

3 Slit the chillies, remove the seeds and chop the flesh into small dice. Place in a blender, add the water and process to a purée.

4 Heat the oil in a heavy pan, add the onions and garlic and cook over a gentle heat for 5 minutes. Add the cumin, Mexican oregano and the chilli purée. Add the sugar and stir until turning syrupy, then add the vinegar and stir well. Bring the mixture to the boil, then lower the heat and simmer for 30 minutes.

5 Meanwhile, heat a griddle on the stove. Roast the peppers, placed with skin-side down so that the skins char. Put the peppers underneath an upturned bowl. When they are cool enough to handle, rub off the skin and finely dice the flesh. Add to the chilli mixture and continue to simmer for about 25 minutes, or until the marmalade thickens. Transfer to a bowl. When cool, cover and chill until 30 minutes before serving.

COOK'S TIP
The aji amarillo marmalade will keep, chilled, for a week. It is also good eaten with hot smoked salmon.

6 Spread out the chicken pieces in a shallow dish and add the garlic, oil and pepper. Turn the fillets in the mixture, cover and set aside in a cool place for 30–45 minutes, turning occasionally.

7 Prepare the barbecue. Position a lightly oiled grill rack over the coals to heat. Grill the chicken pieces over medium-high heat for 2½–3 minutes on each side, or until cooked through and branded with grill marks. Using tongs, carefully move the food about while cooking to avoid over-charring. Transfer to a platter, cover and leave in a warm place for 5 minutes before serving with the marmalade.

Energy 401kcal/1689kJ; Protein 32.2g; Carbohydrate 47.5g, of which sugars 44.9g; Fat 10.4g, of which saturates 1.7g; Cholesterol 88mg; Calcium 56mg; Fibre 2.8g; Sodium 84mg.

HOT TROUT WITH RED VEGETABLES

ROAST THE VEGETABLES IN ADVANCE FOR THIS FLAVOURSOME AND BRIGHTLY COLOURED MEDITERRANEAN-STYLE SANDWICH AND THEN HAVE EVERYTHING READY TO ASSEMBLE WHEN THE TROUT IS COOKED.

SERVES FOUR

INGREDIENTS
  2 red (bell) peppers
  8 cherry tomatoes
  60ml/4 tbsp extra virgin olive oil
  30ml/2 tbsp lemon juice
  4 thin trout fillets, each about
    115g/4oz, skinned
  2 small ciabatta rolls
  15ml/1 tbsp red pesto
  30ml/2 tbsp mayonnaise
  115g/4oz rocket (arugula)
  salt and ground black pepper

1 Preheat the oven to 180°C/350°F/ Gas 4. Place the peppers and tomatoes in a roasting pan and drizzle half the olive oil over. Bake for 25–30 minutes or until the pepper skins are blackened. Set aside to cool.

2 In a small bowl or jug (pitcher), whisk the remaining oil with the lemon juice and a little salt and freshly ground black pepper. Place the trout in a shallow, non-metallic dish and pour over the oil and lemon juice. Turn the fish to make sure they are well coated.

3 Peel the skin off the cooked peppers and discard the core and seeds. Cut the pepper flesh into strips. Slice each ciabatta bread in half vertically, then cut each half in half horizontally.

4 Prepare the barbecue. Heat a griddle on the grill rack over hot coals. Lift the trout fillets carefully out of the marinade and grill them for 1–2 minutes, without adding any oil, until just cooked.

5 Mix the pesto and mayonnaise together and spread over the bread. Divide the rocket among four halves of the bread and top with the trout, pepper strips and roasted tomatoes. Place the remaining bread on top and serve.

COOK'S TIPS
• You can use any bread you like but make sure you slice it thickly.
• This recipe would be delicious using smoked fish fillets as a filling for the sandwich. Try smoking trout or salmon fillets over the barbecue using aromatic wood chips – you can follow the technique for hot smoked salmon that appears in the Fish and Shellfish chapter.
• Small loaves of olive-oil bread, such as ciabatta and focaccia, are ideal for these sandwiches. Try the sun-dried tomato and black olive versions, too.
• If you can't find any red pesto, use 30ml/2 tbsp chopped fresh basil mixed with 15ml/1 tbsp sun-dried tomato paste.

Energy 538kcal/2253kJ; Protein 32.6g; Carbohydrate 46.7g, of which sugars 9.8g; Fat 25.7g, of which saturates 3.8g; Cholesterol 9mg; Calcium 206mg; Fibre 4.2g; Sodium 588mg.

GRILLED CHICKEN BALLS

THESE TASTY JAPANESE CHICKEN BALLS, KNOWN AS TSUKUNE, ARE POPULAR WITH CHILDREN AS WELL AS ADULTS. YOU CAN MAKE THE BALLS IN ADVANCE UP TO THE END OF STEP 2, AND THEY FREEZE VERY WELL.

SERVES FOUR

INGREDIENTS
   300g/11oz skinless chicken,
      minced (ground)
   2 eggs
   2.5ml/½ tsp salt
   10ml/2 tsp plain (all-purpose) flour
   10ml/2 tsp cornflour (cornstarch)
   90ml/6 tbsp dried breadcrumbs
   2.5cm/1in piece of fresh root
      ginger, grated
For the *yakitori* sauce
   60ml/4 tbsp sake
   75ml/5 tbsp shoyu
   15ml/1 tbsp mirin
   15ml/1 tbsp caster (superfine) sugar
   2.5ml/½ tsp cornflour (cornstarch)
      blended with 5ml/1 tsp water
   shichimi togarashi or sansho
      (optional), to serve

1 Soak eight bamboo skewers for 30 minutes in water. Put all the ingredients for the chicken balls, except the ginger, in a food processor and blend well.

2 Wet your hands and scoop about a tablespoonful of the mixture into your palm. Shape it into a small ball about half the size of a golf ball. Make a further 30–32 balls in the same way.

3 Squeeze the juice from the grated ginger into a small mixing bowl. Discard the pulp.

4 Add the ginger juice to a small pan of boiling water. Add the chicken balls, and boil for about 7 minutes, or until the colour of the meat changes and the balls float to the surface. Scoop out using a slotted spoon and drain on a plate covered with kitchen paper.

5 In a small pan, mix all the ingredients for the *yakitori* sauce, except for the cornflour liquid. Bring to the boil, then reduce the heat and simmer for about 10 minutes, or until the sauce has slightly reduced. Add the cornflour liquid and stir until the sauce is thick. Transfer to a small bowl.

6 Prepare the barbecue. Position a lightly oiled grill rack over the hot coals. Thread three to four balls on each skewer and turn over the heat for a few minutes until the balls start to brown. Brush with sauce and return to the heat. Repeat the process twice. Serve, sprinkled with shichimi togarashi or sansho, if you like.

COOK'S TIP
Sansho is a Japanese spice, made by grinding the black seeds of pricky ash berries, that is often sprinkled on soups and stews. It is an important ingredient in the seven-spice blend shichimi togarash, which may also contain ground chilli, sesame seeds, seaweed and citrus peel. Shichimi togarash can be made at home but also bought ready-made.

Energy 263kcal/1111kJ; Protein 24.1g; Carbohydrate 25.9g, of which sugars 4.8g; Fat 4.1g, of which saturates 1g; Cholesterol 148mg; Calcium 54mg; Fibre 0.6g; Sodium 520mg.

GRILLED FOIE GRAS

THE RICH AND LUXURIOUS TEXTURE OF THE FOIE GRAS IS TEAMED HERE WITH A SHARP, TANGY JAPANESE SAUCE, PONZU JOYU. THE CARAMELIZED FLAVOUR OF THE ASIAN PEAR BALANCES THE DISH PERFECTLY.

SERVES FOUR

INGREDIENTS
    2 Asian (nashi) pears, each cut into
      eight wedges
    15ml/1 tbsp clear honey mixed
      with 45ml/3 tbsp water
    225g/8oz duck or goose foie gras,
      chilled and cut into eight
      1cm/½in slices
For the ponzu joyu
    45ml/3 tbsp mirin
    120ml/4fl oz/½ cup tamari
    75ml/5 tbsp dried bonito flakes
    45ml/3 tbsp rice vinegar
    juice of 1 large lemon
    4 strips dried kombu seaweed

1 To make the ponzu joyu, place the mirin in a small pan, bring to the boil and cook for about 30 seconds.

2 Pour into a small bowl and add all the remaining ingredients. Cool, then cover and chill for about 24 hours. Strain the mixture into a screw-topped jar and chill until needed.

COOK'S TIP
You will find the ingredients for the ponzu joyu sauce in a Japanese supermarket. Bonito flakes are the dried shavings or flakes of Pacific bonito (a kind of small tuna). They are used to add flavour and always strained once their flavour has been absorbed. They are often used to season Japanese-style salads and vegetable dishes.

3 Toss the pear wedges in the honey mixture. Heat a griddle on the grill rack over hot coals. Griddle the pear wedges for about 30 seconds on each cut side.

4 Wipe the pan with kitchen paper and heat again. When it is searing hot, grill the foie gras for 30 seconds on each side. Serve immediately with the ponzu joyu and pear wedges.

Energy 238kcal/988kJ; Protein 7.5g; Carbohydrate 11.1g, of which sugars 10.9g; Fat 18.5g, of which saturates 5.4g; Cholesterol 96mg; Calcium 18mg; Fibre 1.7g; Sodium 692mg.

FISH & SHELLFISH

It is not difficult to see why the seafood barbecue is so popular. Most fish and shellfish are quick to cook, and their delicate flesh lends itself well to the smoky flavour contributed by hot coals. Some of these dishes use traditional techniques or suggest specific cooking equipment – such as tying stuffed fish with raffia, or cooking sardine fillets in a wire fish basket – but there are plenty of options and alternatives for those who prefer the simplicity of a kettle barbecue.

CLAMS AND MUSSELS IN BANANA LEAVES

THESE PRETTY RAFFIA-TIED PARCELS CAN EITHER BE COOKED AS SOON AS THEY ARE READY OR CHILLED FOR UP TO 30 MINUTES, OFFERING A MOMENT'S RESPITE BEFORE THE COOKING BEGINS. BANANA LEAVES MAKE NEAT LITTLE PARCELS BUT YOU COULD ALSO USE DOUBLE FOIL.

3 Top a sheet of foil with a piece of banana leaf, placing it smooth-side up. Place another piece of leaf on top, at right angles, so that the leaves form a cross. Don't worry if the leaves are slightly wet – it's more important to work quickly with the leaves at this stage, while they remain soft and pliable.

4 Pile one-sixth of the seafood mixture into the centre, then bring up the leaves and tie them into a money-bag shape, using the raffia. Do the same with the foil, scrunching slightly to seal the top. Make the remaining parcels in the same way, then chill the parcels until needed.

5 Prepare the barbecue. Position a lightly oiled grill rack over the coals to heat. Cook the parcels over medium-high heat for about 15 minutes. Carefully remove the outer layer of foil from each and put the parcels back on the grill rack for 1 minute.

6 Transfer to individual plates. The parcels retain heat for a while, so can be left to stand for up to 5 minutes. Untie the raffia and eat from the leaves. Serve with bread sticks, if you wish.

COOK'S TIP
Have a quick peek into all of the bags to make sure the shells have opened before serving. Discard any shellfish that haven't opened.

SERVES SIX

INGREDIENTS
  15ml/1 tbsp olive oil
  1 large onion, finely chopped
  2 garlic cloves, crushed
  1.5ml/¼ tsp saffron threads
  60ml/4 tbsp Noilly Prat or other
   dry vermouth
  30ml/2 tbsp water
  30ml/2 tbsp chopped fresh flat
   leaf parsley
  500g/1¼lb clams, scrubbed
  900g/2lb mussels, cleaned
  6 banana leaves
  salt and ground black pepper
  raffia, for tying
  bread sticks, for serving

1 Heat the oil in a pan and add the chopped onion and garlic with the saffron threads. Cook over a gentle heat for 4 minutes. Add the vermouth and water, increase the heat and simmer for 2 minutes. Stir in the parsley, with salt and pepper to taste. Transfer to a bowl and leave to cool completely.

2 Tap the clam and mussel shells and discard any that stay open. Stir them into the bowl containing the onion mixture. Trim the hard edge from each banana leaf. Cut the leaves in half lengthways. Soak them in hot water for 10 minutes, then drain. Wipe any white residue from the leaves. Rinse, then pour over boiling water to soften.

Energy 116kcal/488kJ; Protein 14g; Carbohydrate 6.2g, of which sugars 4g; Fat 3.1g, of which saturates 0.5g; Cholesterol 40mg; Calcium 131mg; Fibre 0.9g; Sodium 498mg.

GIANT PRAWNS WRAPPED IN LIME LEAVES

THESE HUGE PRAWNS CAN GROW UP TO 33CM/13IN IN LENGTH, AND ARE PERFECT FOR GRILLING ON A BARBECUE. THIS DISH IS FAST AND EASY, YET IMPRESSIVE; IDEAL FOR A RELAXED POOLSIDE LUNCH WITH SALAD OR FOR SERVING AS AN APPETIZER WHILE THE MAIN COURSE IS COOKING.

SERVES SIX

INGREDIENTS
6 giant Mediterranean prawns
(extra large jumbo shrimp),
total weight about 900g/2lb
juice of 2 limes
60ml/4 tbsp olive oil
12 large kaffir lime leaves
12 pandanus leaves
2 limes, cut into wedges, to serve

VARIATION
Serve these with a really easy dip made by mixing together 150ml/¼ pint/⅔ cup mayonnaise and 20ml/4 tsp Thai sweet chilli sauce.

1 Soak six wooden cocktail sticks (toothpicks) in water for 30 minutes. Make a shallow cut down the curved back of each prawn.

2 Put the giant prawns into a shallow dish, large enough to avoid cramming them on top of each other. In a separate bowl, mix the lime juice and oil together and pour over the prawns. Set aside for 15 minutes to allow the flavour to soak in.

3 Take each marinated prawn, lay two kaffir lime leaves on top, wrap two pandanus leaves around it and skewer with a cocktail stick.

4 Prepare the barbecue. Position a lightly oiled grill rack over the coals to heat. When the coals are medium-hot, grill the wrapped prawns for 3 minutes on each side. Serve with lime wedges. Unwrap the prawns, peel off the shell and remove the black vein with your fingers before eating.

COOK'S TIP
Many barbecue meals are hands-on affairs, so a few finger bowls are often useful. You can scent the water with citrus slices, herbs and flower essences, such as rose. Float fresh petals on top for a decorative touch, if you like.

Energy 122kcal/512kJ; Protein 12.9g; Carbohydrate 0.1g, of which sugars 0.1g; Fat 7.8g, of which saturates 1.2g; Cholesterol 158mg; Calcium 65mg; Fibre 0g; Sodium 900mg.

WHOLE STUFFED SQUID

BEAUTIFULLY FRESH SQUID TASTES WONDERFUL WHEN IT IS BARBECUED, AND THE SQUID BODY IS PERFECT FOR A RICH WALNUT STUFFING. THE TENTACLES ARE PARTICULARLY TASTY, SO BE SURE TO SKEWER THEM AND COOK THEM AS WELL.

SERVES SIX

INGREDIENTS

  12 whole small squid, total weight
    about 675g/1½lb
  45ml/3 tbsp extra virgin olive oil,
    plus extra for coating
  2 onions, finely chopped
  3 garlic cloves, crushed
  25g/1oz/2 tbsp walnuts, finely chopped
  7.5ml/1½ tsp ground sumac or
    a squeeze of lemon juice
  1.5ml/¼ tsp chilli flakes,
    finely chopped
  75–90g/3–3½oz rocket (arugula),
    any tough stalks removed
  115g/4oz/1 cup cooked rice
  salt and ground black pepper
  lemon and lime wedges, to serve

1 To prepare the squid, hold the body firmly in one hand and grasp the tentacles at their base with the other. Pull the head away from the body, bringing the entrails with it. Cut the tentacles (and part of the head above the eyes) away from the entrails. Snip out the hard beak in the middle of the clump of tentacles and discard this, along with the entrails attached to the remainder of the head.

2 Peel the purplish membrane away from the body, then pull out the hard transparent quill and discard. Wash the clumps of tentacles and body well, inside and out, under cold running water.

3 Put the tentacles on a plate, cover and chill. Pull the side flaps or wings away from the body, chop them finely and set aside. Reserve the squid body with the tentacles.

COOK'S TIPS
• You can ask your fishmonger to prepare the squid for you, if you prefer.
• If you stuff the squid in advance and chill them, remember to let them return to room temperature before cooking.

4 Heat a frying pan. Add the oil, onions and garlic and fry for 5 minutes, or until the onions are soft and golden. Add the chopped squid wings and fry for about 1 minute, then stir in the walnuts, sumac and chilli flakes. Add the rocket and continue to stir-fry until it has wilted. Stir in the rice, season well and tip into a bowl to cool. Soak six wooden skewers in water for 30 minutes.

5 Prepare the barbecue. Stuff each squid with the cold mixture and thread two on to each skewer, with two clumps of tentacles. Toss in oil and salt. Position a lightly oiled grill rack over the coals to heat. Grill the squid over medium-high heat for about 1½ minutes on each side.

6 Once they are pale golden, move them to a cooler part of the grill to cook for 1½ minutes more on each side to ensure the filling is hot. Baste with any remaining oil and salt mixture as they are turned. Serve them with the lemon and lime wedges.

Energy 212kcal/887kJ; Protein 19.3g; Carbohydrate 10.3g, of which sugars 2.2g; Fat 10.7g, of which saturates 1.6g; Cholesterol 253mg; Calcium 56mg; Fibre 1g; Sodium 146mg.

MACKEREL WITH NUTTY BACON STUFFING

THIS MACKEREL RECIPE WAS INSPIRED BY A POPULAR TURKISH DISH CALLED USKUMRU DOLMASI.
THE FISH ARE STUFFED, TIED WITH RAFFIA AND THEN GRILLED. THEY TASTE JUST AS GOOD COLD,
SO MAKE EXTRA FOR LUNCH NEXT DAY AND SERVE WITH HORSERADISH MAYONNAISE.

SERVES SIX

INGREDIENTS
  45ml/3 tbsp olive oil
  2 onions, finely chopped
  2 garlic cloves, crushed
  6 rindless smoked bacon rashers
    (strips), diced
  50g/2oz/½ cup pine nuts
  45ml/3 tbsp chopped fresh
    sweet marjoram
  6 mackerel, about 300g/11oz each,
    cleaned but with heads left on
  salt and ground black pepper
  raffia, soaked in water
  lemon wedges, to serve

1 Heat the oil in a large frying pan and sweat the chopped onions and garlic over a medium heat for 5 minutes.

2 Increase the heat and add the bacon and pine nuts. Fry for a further 5–7 minutes, stirring occasionally, until golden. Tip into a bowl to cool. Gently fold in the sweet marjoram, season lightly, cover and chill until needed.

3 To prepare each fish, snip the backbone at the head end. Extend the cavity opening at the tail end so that you can reach the backbone more easily. Turn the fish over and, with the heel of your hand, press firmly along the entire length of the backbone to loosen it. Snip the bone at the tail end and it will lift out surprisingly easily. Season the insides lightly.

4 Stuff the cavity in each mackerel with some of the chilled onion mixture, then tie the mackerel along its entire length with raffia to hold in the stuffing. Chill the fish for at least 15 minutes. They can be chilled for up to 2 hours, but if so, allow them to come to room temperature for about 15 minutes before grilling.

5 Prepare the barbecue. Position a lightly oiled grill rack over the hot coals. Transfer the mackerel to the grill rack and cook for about 8 minutes on each side over medium-high heat, or until cooked and golden.

6 Transfer the cooked fish to warmed serving plates, and snip the raffia in several places, but otherwise leave it wrapped around the fish to add visual appeal. Serve the mackerel with lemon wedges and black pepper.

COOK'S TIPS
• Raffia is a strong, pliable and water-resistant fibre obtained from the raffia palm, native to Madagascar. After being dried in the sun, it is often used in crafts such as weaving or flower arranging.
• If you are cooking these mackerel on a charcoal kettle barbecue, and the heat becomes too intense very suddenly, you can reduce it a little by half-closing the air vents.
• If your barbecue has a lid, it is especially useful for this recipe. This will help you achieve an even golden skin without needing to move the fish about.

Energy 858kcal/3561kJ; Protein 64.5g; Carbohydrate 5.8g, of which sugars 4.3g; Fat 64.1g, of which saturates 12.9g; Cholesterol 175mg; Calcium 69mg; Fibre 1.5g; Sodium 641mg.

GRILLED SALTED SARDINES

WHOLE GRILLED SARDINES ARE CLASSIC MEDITERRANEAN BEACH FOOD, EVOKING MEMORIES OF LAZY LUNCHES UNDER RUSTIC AWNINGS, JUST A STEP AWAY FROM THE SEA. HERE THEY ARE SERVED WITH SALMORIGLIO, AN ITALIAN HERB SALSA POUNDED WITH SEA SALT.

SERVES FOUR TO EIGHT

INGREDIENTS
  8 sardines, total weight about
    800g/1¾lb, scaled and gutted
  50g/2oz/¼ cup salt
  oil, for brushing
  focaccia, to serve
For the salmoriglio
  5ml/1 tsp sea salt flakes
  60ml/4 tbsp chopped fresh tarragon
    leaves
  40g/1½oz/generous 1 cup chopped
    flat leaf parsley
  1 small red onion, very finely
    chopped
  105ml/7 tbsp extra virgin olive oil
  60ml/4 tbsp lemon juice

1 Rub the sardines inside and out with salt. Cover and put in a cool place for 30–45 minutes. Make the salmoriglio by putting the salt in a mortar and pounding all the ingredients one at a time with a pestle.

2 Meanwhile, prepare the barbecue. Rinse the salt off the sardines. Pat them dry with kitchen paper, then leave to air-dry for 15 minutes. Position a lightly oiled grill rack over the hot coals.

3 Brush the sardines with a little oil and put them in a small, hinged, wire barbecue fish basket. Grill them over medium-high heat for about 3 minutes on one side and about 2½ minutes on the other. When ready, lift out of the basket and serve hot with the salmoriglio and focaccia.

COOK'S TIP
Hinged wire fish baskets come in various shapes and sizes, often oval to accommodate a whole fish, square to hold fillets and steaks, or more elaborate in design to hold a number of smaller fish (see left). The idea is that you turn the basket over the barbecue rather than the fish, which is ideal for delicate dishes. If you do not have one, you can of course grill the fish directly on the rack. Do make sure to oil it well first, and only turn the fish when the undersides are crisp.

Energy 210kcal/873kJ; Protein 15.7g; Carbohydrate 0.8g, of which sugars 0.6g; Fat 16g, of which saturates 3.2g; Cholesterol 0mg; Calcium 90mg; Fibre 0.4g; Sodium 87mg.

Tangy Grilled Salmon <u>with</u> Pineapple

Fresh pineapple really brings out the flavour of salmon. Here, it is combined with lime juice to make a light and refreshing dish, which tastes great with wild rice and a simple green salad tossed with a grapefruit vinaigrette dressing.

SERVES FOUR

INGREDIENTS
   4 salmon fillets, each about
      200g/7oz
   1 small pineapple
   30ml/2 tbsp sesame seeds
   fresh chives, to garnish
   wild rice and a green salad,
      to serve
For the marinade
   grated rind and juice of 2 limes
   15ml/1 tbsp olive oil
   1cm/½in piece of fresh root ginger,
      peeled and grated
   1 garlic clove, crushed
   30ml/2 tbsp clear honey
   15ml/1 tbsp soy sauce
   ground black pepper

1 To make the marinade, put the lime rind in a jug (pitcher) and stir in the lime juice, olive oil, ginger, garlic, honey and soy sauce. Taste and add a little ground black pepper. The inclusion of soy sauce in the marinade means that salt will probably not be needed.

2 Place the salmon fillets in a single layer in a shallow, non-metallic dish. Pour the marinade over the salmon. Cover and chill for at least 1 hour, turning the salmon halfway through.

3 Carefully cut the skin off the pineapple, removing as many of the small black "eyes" as possible. Cut the pineapple into four thick rings. Use an apple corer to remove the tough central core from each slice and cut away any remaining eyes with a small knife.

COOK'S TIPS
• To cook wild rice, put it in a pan of cold salted water. Bring to the boil, then simmer for 30–40 minutes, or as directed on the packet, until tender. This would make a perfect salad lightly dressed with oil and vinegar and flavoured with chopped fresh herbs.
• Serve the grilled salmon with a mixed leaf salad. For the dressing, mix 45ml/3 tbsp grapefruit juice with 10ml/2 tsp balsamic vinegar and a pinch each of salt, ground black pepper and sugar, then whisk in 120ml/4fl oz/ ½ cup mild olive oil.

4 Preheat the grill (broiler) to high. Sprinkle the sesame seeds over a piece of foil and place under the grill for a minute or two until they turn golden brown. Set aside.

5 Prepare the barbecue. Position a lightly oiled grill rack over the hot coals. Using a slotted spoon, remove the salmon fillets from the marinade and place them on the grill rack with the pineapple rings.

6 Grill the fish and pineapple for 10 minutes over medium-high heat, brushing occasionally with the marinade and turning everything over once, until the fish is cooked through and the pineapple rings are golden brown. Brush over the final layer of marinade no less than 2 minutes before the end of cooking to ensure it cooks thoroughly.

7 Transfer the fish to serving plates, placing each fillet on a bed of wild rice. Top with the pineapple slices. Sprinkle the sesame seeds over the top and garnish with the chives. Serve with a green salad.

Energy 487kcal/2036kJ; Protein 42.4g; Carbohydrate 17.1g, of which sugars 17.1g; Fat 28.2g, of which saturates 4.6g; Cholesterol 100mg; Calcium 120mg; Fibre 2.4g; Sodium 95mg.

GRILLED SWORDFISH SKEWERS

FOR A TASTE OF THE GREEK ISLANDS, TRY THESE TANTALIZING SWORDFISH KEBABS. BARBECUED WITH PEPPERS AND ONIONS, THEY ALSO HAVE A HINT OF OREGANO. TRY THROWING SOME OREGANO SPRIGS OVER THE COALS AS YOU COOK, FOR ADDED FLAVOUR.

SERVES FOUR

INGREDIENTS

2 red onions, quartered
2 red or green (bell) peppers,
  quartered and seeded
20–24 thick cubes of swordfish,
  prepared weight
  675–800g/1½–1¾lb
75ml/5 tbsp extra virgin olive oil
1 garlic clove, crushed
large pinch of dried oregano
salt and ground black pepper

1 Carefully separate the onion quarters in pieces, each composed of two or three layers. Slice each pepper quarter in half widthways.

2 Make the kebabs by threading five or six pieces of swordfish on to each of four long metal skewers, alternating with pieces of the pepper and onion. Lay the kebabs across a grill pan or roasting tray and set aside while you make the basting sauce.

3 Whisk the olive oil, crushed garlic and oregano in a bowl. Add salt and pepper, and whisk again. Brush the kebabs generously on all sides with the basting sauce.

4 Prepare the barbecue. Position a lightly oiled grill rack over the hot coals. Transfer the skewers to the barbecue. Cook for 8–10 minutes over medium heat, turning the skewers several times, until the fish is cooked and the peppers and onions have begun to scorch around the edges. Every time you turn the skewers, brush them with the basting sauce.

5 Serve the kebabs immediately, with a cucumber, onion and olive salad.

COOK'S TIP
The fishmonger will prepare the cubes of swordfish for you, but if you prefer to do this yourself you will need to buy about 800g/1¾lb swordfish. The cubes should be fairly big – about 5cm/2in square.

Energy 322kcal/1345kJ; Protein 32.5g; Carbohydrate 13.5g, of which sugars 11g; Fat 15.7g, of which saturates 2.8g; Cholesterol 69mg; Calcium 39mg; Fibre 2.8g; Sodium 226mg.

MARINATED SEA TROUT

SEA TROUT HAS A SUPERB TEXTURE AND A FLAVOUR LIKE THAT OF WILD SALMON. IT'S BEST SERVED WITH STRONG BUT COMPLEMENTARY FLAVOURS SUCH AS CHILLIES AND LIME THAT CUT THE RICHNESS OF THE FLESH. USE HINGED WIRE BASKETS TO MAKE COOKING AND TURNING EASIER.

SERVES SIX

INGREDIENTS

    6 sea trout cutlets, about 115g/4oz
      each, or wild or farmed salmon
    2 garlic cloves, chopped
    1 fresh long red chilli, seeded
      and chopped
    45ml/3 tbsp chopped Thai basil
    15ml/1 tbsp palm sugar or
      granulated sugar
    3 limes
    400ml/14fl oz/1⅔ cups coconut milk
    15ml/1 tbsp Thai fish sauce

1 Place the sea trout cutlets in a shallow dish. Using a pestle, pound the garlic and chilli in a large mortar to break it up roughly. Add 30ml/2 tbsp of the Thai basil with the sugar and continue to pound to a rough paste.

2 Grate the rind from 1 lime and squeeze it. Mix the rind and juice into the chilli paste, with the coconut milk. Pour the mixture over the cutlets, cover and chill the mixture for about 1 hour. Cut the remaining limes into wedges.

COOK'S TIP

This recipe uses the marinade as a sauce to accompany the fish. You can do this with most marinades as long as you boil them up thoroughly first. Put a small pan on to the barbecue to boil up the marinade and then move it to the side while it simmers for about 5 minutes. Never use a marinade to brush over food just before serving or as a sauce unless it has been thoroughly cooked first.

3 Remove the fish from the refrigerator so that it can return to room temperature before you cook it on the barbecue. Prepare the barbecue. Position a lightly oiled grill rack over the hot coals. Remove the cutlets from the marinade and reserve the marinade. Place them in an oiled hinged wire fish basket or directly on the grill rack. Cook the fish over medium-high heat for 4 minutes on each side, trying not to move them. They may stick to the grill rack if not seared first.

4 Strain the remaining marinade into a pan, reserving the contents of the sieve. Bring the marinade to the boil, simmer gently for 5 minutes, then stir in the contents of the sieve and continue to simmer for 1 minute more.

5 Add the Thai fish sauce and the remaining Thai basil. Lift each fish cutlet on to a plate, pour over the sauce and serve with the lime wedges.

Energy 157kcal/662kJ; Protein 23.1g; Carbohydrate 5.9g, of which sugars 5.9g; Fat 4.7g, of which saturates 0.1g; Cholesterol 0mg; Calcium 46mg; Fibre 0.4g; Sodium 141mg.

BARBECUED RED SNAPPER

THE RED SNAPPER IS A LINE-CAUGHT REEF FISH FROM THE INDIAN OCEAN AND THE CARIBBEAN. ALTHOUGH BEAUTIFUL TO LOOK AT, IT HAS VICIOUS SPINES AND A FAIRLY IMPENETRABLE ARMOUR OF SCALES, SO PERHAPS IT WOULD BE BEST IF YOU ASK THE FISHMONGER TO SCALE IT. LEAVE THE FINS ON, HOWEVER, SO THAT IT RETAINS ITS LOVELY APPEARANCE.

SERVES FOUR

INGREDIENTS
   2 red snapper, about 900g/2lb each,
      cleaned and scaled, or tilapia
   15ml/1 tbsp olive oil
   5cm/2in piece of fresh root ginger,
      thinly sliced
   4 banana shallots, total weight about
      150g/5oz, thinly sliced
   3 garlic cloves, thinly sliced
   30ml/2 tbsp sugar
   3 lemon grass stalks, 1 thinly sliced
   grated rind and juice of 1 lime
   5ml/1 tsp salt
   4 small fresh green or red chillies,
      thinly sliced
   2 whole banana leaves
   30ml/2 tbsp chopped fresh coriander
      (cilantro)
For the dipping sauce
   1 large fresh red chilli, seeded and
      finely chopped
   juice of 2 limes
   30ml/2 tbsp fish sauce
   5ml/1 tsp sugar
   60ml/4 tbsp water

1 Soak six wooden skewers in cold water for 30 minutes. Make four slashes in either side of each fish and rub the skin with oil.

2 Make the dipping sauce by mixing together all the ingredients in a bowl. Cover and chill until needed.

3 Place half the ginger and shallots and the garlic in a mortar. Add half the sugar, the thinly sliced lemon grass, a little of the lime juice, the salt and the chillies and pound to break up and bruise. Mix in the remaining sugar and lime juice, with the lime rind. Rub a little of the mixture into the slashes and the bulk of it into the cavity of each fish.

4 Trim the hard edge from each banana leaf and discard it. Soak the banana leaves in hot water for 10 minutes, then drain. Wipe any white residue from the leaves. Rinse, then pour over boiling water to soften. Drain again.

5 Lay a fish on each leaf and scatter the remaining ginger and shallots over them. Split the whole lemon grass stalks lengthways and lay the pieces over each fish. Bring the sides of the leaves up over the fish and secure using three wooden skewers for each envelope. Wrap in clear film (plastic wrap) to keep the wooden skewers moist, and chill for at least 30 minutes, but no more than 6 hours.

COOK'S TIPS
• Serve leaf-wrapped rice parcels with the fish. Heat them up in foil next to the fish for the last 5 minutes. They can be found in larger Asian food stores.
• Banana shallots have longer bulbs than most shallots or onions, and varieties include Long Red Florence and Longor.

6 Prepare the barbecue. Bring the dipping sauce to room temperature. Remove the clear film from each banana leaf envelope and place each on a sheet of foil. Bring the sides of the foil up around each envelope to enclose it loosely. This will protect the base of each banana leaf wrapper.

7 Position a lightly oiled grill rack over the hot coals. Lay the envelopes on the grill rack and cook for 15 minutes over medium-high heat. Turn the envelopes around 180 degrees and cook for about 10 minutes more, opening up the foil for the last 5 minutes.

8 Remove from the barbecue and leave to stand for a further 5 minutes, then check to see if the fish is cooked by inserting a skewer – it should flake easily when the skewer is removed. Place on a large serving dish, open the envelopes and sprinkle the fish with the chopped coriander. Serve the fish in individual serving bowls, with smaller bowls for the dipping sauce.

Energy 305kcal/1293kJ; Protein 57.3g; Carbohydrate 2.9g, of which sugars 2.9g; Fat 7.5g, of which saturates 1.4g; Cholesterol 104mg; Calcium 157mg; Fibre 1.2g; Sodium 541mg.

POULTRY

From classics such as Chargrilled Cajun Drummers to superb street food such as Chicken with Lemon Grass and Ginger, there are so many different ways to barbecue chicken. Try tender morsels wrapped as Chicken Fajitas, Spicy Indonesian Chicken Satay – simply oozing piquant sweetness – or the fresh and healthy Griddled Chicken with Salsa. Other poultry meats lend themselves just as well to the barbecue, such as Turkey Sosaties with Apricot Sauce or Glazed Duck Breasts.

CARIBBEAN CHICKEN KEBABS

RUM, LIME JUICE AND CINNAMON MAKE A ROBUST MARINADE FOR CHICKEN, WHICH IS THEN BARBECUED WITH MANGOES TO MAKE AN UNUSUAL AND FRESH-TASTING DISH. YOU CAN SERVE THE KEBABS WITH RICE, OR SLIDE THEM OFF THE SKEWERS STRAIGHT INTO PITTA BREAD FOR AN INFORMAL BARBECUE MEAL.

2 Soak four wooden skewers in water for 30 minutes. Cut the mangoes into cubes by cutting slices, scoring into cubes and slicing away from the skin.

3 Prepare the barbecue. Position a lightly oiled grill rack over the hot coals. Drain the chicken, saving the juices, and thread on to the wooden skewers, alternating with the mango cubes.

SERVES FOUR

INGREDIENTS
 500g/1¼lb skinless chicken
   breast fillets
 finely grated rind of 1 lime
 30ml/2 tbsp fresh lime juice
 15ml/1 tbsp rum or sherry
 15ml/1 tbsp light muscovado
   (brown) sugar
 5ml/1 tsp ground cinnamon
 2 mangoes, peeled and cubed
 rice and salad, to serve

1 Cut the chicken into bitesize chunks, and place in a bowl with the lime rind and juice, rum or sherry, sugar and cinnamon. Toss well, cover and leave to stand for 1 hour in a cool place.

4 Grill the skewers over high heat for 8–10 minutes, turning occasionally and basting with the juices, until the chicken is tender and golden brown. Serve at once with rice and a salad.

Energy 195kcal/826kJ; Protein 30.6g; Carbohydrate 14.6g, of which sugars 14.3g; Fat 1.5g, of which saturates 0.5g; Cholesterol 88mg; Calcium 18mg; Fibre 2g; Sodium 77mg.

BARBECUED CHICKEN TIKKA

MARINATED IN LOW-FAT YOGURT AND SPICES, THE CHICKEN HAS ALL THE FLAVOUR YOU WOULD EXPECT FROM A BARBECUED DISH AND YET IT IS A HEALTHY LOW-FAT MEAL. LEAVE IT OVERNIGHT TO MARINATE, IF YOU CAN, FOR THE BEST FLAVOUR. RED FOOD COLOURING ADDS A DASH OF TRADITIONAL COLOUR.

SERVES FOUR

INGREDIENTS

4 skinless chicken breast fillets
lemon wedges and mixed salad
  leaves, such as frisée and oakleaf
  lettuce or radicchio, to serve
For the marinade
  150ml/¼ pint/⅔ cup low-fat natural
    (plain) yogurt
  5ml/1 tsp paprika
  10ml/2 tsp grated fresh root ginger
  1 garlic clove, crushed
  10ml/2 tsp garam masala
  2.5ml/½ tsp salt
  few drops of red food
    colouring (optional)
  juice of 1 lemon

3 Remove the chicken pieces from the marinade and cook over high heat for 30–40 minutes, or until tender, turning occasionally and basting with a little of the marinade.

4 Arrange the chicken pieces on a bed of salad leaves with two lemon wedges and serve either hot or cold.

1 Mix all the marinade ingredients in a large dish. Add the chicken pieces to coat for at least 4 hours or overnight in the refrigerator to allow the flavours to penetrate the flesh.

2 Prepare the barbecue. Position a lightly oiled grill rack over the hot coals.

COOK'S TIP
This is an example of a dish that is usually very high in fat, but with a few basic changes this level can be dramatically reduced. This can also be achieved with other similar dishes, by substituting low-fat yogurt for full-fat versions and creams, and by removing the skin from the chicken, as well as by reducing the amount of oil.

Energy 169kcal/716kJ; Protein 36.8g; Carbohydrate 1.3g, of which sugars 1.3g; Fat 1.9g, of which saturates 0.5g; Cholesterol 105mg; Calcium 38mg; Fibre 0.2g; Sodium 199mg.

JERK CHICKEN

Traditionally jerk refers to the blend of herb and spice seasoning rubbed into meat before it is roasted over charcoal sprinkled with pimiento berries. In Jamaica, jerk seasoning was originally used only for pork, but jerked chicken is equally good.

SERVES FOUR

INGREDIENTS
  8 chicken pieces
  salad leaves, to serve
For the marinade
  5ml/1 tsp ground allspice
  5ml/1 tsp ground cinnamon
  5ml/1 tsp dried thyme
  1.5ml/¼ tsp freshly grated nutmeg
  10ml/2 tsp demerara (raw) sugar
  2 garlic cloves, crushed
  15ml/1 tbsp finely chopped onion
  15ml/1 tbsp chopped spring onion
    (scallion)
  15ml/1 tbsp vinegar
  30ml/2 tbsp oil, plus extra for
    brushing
  15ml/1 tbsp lime juice
  1 hot chilli, chopped
  salt and ground black pepper

1 Combine all the marinade ingredients in a small bowl. Using a fork, mash them together thoroughly to form a thick paste.

2 Lay the chicken pieces on a plate or board and make several lengthways slits in the flesh. Rub the marinade all over the chicken and into the slits.

3 Place the chicken in a dish, cover with clear film (plastic wrap) and leave to marinate in the refrigerator for 2 hours or overnight.

4 Prepare the barbecue. Position a lightly oiled grill rack over the hot coals. Shake off any excess marinade from the chicken and brush with oil. Place on the grill rack.

5 Cook over medium heat for 30 minutes, turning often until done. Serve hot with salad leaves.

COOK'S TIP
Always use tongs to turn meat over rather than using a fork, as the tines can easily pierce the meat and so allow the juices to escape.

Energy 298kcal/1257kJ; Protein 54.2g; Carbohydrate 2.5g, of which sugars 2.2g; Fat 8g, of which saturates 1.5g; Cholesterol 158mg; Calcium 16mg; Fibre 0.2g; Sodium 136mg.

SPICY MASALA CHICKEN

SPICES, HERBS AND HONEY MAKE A LOVELY SWEET-AND-SOUR MARINADE FOR CHICKEN PIECES, WHICH TASTE GREAT WHEN COOKED OVER THE COALS. SERVE WITH SALADS AND CRUSTY BREAD OR RICE. REMEMBER YOU CAN ALWAYS ADD SOME HERB SPRIGS TO THE COALS TO ADD TO THE SMOKY FLAVOUR.

SERVES SIX

INGREDIENTS

    12 chicken thighs
    90ml/6 tbsp lemon juice
    5ml/1 tsp chopped fresh root ginger
    5ml/1 tsp chopped garlic
    5ml/1 tsp crushed dried red chillies
    5ml/1 tsp salt
    5ml/1 tsp soft light brown sugar
    30ml/2 tbsp clear honey
    30ml/2 tbsp chopped fresh
      coriander (cilantro)
    1 green chilli, finely chopped
    30ml/2 tbsp vegetable oil
    fresh coriander sprigs, to garnish

1 Prick the chicken thighs with a fork, rinse, pat dry and set aside.

2 In a large mixing bowl, make the marinade by mixing together the lemon juice, ginger, garlic, crushed dried red chillies, salt, sugar and honey.

3 Transfer the chicken thighs to the spice mixture and coat well. Set aside for about 45 minutes.

4 Prepare the barbecue. Position a lightly oiled grill rack over the hot coals. Add the coriander and green chilli to the chicken thighs and place them in a flameproof dish.

5 Pour any remaining marinade over the chicken and baste lightly with the oil, taking care not to remove the marinade. Transfer to the grill rack.

6 Grill the chicken thighs over medium heat for 15–20 minutes, turning and basting with the marinade occasionally, until they are cooked. Add the final basting no less than 5 minutes before the end of the cooking time to ensure the marinade is fully cooked.

7 Serve the chicken garnished with a few sprigs of fresh coriander and accompanied with rice or barbecued potatoes and a salad.

COOK'S TIP

If you are cooking by gas and don't have a smoke box but want to add some aromatics, you can use a foil container and cover it with a piece of foil. Make some holes in the top for the smoke to escape.

Energy 165kcal/694kJ; Protein 18.9g; Carbohydrate 9.1g, of which sugars 9.1g; Fat 6.2g, of which saturates 1.2g; Cholesterol 95mg; Calcium 9mg; Fibre 0g; Sodium 409mg.

GRIDDLED CHICKEN WITH SALSA

THINLY POUNDED CHICKEN BREAST FILLETS COOK IN THE MINIMUM OF TIME WHEN USING THE GRIDDLE. MARINATE THEM FIRST TO MAKE THEM EXTRA DELICIOUS AND MOIST, AND THEN SERVE WITH A SALSA OF FRESH SUMMER INGREDIENTS WITH ROASTED CHILLI TO MAKE A SIMPLE DISH THAT IS FULL OF FLAVOUR.

SERVES FOUR

INGREDIENTS
   4 boneless, skinless chicken breast
     fillets, about 175g/6oz each
   30ml/2 tbsp fresh lemon juice
   30ml/2 tbsp olive oil
   10ml/2 tsp ground cumin
   10ml/2 tsp dried oregano
   15ml/1 tbsp coarse black pepper
For the salsa
   1 green chilli
   450g/1lb plum tomatoes, seeded
     and chopped
   3 spring onions (scallions), chopped
   15ml/1 tbsp chopped fresh parsley
   30ml/2 tbsp chopped fresh coriander
     (cilantro)
   30ml/2 tbsp fresh lemon juice
   45ml/3 tbsp olive oil

1 With a meat mallet, pound the chicken fillets between two sheets of clear film (plastic wrap) until thin.

2 In a shallow dish, combine the lemon juice, oil, cumin, oregano and pepper. Add the chicken and turn to coat. Cover and leave to marinate for 2 hours, or in the refrigerator overnight.

3 To make the salsa, char the chilli skin either over a gas flame or under the grill (broiler). Leave to cool for 5 minutes. Carefully rub off the charred skin, taking care to wash your hands afterwards. For a less hot flavour, discard the seeds.

4 Chop the chilli very finely and place in a bowl. Add the tomatoes, the spring onions, parsley and coriander, lemon juice and olive oil, and mix well.

5 Prepare the barbecue. Heat a griddle on the grill rack over hot coals. Remove the chicken from the marinade. Griddle the chicken on one side until browned, for about 3 minutes. Turn over and cook for a further 4 minutes. Serve with the chilli salsa.

Energy 312kcal/1309kJ; Protein 43.4g; Carbohydrate 4.5g, of which sugars 4.4g; Fat 13.5g, of which saturates 2.2g; Cholesterol 123mg; Calcium 46mg; Fibre 2g; Sodium 121mg.

CHICKEN WITH LEMON GRASS AND GINGER

CHICKEN COOKED ON A BARBECUE IS SERVED AS STREET FOOD IN COMMUNITIES ALL OVER THE WORLD, FROM ROADSIDE STALLS TO SPORTS STADIA. THIS DISH USES TYPICAL THAI FLAVOURINGS THAT ARE NOT TOO SPICY FOR KIDS. THE CHICKEN PIECES ARE PERFECT TO NIBBLE ON AT PARTIES.

SERVES FOUR TO SIX

INGREDIENTS
    1 chicken, about 1.3–1.6kg/3–3½ lb,
        cut into 8–10 pieces
    lime wedges and fresh red chillies,
        to garnish
For the marinade
    2 lemon grass stalks, roots trimmed
    2.5cm/1in piece fresh root ginger,
        peeled and thinly sliced
    6 garlic cloves, coarsely chopped
    4 shallots, coarsely chopped
    ½ bunch coriander (cilantro)
        roots, chopped
    15ml/1 tbsp palm sugar or light
        muscovado (brown) sugar
    120ml/4fl oz/½ cup coconut milk
    30ml/2 tbsp Thai fish sauce
    30ml/2 tbsp light soy sauce

1 To make the marinade, cut off the lower 5cm/2in of the lemon grass stalks and chop them coarsely. Put into a food processor with the ginger, garlic, shallots, coriander, sugar, coconut milk and sauces, and process until smooth.

2 Place the chicken pieces in a dish, pour over the marinade and stir to mix well. Cover the dish and leave in a cool place to marinate for at least 4 hours, or leave in the refrigerator overnight.

3 Prepare the barbecue. Position a lightly oiled grill rack over the hot coals. Drain the chicken, reserving the marinade, and transfer to the grill rack.

4 Cook over medium heat for 20–30 minutes. Turn the pieces frequently and brush with the reserved marinade once or twice during cooking but add the final basting no less than 5 minutes before the end of the cooking time to ensure the marinade is fully cooked.

5 As soon as the chicken pieces are golden brown and cooked through, transfer them to a serving platter, garnish with the lime wedges and red chillies and serve immediately.

COOK'S TIPS
• Coconut milk is available fresh or in cans or cartons from Asian food stores and most supermarkets and you may also find it in powdered form. Alternatively, use 50g/2oz creamed coconut from a packet and add warm water, stirring all the time, until it has completely dissolved.
• Coriander roots are more intensely flavoured than the leaves, but the herb is not always available with the roots intact.

Energy 361kcal/1502kJ; Protein 28.8g; Carbohydrate 8.3g, of which sugars 6.7g; Fat 23.9g, of which saturates 18.4g; Cholesterol 140mg; Calcium 28mg; Fibre 0.9g; Sodium 478mg.

TURKEY SOSATIES WITH APRICOT SAUCE

CHUNKS OF TURKEY FILLET ARE MARINATED IN A FABULOUS SWEET-AND-SOUR SPICED SAUCE IN THIS RECIPE FROM SOUTH AFRICA. MOP IT UP WITH SOME CRUSTY BREAD.

SERVES FOUR

INGREDIENTS
5ml/1 tsp vegetable oil
1 onion, finely chopped
1 garlic clove, crushed
2 bay leaves
juice of 1 lemon
30ml/2 tbsp curry powder
60ml/4 tbsp apricot jam
60ml/4 tbsp apple juice
675g/1½lb turkey fillet
30ml/2 tbsp low-fat crème fraîche
salt

COOK'S TIP
If serving the sosaties indoors, serve with couscous and grilled vegetables.

1 Heat the oil in a pan. Add the onion, garlic and bay leaves and cook over a low heat for 10 minutes, or until the onions are soft. Add the lemon juice, curry powder, apricot jam and apple juice, with salt to taste. Cook gently for 5 minutes. Transfer to a bowl and cool.

2 Cut the turkey into 2cm/³/₄in cubes and add to the bowl. Mix well, cover and leave to marinate for at least 2 hours or chill overnight.

3 Prepare the barbecue. Position a lightly oiled grill rack over the hot coals. Thread the turkey on to four metal skewers, allowing the marinade to run back into the bowl. Cook the sosaties for 6–8 minutes over medium heat, turning several times, until done.

4 Meanwhile, transfer the marinade to a pan and simmer on the grill rack for 2 minutes. Stir in the crème fraîche, allow to heat through gently, and serve the sauce with the sosaties.

SPICY INDONESIAN CHICKEN SATAY

CHILLIES, GARLIC AND SOY SAUCE GIVE THESE INDONESIAN CHICKEN SATAYS PIQUANCY, AND THE REMAINING MARINADE IS COOKED TO MAKE A TASTY ACCOMPANYING DIP.

SERVES FOUR

INGREDIENTS
½ onion, sliced
oil, for deep-frying
4 chicken breast fillets, about
175g/6oz each, skinned and cut
into 2.5cm/1in cubes
For the sambal kecap
1 fresh red chilli, seeded and finely
chopped
2 garlic cloves, crushed
60ml/4 tbsp dark soy sauce
20ml/4 tsp lemon juice or 15–25ml/
1–1½ tbsp tamarind juice
30ml/2 tbsp hot water

1 Deep-fry the onion until golden. Set aside.

2 To make the sambal kecap, mix all the ingredients in a bowl. Leave to stand for 30 minutes.

3 Place the chicken breast cubes in a bowl with the sambal kecap. Mix thoroughly. Cover and leave in a cool place to marinate for 1 hour.

4 Meanwhile, soak eight wooden skewers in water for 30 minutes.

5 Tip the chicken and marinade into a sieve placed over a pan and leave to drain for a few minutes. Set the sieve with the chicken aside.

6 Add 30ml/2 tbsp hot water to the marinade and bring to the boil. Lower the heat and simmer for 2 minutes, then pour into a bowl and leave to cool. When cool, add the deep-fried onion.

7 Prepare the barbecue. Position a lightly oiled grill rack over the hot coals. Thread the skewers with the chicken and cook over medium heat for about 10 minutes, turning regularly, until golden brown and cooked through. Serve with the sambal kecap as a dip.

Above: Energy 325kcal/1381kJ; Protein 59.4g; Carbohydrate 12.2g, of which sugars 12.1g; Fat 4.8g, of which saturates 1.9g; Cholesterol 125mg; Calcium 18mg; Fibre 0g; Sodium 162mg.
Below: Energy 197kcal/835kJ; Protein 42.5g; Carbohydrate 2.5g, of which sugars 2g; Fat 2g, of which saturates 0.5g; Cholesterol 123mg; Calcium 15mg; Fibre 0.4g; Sodium 640mg.

DUCK SAUSAGES WITH SPICY PLUM SAUCE

THE RICH FLAVOUR OF DUCK SAUSAGES GOES EXTREMELY WELL WITH SWEET POTATO MASH AND A PLUM SAUCE. THE RECIPE WOULD ALSO WORK WELL WITH PORK OR GAME SAUSAGES — OR A LUXURIOUS HICKORY-SMOKED SAUSAGE FOR A REAL BOOST TO FLAVOUR.

SERVES FOUR

INGREDIENTS
8–12 duck sausages
For the sweet potato mash
  1.5kg/3¼lb sweet potatoes, cut
    into chunks
  25g/1oz/2 tbsp butter or 30ml/2 tbsp
    olive oil
  60ml/4 tbsp milk
  sea salt and ground black pepper
For the plum sauce
  30ml/2 tbsp olive oil
  1 small onion, chopped
  1 small red chilli, seeded
    and chopped
  450g/1lb plums, stoned (pitted)
    and chopped
  30ml/2 tbsp red wine vinegar
  45ml/3 tbsp clear honey

1 Put the sweet potatoes in a pan and add water to cover. Bring to the boil, then reduce the heat and simmer for 20 minutes, or until tender.

2 To make the plum sauce, heat the oil in a small pan and fry the onion and chilli gently for 5 minutes. Stir in the plums, vinegar and honey, then simmer gently for 10 minutes.

3 Drain and mash the potatoes and leave them in the pan.

VARIATION
If you'd rather not go to the bother of cooking the sweet potato mash, try a quick and easy polenta mash, perhaps combined with steamed spinach.

4 Prepare the barbecue. Arrange the duck sausages on the grill rack and cook over medium heat for 25–30 minutes, turning the sausages two or three times during cooking to ensure that they brown and cook evenly.

5 Place the pan with the mash on the grill rack and reheat. Stir frequently for about 5 minutes to dry out the mashed potato. Beat in the butter or oil and milk, and season to taste.

6 Serve the freshly cooked sausages accompanied by the sweet potato mash and plum sauce.

Energy 894kcal/3755kJ; Protein 17.8g; Carbohydrate 110.8g, of which sugars 42.9g; Fat 45.5g, of which saturates 17.9g; Cholesterol 67mg; Calcium 170mg; Fibre 11.6g; Sodium 1052mg.

GLAZED DUCK BREASTS

In this Cajun recipe, sliced and barbecued sweet potatoes go particularly well with duck breasts that have been brushed with a sweet glaze. The dish is quick to prepare and cook, making it ideal for a fuss-free barbecue.

SERVES TWO

INGREDIENTS

2 duck breast portions
1 sweet potato, about 400g/14oz
30ml/2 tbsp red pepper jelly
15ml/1 tbsp sherry vinegar
50g/2oz/4 tbsp butter, melted
coarse sea salt and ground
  black pepper

COOK'S TIP
Choose cylindrical sweet potatoes for the neatest slices.

1 Prepare the barbecue. Position a lightly oiled grill rack over the hot coals. Slash the skin of the duck breast portions diagonally at 2.5cm/1in intervals and rub plenty of salt and pepper over the skin and into the cuts.

2 Scrub the sweet potato and cut into 1cm/½in slices, discarding the ends.

3 Cook the duck breast portions over medium heat, skin side down, for 5 minutes. Turn and cook for a further 8–10 minutes, according to preference.

4 Meanwhile, brush the sweet potato slices with melted butter and sprinkle with coarse sea salt. Cook on the hottest part of the barbecue for 8–10 minutes until soft, brushing regularly with more butter and sprinkling liberally with salt and pepper every time you turn them. Keep an eye on them so that they do not char.

5 Warm the red pepper jelly and sherry vinegar together in a bowl set over a pan of hot water, stirring to mix them as the jelly melts. Brush the skin of the duck with the jelly and return to the barbecue, skin side down, for 2–3 minutes to caramelize it. Slice and serve with the sweet potatoes.

Energy 643kcal/2702kJ; Protein 42.1g; Carbohydrate 53.1g, of which sugars 21.9g; Fat 34.2g, of which saturates 15.8g; Cholesterol 273mg; Calcium 79mg; Fibre 4.8g; Sodium 456mg.

QUAIL WITH A FIVE-SPICE MARINADE

BLENDING AND GRINDING YOUR OWN FIVE-SPICE POWDER WILL GIVE THE FRESHEST-TASTING RESULTS FOR THIS Vietnamese-STYLE DISH OF SPATCHCOCKED QUAIL. IF YOU ARE SHORT OF TIME, BUY A GOOD-QUALITY READY-MIXED BLEND FROM THE SUPERMARKET.

SERVES FOUR TO SIX

INGREDIENTS
  6 quails, cleaned
To garnish
    mandarin orange or satsuma
    2 spring onions (scallions),
      roughly chopped
    banana leaves, to serve
For the marinade
    2 pieces star anise
    10ml/2 tsp ground cinnamon
    10ml/2 tsp fennel seeds
    10ml/2 tsp Sichuan pepper
    a pinch ground cloves
    1 small onion, finely chopped
    1 garlic clove, crushed
    60ml/4 tbsp clear honey
    30ml/2 tbsp dark soy sauce

COOK'S TIP
If you prefer, or if quails are not available, you could use other small poultry such as poussins. Poussins will take around 25–30 minutes to cook using the method given in this recipe.

1 Soak 12 wooden skewers in water for 30 minutes. Remove the backbones from the quails by cutting down either side with a pair of strong kitchen scissors.

2 Flatten the birds with the palm of your hand and secure each bird using two bamboo skewers.

3 To make the marinade, place the spices in a mortar or spice mill and grind into a fine powder. Add the onion, garlic, clear honey and soy sauce, and combine until thoroughly mixed.

4 Arrange the quails on a flat dish and pour over the marinade. Cover with clear film (plastic wrap) and leave in the refrigerator for 8 hours or overnight for the flavours to mingle.

5 Preheat the barbecue. Position a lightly oiled grill rack over the hot coals. Cook the quails over medium-high heat for 5 minutes then cover with a lid or tented heavy-duty foil and cook for 10 minutes more until golden brown. Baste occasionally with the marinade during cooking.

6 To make the garnish, remove the outer zest from the mandarin orange or satsuma, using a vegetable peeler. Shred the zest finely and combine with the chopped spring onions. Arrange the quails on a bed of banana leaves and garnish with the orange zest and spring onions.

Energy 159kcal/664kJ; Protein 13.2g; Carbohydrate 5.6g, of which sugars 5.6g; Fat 9.5g, of which saturates 2.6g; Cholesterol 68mg; Calcium 7mg; Fibre 0.1g; Sodium 404mg.

MEAT

Barbecuing meat is an age-old method of cooking: our ancestors roasted joints of red meat and game over hot coals thousands of years ago. In addition to some of the great grilled classics here, there is some fresh inspiration. Belmont Sausage with Mushroom Relish – quality meat curled into rounds and skewered over a metal rack – is bound to whet the appetite of any meat-eating guest. Or, if you have a spit, try Barbecue Roast Beef: a meaty fillet brushed with horseradish and beer.

SHISH KEBABS

SUMAC IS A SPICE, GROUND FROM A DRIED PURPLE BERRY WITH A SOUR, FRUITY FLAVOUR. IN THIS RECIPE IT BLISSFULLY COMPLEMENTS THE RICHNESS OF THE LAMB AND YOGURT. THESE KEBABS ARE EXCELLENT SERVED WITH LITTLE BOWLS OF INDIVIDUAL HERBS DRESSED AT THE LAST MINUTE.

MAKES EIGHT

INGREDIENTS
675g/1½lb lamb neck (US shoulder or breast) fillet, trimmed and cut into 2.5cm/1in pieces
5ml/1 tsp each fennel, cumin and coriander seeds, roasted and crushed
1.5ml/¼ tsp cayenne pepper
5cm/2in piece of fresh root ginger
150ml/¼ pint/⅔ cup Greek (US strained plain) yogurt
2 small red (bell) peppers
2 small yellow (bell) peppers
300g/11oz small or baby (pearl) onions
30ml/2 tbsp olive oil
15ml/1 tbsp ground sumac
salt and ground black pepper
To serve
8 Lebanese flat breads
150ml/¼ pint/⅔ cup Greek (US strained plain) yogurt
5ml/1 tsp ground sumac
1 bunch rocket (arugula), about 50g/2oz
50g/2oz/2 cups fresh flat leaf parsley
10ml/2 tsp olive oil
juice of ½ lemon

COOK'S TIP
If you want to use a griddle on the barbecue, cook the kebabs over a high heat to begin with, then lower the heat, and turn them frequently.

1 Place the lamb pieces in a bowl and sprinkle over the crushed seeds and the cayenne pepper. Grate the ginger and squeeze it over the lamb. When all the juices have been extracted, discard the pulp. Pour over the yogurt. Mix well, then cover and marinate overnight in the refrigerator.

2 Prepare the barbecue. Stand a large sieve over a bowl and pour in the lamb mixture. Leave to drain well. Cut the peppers in half, remove the cores and seeds, then cut the flesh into rough chunks. Place in a bowl. Add the onions and the olive oil.

3 Pat the drained lamb with kitchen paper to remove excess marinade. Add the lamb to the bowl, season and toss well. Divide the lamb, peppers and onions into eight equal portions and thread on to eight long metal skewers.

4 Position a lightly oiled grill rack over the coals to heat. Grill the kebabs for about 10 minutes over medium-high heat, turning every 2 minutes to prevent the meat and vegetables from getting too charred. When cooked, transfer the kebabs to a platter, lightly sprinkle with the sumac, cover loosely with foil, and leave to rest for a few minutes.

5 Wrap the breads in foil and put them on the barbecue to warm. Place the yogurt in a small serving bowl and sprinkle the surface with sumac. Arrange the rocket and parsley in separate bowls and pour over the oil and lemon juice. Serve with the kebabs and the warmed flat bread.

COOK'S TIP
Take care not to pack the lamb pieces too tightly on the skewers because they will not brown properly.

Energy 361kcal/1515kJ; Protein 22.5g; Carbohydrate 38.4g, of which sugars 8.1g; Fat 14.1g, of which saturates 5.1g; Cholesterol 64mg; Calcium 133mg; Fibre 3g; Sodium 249mg.

LAMB BURGERS <u>WITH</u> REDCURRANT CHUTNEY

THESE RATHER SPECIAL BURGERS TAKE A LITTLE EXTRA TIME TO PREPARE BUT ARE WELL WORTH IT, BECAUSE EACH CONTAINS SOME MELTINGLY SOFT MOZZARELLA CHEESE. THE REDCURRANT CHUTNEY IS THE PERFECT COMPLEMENT TO THE MINTY LAMB TASTE OF THE BURGERS.

SERVES FOUR

INGREDIENTS
  500g/1¼lb/2½ cups minced
    (ground) lean lamb
  1 small onion, finely chopped
  30ml/2 tbsp finely chopped fresh mint
  30ml/2 tbsp finely chopped
    fresh parsley
  115g/4oz mozzarella cheese
  30ml/2 tbsp oil, for basting
  salt and freshly ground black pepper
For the redcurrant chutney
  115g/4oz/1½ cups fresh or
    frozen redcurrants
  10ml/2 tsp clear honey
  5ml/1 tsp balsamic vinegar
  30ml/2 tbsp finely chopped mint

1 In a large bowl, mix together the lamb, onion, mint and parsley until evenly combined. Season well with plenty of salt and pepper.

2 Roughly divide the minced meat mixture into eight equal pieces and use your hands to press each of the pieces into flat rounds.

3 Cut the mozzarella cheese into four chunks. Place one chunk of cheese on half the lamb rounds. Top each with another round of meat mixture.

4 Press each of the two rounds of meat together firmly, making four flattish burger shapes. Use your fingers to blend the edges and seal in the cheese completely.

5 Prepare the barbecue. Position a lightly oiled grill rack over the hot coals. Place all the ingredients for the chutney in a bowl and mash them together with a fork. Season well with salt and freshly ground black pepper.

6 Brush the lamb burgers with olive oil and cook them over a medium-high heat for about 15 minutes, turning once, until golden brown. Serve with the redcurrant chutney.

Energy 344kcal/1432kJ; Protein 30.1g; Carbohydrate 5g, of which sugars 4.6g; Fat 22.8g, of which saturates 11.7g; Cholesterol 113mg; Calcium 171mg; Fibre 1.9g; Sodium 206mg.

MIXED GRILL SKEWERS

THIS HEARTY SELECTION OF MEATS, COOKED ON A SKEWER AND DRIZZLED WITH HORSERADISH SAUCE, MAKES A POPULAR MAIN COURSE. KEEP ALL THE PIECES OF MEAT ABOUT THE SAME THICKNESS SO THAT THEY WILL COOK EVENLY. THROW SOME BAY LEAVES ON TO THE COALS IF YOU LIKE.

SERVES FOUR

INGREDIENTS
   4 small lamb noisettes, each about
     2.5cm/1in thick
   4 lamb's kidneys
   4 streaky (fatty) bacon rashers (strips)
   8 cherry tomatoes
   8 chipolata sausages
   12–16 bay leaves
   salt and ground black pepper
For the horseradish sauce
   30ml/2 tbsp horseradish relish
   45ml/3 tbsp melted butter

1 Trim any excess fat from the lamb noisettes with a sharp knife. Halve the kidneys and remove the cores, using kitchen scissors.

2 Cut each bacon rasher in half and wrap around the tomatoes or kidneys.

3 Thread the lamb noisettes, bacon-wrapped kidneys and cherry tomatoes, chipolatas and bay leaves on to four long metal skewers. Set aside while you prepare the sauce.

4 Mix the horseradish relish with the melted butter and stir until thoroughly mixed. Put half the sauce into a serving bowl.

5 Brush a little of the horseradish sauce from the pan over the meat and sprinkle with salt and freshly ground black pepper.

6 Prepare the barbecue. Position a lightly oiled grill rack over the hot coals. Cook the skewers over medium heat for 12 minutes, turning occasionally, until the meat is golden brown and thoroughly cooked. Serve hot, drizzled with the sauce from the bowl.

Energy 422kcal/1756kJ; Protein 27.2g; Carbohydrate 7g, of which sugars 3.4g; Fat 31.9g, of which saturates 14.2g; Cholesterol 323mg; Calcium 68mg; Fibre 1g; Sodium 955mg.

BACON KOFTAS

Kofta kebabs can be made with any type of minced meat, but bacon is very successful. You will need a food processor for the best result as the ingredients need to be chopped finely. They go very nicely with a bulgur wheat salad, which is substantial and quick to make.

SERVES FOUR

INGREDIENTS
 250g/9oz streaky (fatty) bacon
  rashers (strips), roughly chopped
 1 small onion, roughly chopped
 1 celery stick, roughly chopped
 75ml/5 tbsp fresh wholemeal
  (whole-wheat) breadcrumbs
 45ml/3 tbsp chopped fresh thyme
 30ml/2 tbsp Worcestershire sauce
 1 egg, beaten
 salt and ground black pepper
 olive oil, for brushing
For the salad
 115g/4oz/¾ cup bulgur wheat
 60ml/4 tbsp toasted sunflower seeds
 15ml/1 tbsp olive oil
 salt and freshly ground black pepper
 handful of celery leaves, chopped

1 Soak eight bamboo skewers in water for 30 minutes. Place the bacon, onion, celery and breadcrumbs in a food processor and process until chopped. Add the thyme, Worcestershire sauce and seasoning. Bind to a firm mixture with the egg.

2 Divide the mixture into eight equal portions and use your hands to shape them around eight bamboo skewers.

3 For the salad, place the bulgur wheat in a bowl and pour over boiling water to cover. Leave to stand for 30 minutes, until the grains are tender. Prepare the barbecue. Position a lightly oiled grill rack over the hot coals.

4 Drain the bulgur wheat well, then stir in the sunflower seeds, olive oil, salt and pepper. Stir in the celery leaves.

5 Cook the kofta skewers over medium-high heat for 8–10 minutes, turning occasionally, until golden brown. Serve with the salad.

Energy 340kcal/1417kJ; Protein 14g; Carbohydrate 31.7g, of which sugars 2.5g; Fat 18.2g, of which saturates 5.5g; Cholesterol 41mg; Calcium 55mg; Fibre 0.7g; Sodium 1025mg.

PORK SATAY KEBABS

MACADAMIA NUTS HAVE AN UNMISTAKABLY RICH FLAVOUR AND ARE USED HERE WITH ASIAN FLAVOURINGS AND CHILLIES TO MAKE A HOT AND SPICY MARINADE FOR BITE SIZE PIECES OF TENDER PORK. SERVE THE SATAY KEBABS WITH A REFRESHING LEAF SALAD AND A RICE SALAD OR BARBECUED VEGETABLES.

MAKES EIGHT TO TWELVE

INGREDIENTS
    450g/1lb pork fillet (tenderloin)
    15ml/1 tbsp light muscovado
        (brown) sugar
    1cm/½in cube shrimp paste
    1–2 lemon grass stalks
    30ml/2 tbsp coriander seeds, dry-fried
    6 macadamia nuts or
        blanched almonds
    2 onions, roughly chopped
    3–6 fresh red chillies, seeded and
        roughly chopped
    2.5ml/½ tsp ground turmeric
    300ml/½ pint/1¼ cups canned
        coconut milk
    30ml/2 tbsp groundnut (peanut) oil
        or sunflower oil
    salt

1 Soak 8–12 bamboo skewers in water for 30 minutes to prevent them scorching on the barbecue.

2 Cut the pork into small, bite size chunks, then spread it out in a single layer in a shallow dish. Sprinkle with the sugar, to help release the juices, and then set aside.

3 Fry the shrimp paste briefly in a foil parcel in a dry frying pan. Alternatively, warm the foil parcel on a skewer held over the gas flame.

4 Cut off the lower 5cm/2in of the lemon grass stalks and chop finely. Process the dry-fried coriander seeds to a powder in a food processor.

5 Add the nuts and chopped lemon grass, process briefly, then add the onions, chillies, shrimp paste, turmeric and a little salt; process to a fine paste.

6 Pour in the coconut milk and oil. Switch the machine on very briefly to mix. Pour the mixture over the pork and leave to marinate for 1–2 hours.

7 Prepare the barbecue. Position a lightly oiled grill rack over the hot coals. Thread three or four pieces of marinated pork on to each bamboo skewer and grill over medium heat for 8–10 minutes, or until tender, basting frequently with the remaining marinade up until the final 5 minutes. Serve the skewers immediately while hot.

Energy 103kcal/432kJ; Protein 13.1g; Carbohydrate 5.2g, of which sugars 4.4g; Fat 3.5g, of which saturates 0.8g; Cholesterol 33mg; Calcium 20mg; Fibre 0.5g; Sodium 54mg.

PORK RIBS WITH GINGER RELISH

THIS DISH WORKS BEST WHEN THE PORK RIBS ARE GRILLED IN WHOLE, LARGE SLABS, THEN SLICED TO SERVE. NOT ONLY DOES THIS KEEP THE MEAT SUCCULENT, BUT IT ALSO CREATES PERFECT-SIZED PORTIONS FOR GUESTS TO GRAB! MAKE THE GINGER RELISH THE DAY BEFORE IF POSSIBLE.

SERVES FOUR

INGREDIENTS

    4 pork rib slabs, each with 6 ribs,
      total weight about 2kg/4½lb
    40g/1½oz/3 tbsp light muscovado
      (brown) sugar
    3 garlic cloves, crushed
    5cm/2in piece of fresh root ginger,
      finely grated
    10ml/2 tsp Sichuan peppercorns,
      finely crushed
    2.5ml/½ tsp ground black pepper
    5ml/1 tsp finely ground star anise
    5ml/1 tsp Chinese five-spice powder
    90ml/6 tbsp dark soy sauce
    45ml/3 tbsp sunflower oil
    15ml/1 tbsp sesame oil
For the relish
    60ml/4 tbsp sunflower oil
    300g/11oz banana shallots,
      finely chopped
    9 garlic cloves, crushed
    7.5cm/3in piece of fresh root ginger,
      finely grated
    60ml/4 tbsp seasoned rice
      wine vinegar
    45ml/3 tbsp sweet chilli sauce
    105ml/7 tbsp tomato ketchup
    90ml/6 tbsp water
    60ml/4 tbsp chopped fresh coriander
      (cilantro) leaves
    salt

1 Lay the slabs of pork ribs in a large shallow dish. Mix the remaining ingredients in a bowl and pour the marinade over the ribs, making sure they are evenly coated. Cover and chill the ribs overnight.

2 To make the relish, heat the oil in a heavy pan, add the shallots and cook them gently for 5 minutes. Add the garlic and ginger and cook for about 4 minutes more. Increase the heat and add all the remaining ingredients except the coriander. Cover and simmer gently for 10 minutes until thickened. Tip into a bowl and stir in the coriander. When completely cold, chill until needed.

3 Remove the ribs from the refrigerator 1 hour before cooking. Prepare the barbecue. Remove the ribs from the marinade and pat them dry with kitchen paper. Pour the marinade into a pan. Bring it to the boil on the stove, then simmer for 3 minutes.

4 Once the flames have died down, rake the hot coals to one side and insert a large drip tray beside them. Position a lightly oiled grill rack over the hot coals. Lay the ribs over high heat directly over the coals and cook them for 3 minutes on each side, then move over the drip tray. Cover with a lid or tented heavy-duty foil and cook for a further 30–35 minutes, turning and basting occasionally with the marinade.

5 The meat should be ready when it is golden-brown in appearance. If, towards the end of the cooking time, the ribs need crisping up a bit, move them quickly back over the coals. Stop basting with the marinade 5 minutes before cooking time. Cut into single ribs to serve, with the relish.

Energy 665kcal/2761kJ; Protein 46.6g; Carbohydrate 17g, of which sugars 14.8g; Fat 45.9g, of which saturates 14.2g; Cholesterol 155mg; Calcium 59mg; Fibre 1.4g; Sodium 1111mg.

FIVE-SPICED PORK RIBS

BARBECUED PORK SPARE RIBS MARINATED WITH CHINESE FLAVOURINGS HAVE GOT TO BE ONE OF THE ALL-TIME FAVOURITES. CHOOSE THE MEATIEST SPARE RIBS YOU CAN FIND TO MAKE THE DISH A REAL SUCCESS AND HAVE PLENTY OF NAPKINS HANDY.

SERVES FOUR

INGREDIENTS

    1kg/2¼lb Chinese-style pork
      spare ribs
    10ml/2 tsp Chinese five-spice powder
    2 garlic cloves, crushed
    15ml/1 tbsp grated fresh
      root ginger
    2.5ml/½ tsp chilli sauce
    60ml/4 tbsp dark soy sauce
    45ml/3 tbsp muscovado
      (brown) sugar
    15ml/1 tbsp sunflower oil
    4 spring onions (scallions)

1 If the spare ribs are still attached to each other, cut between them to separate them (or you could ask your butcher to do this when you buy them). Place the spare ribs in a large bowl.

2 Mix together all the remaining ingredients, except the spring onions, and pour over the ribs. Toss well to coat evenly. Cover the bowl and leave to marinate in the refrigerator overnight.

3 Prepare the barbecue. Position a lightly oiled grill rack over the hot coals. Cook the ribs over medium-high heat, turning frequently, for about 30–40 minutes. Brush occasionally with the remaining marinade up until the final 5 minutes.

4 While the ribs are cooking, finely slice the spring onions. Scatter them over the ribs and serve immediately.

Energy 562kcal/2346kJ; Protein 47.2g; Carbohydrate 12.7g, of which sugars 12.6g; Fat 36.3g, of which saturates 13.3g; Cholesterol 165mg; Calcium 46mg; Fibre 0g; Sodium 1047mg.

BELMONT SAUSAGE <u>WITH</u> MUSHROOM RELISH

NOTHING QUITE BEATS GOOD QUALITY SAUSAGE, AND THIS RECIPE ENSURES YOU GET JUST THAT. YOU CAN CHANGE THE COMBINATION OF HERBS AND SPICES OR TWIST THE SAUSAGE INTO SMALL LENGTHS. IT REALLY IS A VERY ADAPTABLE RECIPE, AND THE MUSHROOM RELISH IS PERFECT TO GO WITH IT.

SERVES SIX TO EIGHT

INGREDIENTS

450g/1lb skinless and boneless belly pork, cut into large pieces
450g/1lb pork shoulder, cut into large pieces
300–400g/11–14oz back fat, cut into large pieces
50g/2oz/1 cup freshly made breadcrumbs
2 garlic cloves, crushed
10ml/2 tsp salt
10ml/2 tsp ground coriander
5ml/1 tsp ground black pepper
5ml/1 tsp ground cumin
1.5ml/¼ tsp cayenne pepper
1.5ml/¼ tsp ground cinnamon
45ml/3 tbsp chopped fresh basil
60ml/4 tbsp chopped fresh marjoram
60ml/4 tbsp chopped fresh flat leaf parsley
enough cleaned sausage casing for just over 900g/2lb sausage: about 50g/2oz or 2.7m/9ft
30ml/2 tbsp olive oil for brushing
6 metal skewers

For the relish
45ml/3 tbsp extra virgin olive oil
2 onions, finely chopped
2 garlic cloves, finely chopped
150g/5oz/2 cups finely chopped chestnut mushrooms
25g/1oz/3 tbsp drained sun-dried tomatoes in oil, finely chopped
90ml/6 tbsp water
20ml/4 tsp sugar
30ml/2 tbsp chopped fresh flat leaf parsley
30ml/2 tbsp sherry vinegar
salt and ground black pepper

1 Pass both meats through the mincer (grinder) once and the back fat twice, using the plate with the widest holes. Place in a large bowl and add the breadcrumbs. Add the garlic with a pinch of the salt, and the remaining sausage ingredients except the remaining salt, the casings and the oil. Mix thoroughly. Cover and chill overnight.

2 Rinse the casing by running cold water through it. Fit the casing on to the sausage-making attachment of the mincer, or use a piping bag with a wide nozzle. Add the remaining salt to the mixture and mix well. Fill the casing in one continuous length, leaving a gap of 13cm/5in of empty casing halfway. Separate into two sausages, securing by tying the ends. Curl each sausage into a round, cover and chill.

3 To make the relish, heat the oil in a pan and fry the onions and garlic for about 10 minutes. Add the mushrooms and tomatoes and fry for 1 minute. Stir in the measured water and boil until it has evaporated. Stir in the sugar, parsley and vinegar. Season, cover and cool.

4 Prepare the barbecue. Skewer the sausages to maintain the round shape. Once the flames have died down, rake the hot coals to one side and insert a drip tray beside them. Position a lightly oiled grill rack over the hot coals. Brush the sausages with a little oil and place them on the grill rack over the drip tray. Cover with a lid or tented heavy-duty foil, and cook for 5–7 minutes on each side, or until cooked and golden. Serve with the relish.

Energy 765kcal/3159kJ; Protein 21.9g; Carbohydrate 6.1g, of which sugars 4.9g; Fat 72.7g, of which saturates 26.8g; Cholesterol 117mg; Calcium 38mg; Fibre 1.4g; Sodium 87mg.

PEPPERED STEAKS IN BEER AND GARLIC

STEAKS GO VERY WELL WITH A ROBUST MARINADE OF GARLIC, WORCESTERSHIRE SAUCE AND BEER. MARINADES HAVE A DUAL PURPOSE OF FLAVOURING AS WELL AS TENDERIZING MEAT AND SO WILL IMPROVE THE TEXTURE AS WELL AS THE TASTE. SERVE WITH A BAKED POTATO AND CRISP MIXED SALAD.

SERVES FOUR

INGREDIENTS

  4 beef sirloin or rump steaks, about
    175g/6oz each
  2 garlic cloves, crushed
  120ml/4fl oz/½ cup brown ale
    or stout
  30ml/2 tbsp muscovado
    (molasses) sugar
  30ml/2 tbsp Worcestershire sauce
  15ml/1 tbsp corn oil
  15ml/1 tbsp crushed
    black peppercorns

1 Place the steaks in a dish and add the garlic, ale or stout, sugar, Worcestershire sauce and oil. Turn to coat evenly, then leave to marinate in the refrigerator for 2–3 hours or overnight.

2 Prepare the barbecue. Position a lightly oiled grill rack over the hot coals. Remove the steaks and reserve the marinade. Sprinkle the peppercorns over the steaks and press them into the surface.

3 Cook the steaks over high heat, basting them occasionally with the reserved marinade during cooking. (Take care when basting, as the alcohol will tend to flare up: spoon or brush on just a small amount at a time and allow the final basting to cook through.)

4 Turn the steaks once during cooking, and cook them for about 3–6 minutes on each side, depending on how rare you like them.

Energy 355kcal/1480kJ; Protein 39.8g; Carbohydrate 4.7g, of which sugars 4.7g; Fat 19g, of which saturates 7.1g; Cholesterol 102mg; Calcium 13mg; Fibre 0g; Sodium 114mg.

HOME-MADE BURGERS <u>WITH</u> RELISH

*MAKING YOUR OWN BURGERS MEANS YOU CONTROL WHAT GOES INTO THEM. THESE ARE FULL OF
FLAVOUR AND ALWAYS PROVE POPULAR. SERVE IN BUNS WITH LETTUCE AND THE TANGY RATATOUILLE
RELISH, WHICH IS VERY EASY TO MAKE.*

<u>SERVES FOUR</u>

INGREDIENTS
  2 shallots, unpeeled
  450g/1lb/2 cups fresh lean minced
    (ground) beef
  30ml/2 tbsp chopped parsley
  30ml/2 tbsp tomato ketchup
  1 garlic clove, crushed
  1 fresh green chilli, seeded and
    finely chopped
  15ml/1 tbsp olive oil
  400g/14oz can ratatouille
  4 burger buns
  lettuce leaves
  salt and ground black pepper

VARIATION
These burgers also taste great with spicy
corn relish on the side. To make the
relish, heat 30ml/2 tbsp oil in a pan and
fry 1 onion, 2 crushed garlic cloves and
1 seeded and finely chopped red chilli
until soft. Add 10ml/2 tsp garam masala
and cook for 2 minutes, then mix in a
320g/11¼oz can of corn kernels and the
grated rind and juice of 1 lime.

1 Prepare the barbecue. Put the
shallots in a bowl with boiling water
to cover. Leave for 1–2 minutes, then
slip off the skins and chop the
shallots finely.

2 Mix 1 shallot with the beef in a bowl.
Add the parsley and tomato ketchup,
with salt and pepper to taste. Mix well
with clean hands. Divide the mixture
into four. Knead each portion into a ball,
then flatten it into a burger.

3 Make a spicy relish by cooking the
remaining shallot with the garlic and
green chilli in the olive oil for
2–3 minutes, or until softened.

4 Add the canned ratatouille to the pan
containing the vegetables. Bring to the
boil, then simmer for 5 minutes.
Position a lightly oiled grill rack over the
hot coals.

5 Transfer the pan to the edge of the
barbecue. Cook the burgers over high
heat for about 5 minutes on each side,
until browned and cooked through.

6 Split the burger buns. Arrange the
lettuce leaves on the bun bases, add
the burgers and top with warm relish
and the bun tops.

Energy 487kcal/2037kJ; Protein 27.9g; Carbohydrate 31.7g, of which sugars 7.8g; Fat 28.6g, of which saturates 9g; Cholesterol 68mg; Calcium 92mg; Fibre 2g; Sodium 492mg.

THE GAUCHO BARBECUE

This delicious traditional pampas beef dish consists of short ribs and rump steak accompanied by pork sausages. It involves no marinating, but the meat is brushed with brine during cooking to keep it moist. Serve each meat as it is cooked, accompanied by a selection of salads and salsas.

SERVES SIX

INGREDIENTS

50g/2oz/¼ cup coarse sea salt
200ml/7fl oz/scant 1 cup
 warm water
6 pork sausages
1kg/2¼lb beef short ribs
1kg/2¼lb rump (round) steak, in
 one piece
salads, salsas and breads, to serve

1 Dissolve the sea salt in the measured water in a bowl. Leave to cool.

2 Prepare the barbecue. Position a lightly oiled grill rack over the hot coals.

3 Start by cooking the sausages, which should take 15–20 minutes over medium heat, depending on their size. Once cooked on all sides, slice the sausages thickly and arrange them on a plate. Let guests help themselves while you cook the remaining meats.

4 Place the short ribs bony side down on the grill rack. Cook for 15 minutes, turn, brush the cooked side of each rib with brine and grill for a further 25–30 minutes and continue basting. Slice the meat and transfer to a plate for guests to help themselves.

5 Place the whole rump steak on the grill rack and cook for 5 minutes, then turn over and baste the browned side with brine.

6 Continue turning and basting in this way for 20–25 minutes in total, until the meat is cooked to your liking. Allow the meat to rest for 5 minutes under tented heavy-duty foil, then slice thinly and serve with salads, salsa and bread.

COOK'S TIPS

• This dish is quick to cook over the barbecue, but don't be tempted to partially precook any meat and then to finish it off on the barbecue, as this will encourage bacteria to grow.
• Remember that if you are not cooking at home you will need to transport meat in a cooler bag or box and take out what you need as and when you need it to avoid it becoming warm before it is cooked.
• Always pack the cooler with the foods you are going to cook first on the top and close the cooler completely each time you take an item of food out.

VARIATION

A selection of meat cuts can be used, from sirloin to flank steak or chuck steak. Sweetbreads, skewered chicken hearts and kidneys are popular additions to the Gaucho barbecue, as well as chicken, lamb and pork. The star of the show, however, will always be the beef.

Energy 873kcal/3637kJ; Protein 84.4g; Carbohydrate 6.3g, of which sugars 0.9g; Fat 56.7g, of which saturates 23.8g; Cholesterol 246mg; Calcium 46mg; Fibre 0.3g; Sodium 1333mg.

VEGETARIAN

Some vegetarians rather despair of a barbecue, which is a shame when so many exciting options exist. Vegetables can, in fact, be cooked using similar methods to meat recipes: roasted vegetables, for example, make a perfect topping for toasted tortillas and even barbecue-style pizza. Potato and Cheese Polpettes are a nice variation on vegetarian burgers, while sumptuous filled vegetables include Onions Stuffed with Goat's Cheese and Grilled Aubergine Parcels.

ROASTED VEGETABLE QUESADILLAS

THIS RECIPE IS A WONDERFUL EXAMPLE OF HOW THE GRIDDLE AND GRILL RACK CAN BE USED SIMULTANEOUSLY TO COPE WITH A RANGE OF INGREDIENTS. HAVE A LONG GRIDDLE ON ONE SIDE OF THE GRILL RACK FOR THE ONIONS AND PEPPERS; THE AUBERGINES CAN COOK ON THE GRILL RACK.

SERVES SIX TO EIGHT

INGREDIENTS
    1 yellow and 1 orange (bell) pepper,
        each quartered and seeded
    2 red (bell) peppers, quartered
        and seeded
    2 red onions, cut into wedges with
        root intact
    8 long baby aubergines (eggplants),
        total weight about 175g/6oz,
        halved lengthways
    30ml/2 tbsp olive oil
    400g/14oz mozzarella
    2 fresh green chillies, seeded and
        sliced into rounds
    15ml/1 tbsp Mexican tomato sauce
    8 corn or wheat flour tortillas
    handful of fresh basil leaves
    salt and ground black pepper

1 Prepare the barbecue. Position a lightly oiled grill rack over the hot coals. Heat a griddle on the grill rack.

COOK'S TIPS
• The quesadillas can be cut into wedges and eaten as they come off the griddle or wrapped in foil to keep warm while the rest are cooked.
• When cooking for vegetarians as well as non-vegetarians, always remember to keep one side of the barbecue for cooking the vegetarian dishes only so that they do not come in contact with meat.

2 Toss the peppers, onions and aubergines in the oil on a large baking tray. Place the peppers, skin-side down, on the griddle or directly on the grill rack over medium-high heat and cook until seared and browned underneath. If the food starts to char, remove the griddle until the coals cool down. Put the peppers under an upturned bowl and set aside to cool slightly so that the skins will loosen.

3 Grill the onions and aubergines until they have softened slightly and are branded with brown grill marks, then set them aside. Rub the skins off the peppers with your fingers, cut each piece of pepper in half and add to the other vegetables.

4 Cut the mozzarella into 20 slices. Place them, along with the roasted vegetables, in a large bowl and add the chillies and tomato sauce. Stir well to mix, and season with salt and pepper to taste. Place the griddle over a medium heat and cook all the tortillas on one side only.

5 Lay a tortilla on the griddle, cooked-side up, and pile about a quarter of the vegetable mixture into the centre of the tortilla. Scatter over some basil leaves. When the tortilla browns underneath, put another tortilla on top, cooked side down. Carefully turn the quesadilla over using a wide pizza server with a tubular handle and continue to cook until the underside has browned and the cheese just starts to melt. Remove from the pan with the pizza server and either serve immediately or wrap in foil to keep warm while you cook the remaining three quesadillas.

VARIATION
Thinly sliced courgettes (zucchini) are also delicious when griddled and can be added to the mixture here or used instead of the aubergines.

Energy 233kcal/971kJ; Protein 11.8g; Carbohydrate 17g, of which sugars 8.5g; Fat 13.5g, of which saturates 7.4g; Cholesterol 29mg; Calcium 214mg; Fibre 2.7g; Sodium 268mg.

GRILLED GOAT'S CHEESE PIZZA

A PIZZA WITH A THIN CRUST CAN BE COOKED ON THE BARBECUE, AND IT PRODUCES A GOOD, CRISPY AND GOLDEN BASE. A FINE WIRE MESH RACK IS USEFUL FOR GRILLING THE BASE.

SERVES FOUR

INGREDIENTS
150g/5oz packet pizza-base mix
olive oil, for brushing
150ml/¼ pint/⅔ cup passata
30ml/2 tbsp red pesto
1 small red onion, thinly sliced
8 cherry tomatoes, halved
115g/4oz firm goat's cheese,
  thinly sliced
handful shredded fresh basil leaves
salt and ground black pepper

1 Prepare the barbecue. Position a lightly oiled grill rack over the hot coals. Make up the pizza dough according to the directions on the packet. Roll out the dough on a lightly floured surface to a round of about 25cm/10in diameter.

2 Brush the dough round with olive oil and place, oiled side down, on the grill rack over medium heat. Cook for about 6–8 minutes until firm and golden underneath. Brush the uncooked side with olive oil and turn the pizza over.

3 Mix together the passata and red pesto, and quickly spread over the cooked side of the pizza, to within about 1cm/½in of the edge. Arrange the onion, tomatoes and cheese on top, and sprinkle with salt and pepper.

4 Cook the pizza for 10 minutes more, until golden brown and crisp. Sprinkle with fresh basil and serve.

COOK'S TIP
For home-made pizza dough, sift 175g/6oz/1½ cups strong white bread flour and 1.5ml/¼ tsp salt in a bowl. Stir in 5ml/1 tsp easy-blend (rapid-rise) dried yeast. Pour in about 120ml/4fl oz/½ cup lukewarm water and 15ml/1 tbsp olive oil. Mix to form a dough. Knead until smooth. Place in a greased bowl, cover and leave to rise for 1 hour. Knock back (punch down) the dough and use as required.

Energy 338kcal/1420kJ; Protein 11g; Carbohydrate 46g, of which sugars 5g; Fat 13.5g, of which saturates 3.5g; Cholesterol 13mg; Calcium 218mg; Fibre 1.9g; Sodium 327mg.

POTATO AND CHEESE POLPETTES

THESE LITTLE MORSELS OF POTATO AND GREEK FETA CHEESE, FLAVOURED WITH DILL AND LEMON JUICE, ARE EXCELLENT WHEN GRILLED ON THE BARBECUE. THEY CAN BE ACCOMPANIED WITH A TOMATO SAUCE, IF YOU LIKE, OR A NICELY DRESSED SALAD OF TOMATOES, SALAD LEAVES AND ONIONS.

SERVES FOUR

INGREDIENTS
    500g/1¼lb potatoes
    115g/4oz feta cheese
    4 spring onions (scallions),
        chopped
    45ml/3 tbsp chopped fresh dill
    1 egg, beaten
    15ml/1 tbsp lemon juice
    15ml/1 tbsp olive oil
    salt and ground black pepper

1 Boil the potatoes in their skins in salted water until soft. Drain, then peel while still warm.

2 Place the cooked potatotes in a bowl and mash. Crumble the feta cheese into the potatoes and add the spring onions, dill, egg and lemon juice, and season with pepper and a little salt. Stir well, then cover and chill until firm.

3 Divide the mixture into walnut-size balls, then flatten them slightly. Brush lightly with olive oil. Prepare the barbecue. Position a lightly oiled grill rack over the hot coals. Arrange the polpettes on the grill rack and cook over medium heat, turning once, until golden brown. Serve at once.

Energy 230kcal/960kJ; Protein 8.4g; Carbohydrate 20.9g, of which sugars 2.3g; Fat 13.1g, of which saturates 5.3g; Cholesterol 68mg; Calcium 122mg; Fibre 1.4g; Sodium 446mg.

GRILLED VEGETABLES WITH YOGURT PESTO

CHARGRILLED SUMMER VEGETABLES MAKE A MEAL ON THEIR OWN, OR ARE DELICIOUS SERVED AS A MEDITERRANEAN-STYLE SIDE DISH WITH GRILLED MEATS AND FISH. THE YOGURT PESTO MAKES A CREAMY ACCOMPANIMENT TO THE RICH FLAVOURS OF THE GRILLED VEGETABLES.

3 Slice the fennel bulbs and the red onions into thick wedges, using a sharp kitchen knife.

4 Prepare the barbecue. Position a lightly oiled grill rack over the hot coals. Stir the yogurt and pesto lightly together in a bowl, to make a marbled sauce. Spoon into a serving bowl and set aside.

SERVES EIGHT

INGREDIENTS
4 small aubergines (eggplants)
4 large courgettes (zucchini)
2 red and 2 yellow (bell) peppers
2 fennel bulbs
2 red onions
300ml⁄½ pint/1¼ cups Greek
 (US strained plain) yogurt
90ml/6 tbsp pesto
olive oil, for brushing
salt and ground black pepper

1 Cut the aubergines into 1cm/½in slices. Sprinkle with salt and leave to drain for about 30 minutes. Rinse well in cold running water and pat dry.

2 Use a sharp kitchen knife to cut the courgettes in half lengthways. Cut the peppers in half, removing the seeds but leaving the stalks in place.

5 Arrange the vegetables on the grill rack over high heat. Brush generously with olive oil and sprinkle with plenty of salt and ground black pepper.

6 Cook the vegetables until golden brown and tender, turning occasionally. The aubergines and peppers will take 6–8 minutes to cook, the courgettes, onion and fennel 4–5 minutes. Serve the vegetables as soon as they are cooked, with the yogurt pesto.

COOK'S TIP
Baby vegetables are excellent for grilling whole on the barbecue, so look out for baby aubergines and peppers, in particular. There's no need to salt the aubergines if they are small.

VARIATION
Barbecue some halloumi cheese, sliced and brushed with oil, to serve with the vegetables, if you like.

Energy 146kcal/606kJ; Protein 6.9g; Carbohydrate 12.3g, of which sugars 11.8g; Fat 8g, of which saturates 1.9g; Cholesterol 4mg; Calcium 163mg; Fibre 5.1g; Sodium 86mg.

SQUASH STUFFED WITH GOAT'S CHEESE

GEM SQUASH HAS A SWEET, SUBTLE FLAVOUR THAT CONTRASTS WELL WITH OLIVES AND SUN-DRIED TOMATOES IN THIS RECIPE. THE RICE ADDS SUBSTANCE WITHOUT CHANGING ANY OF THE FLAVOURS.

SERVES TWO

INGREDIENTS
 4 whole gem squashes
 225g/8oz/2 cups cooked white
  long grain rice
 75g/3oz/1½ cups sun-dried
  tomatoes, chopped
 40g/1½ oz/⅓ cup pitted black
  olives, chopped
 50g/2oz/¼ cup soft goat's cheese
 10ml/2 tsp olive oil
 15ml/1 tbsp chopped fresh basil
  leaves, plus basil sprigs,
  to serve
 green salad, to serve (optional)

3 Divide the rice mixture evenly between the squashes and place them individually on pieces of oiled, double thickness heavy-duty foil. Wrap the foil around the squashes and place them in among the coals of a medium-hot barbecue.

4 Bake for 45 minutes–1 hour, or until the squashes are tender when pierced with a skewer. Garnish with basil sprigs and serve with a green salad, if you like.

COOK'S TIP
The amount of time required to cook these vegetable parcels depends on the size of the squashes, and the heat of the coals. To maintain a medium-to-high temperature throughout the cooking time, keep rearranging the coals so that the hotter ones are nearest to the vegetable parcels. You can gauge the heat by the layer of ash that gathers on the coals.

1 Prepare the barbecue. Trim away the base of each squash, slice off the top and scoop out and discard the seeds.

2 Mix together the rice, tomatoes, olives, goat's cheese, olive oil and basil in a bowl.

Energy 337kcal/1416kJ; Protein 11.5g; Carbohydrate 43.5g, of which sugars 7.1g; Fat 14.2g, of which saturates 5.9g; Cholesterol 23mg; Calcium 206mg; Fibre 5.3g; Sodium 613mg.

PASTA SALAD WITH CHARGRILLED PEPPERS

ONE OF THE MANY WONDERFUL THINGS ABOUT SUMMER IS THE ABUNDANCE OF FRESH HERBS. LOTS OF BASIL AND CORIANDER MAKE THIS SALAD ESPECIALLY TASTY. LEAVE THE PASTA TO SOAK UP THE DRESSING AND THEN ADD THE HERBS JUST BEFORE YOU ARE READY TO BARBECUE THE PEPPERS.

SERVES FOUR

INGREDIENTS
  250g/9oz/2¼ cups dried
    fusilli tricolore
  1 handful fresh basil leaves, chopped
  1 handful fresh coriander (cilantro)
    leaves, chopped
  1 garlic clove, chopped
  1 large red and 1 large green
    (bell) pepper
  salt and ground black pepper
For the dressing
  30ml/2 tbsp pesto
  juice of ½ lemon
  60ml/4 tbsp extra virgin olive oil

VARIATION
Dry-roast some pine nuts over the barbecue to add crunch to the salad.

1 Bring a large pan of salted water to the boil. Add the pasta and cook for 10–12 minutes or according to the instructions on the packet.

2 Whisk the dressing ingredients together in a large mixing bowl. Drain the cooked pasta and tip it into the bowl of dressing. Toss well to mix and set aside to cool. Add the basil, coriander and garlic to the pasta and toss well to mix.

3 Prepare the barbecue. Position a lightly oiled grill rack over the hot coals. Put the peppers on the grill rack over high heat for about 10 minutes, turning frequently until they are charred on all sides. Put the hot peppers under an upturned bowl and leave to cool a little and for the skins to loosen.

4 Peel off the skins with your fingers, split the peppers open and pull out the cores. Remove all the seeds.

5 Chop the peppers and add them to the pasta. Taste and adjust the seasoning, if necessary, and serve.

Energy 402kcal/1688kJ; Protein 10.1g; Carbohydrate 51.6g, of which sugars 7.1g; Fat 18.7g, of which saturates 2.9g; Cholesterol 3mg; Calcium 75mg; Fibre 3.7g; Sodium 36mg.

GRILLED AUBERGINE PARCELS

AUBERGINES ARE VERSATILE VEGETABLE FRUITS WITH SOFT FLESH THAT ABSORBS OTHER FLAVOURS.
PREPARE THEM IN ADVANCE, BARBECUE THEM QUICKLY TO GET THAT LOVELY SMOKY FLAVOUR AND
THEN ENJOY THEM WITH A BALSAMIC VINEGAR AND TOMATO DRESSING FOR A REAL TASTE OF ITALY.

SERVES FOUR

INGREDIENTS
2 large, long aubergines (eggplants)
225g/8oz mozzarella
2 plum tomatoes
16 large fresh basil leaves
30ml/2 tbsp olive oil
salt and ground black pepper
For the dressing
60ml/4 tbsp olive oil
5ml/1 tsp balsamic vinegar
15ml/1 tbsp sun-dried tomato paste
15ml/1 tbsp lemon juice
For the garnish
30ml/2 tbsp toasted pine nuts
torn fresh basil leaves

COOK'S TIP
The best cheese to use in these
delectable little parcels is undoubtedly
mozzarella. Look for the authentic moist
cheese, made from buffalo's milk, which
is sold packed in whey. If you can find it,
lightly smoked mozzarella would also
work well, and would add additional
flavour to the dish. It is labelled
mozzarella affumicata. Alternatively, you
could use a plain or smoked goat's
cheese. Look for one with a similar
texture to mozzarella.

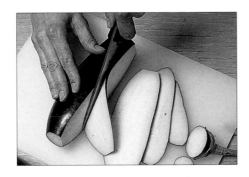

1 Remove the stalks from the
aubergines and cut the aubergines
lengthways into thin slices – the aim is
to get 16 slices in total, disregarding the
outer two slices, which consist largely of
skin. (If you have a mandolin, it will cut
perfect, even slices for you – otherwise,
use a sharp, long-bladed cook's knife.)

2 Bring a large pan of salted water to
the boil and cook the aubergine slices
for about 2 minutes. Drain the slices
thoroughly, then dry on kitchen paper.
Cut the mozzarella cheese into eight
slices. Cut each tomato into eight slices,
not counting the first and last slices.

3 Take two aubergine slices and place
on a tray, in a cross. Place a slice of
tomato in the centre, season with salt
and pepper, then add a basil leaf,
followed by a slice of mozzarella,
another basil leaf, a slice of tomato and
more seasoning.

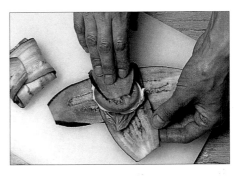

4 Fold the ends of the aubergine slices
around the mozzarella and tomato
filling. Repeat to make eight parcels.
Chill for about 20 minutes.

5 To make the tomato dressing, whisk
together the oil, vinegar, tomato paste
and lemon juice. Season to taste.

6 Prepare the barbecue. Position a
lightly oiled grill rack over the hot coals.
Brush the parcels with olive oil and
cook over high heat for about 5 minutes
on each side until golden. Garnish and
serve hot, with the dressing.

Energy 350kcal/1449kJ; Protein 12.7g; Carbohydrate 5g, of which sugars 4.7g; Fat 31.2g, of which saturates 10.5g; Cholesterol 33mg; Calcium 223mg; Fibre 3.6g; Sodium 230mg.

ONIONS STUFFED WITH GOAT'S CHEESE

CHARGRILLED ONIONS HAVE A SWEET TASTE AND GO VERY WELL WITH A GOAT'S CHEESE, SUN-DRIED TOMATO AND PINE NUT FILLING. COOK THEM OVER INDIRECT HEAT TO ENSURE THEY COOK THROUGH WITHOUT BURNING. SERVE THEM WITH A SELECTION OF SALADS AND BREADS.

SERVES FOUR

INGREDIENTS
4 large onions
150g/5oz goat's cheese, crumbled
  or cubed
50g/2oz/1 cup fresh breadcrumbs
8 sun-dried tomatoes in olive oil,
  drained and chopped
1–2 garlic cloves, finely chopped
2.5ml/½ tsp chopped fresh
  thyme leaves
30ml/2 tbsp chopped fresh parsley
1 small egg, beaten
45ml/3 tbsp pine nuts, toasted
45ml/3 tbsp olive oil (from the jar of
  sun-dried tomatoes)
salt and ground black pepper

1 Bring a large pan of lightly salted water to the boil. Add the whole onions in their skins and boil them for about 10 minutes. Drain and cool, then cut each onion in half horizontally and slip off the skins, taking care to keep the onion halves from unravelling.

2 Using a teaspoon to scoop out the flesh, remove the centre of each onion, leaving a thick shell.

3 Chop the scooped-out onion flesh and place it in a bowl. Add the goat's cheese, breadcrumbs, sun-dried tomatoes, garlic, thyme, half the parsley and the egg. Mix well, then season to taste with salt and pepper, and add the toasted pine nuts.

4 Brush the outside of the onion shells with oil and divide the stuffing among the onions. Drizzle a little oil over the top.

5 Prepare the barbecue. Part the coals in the centre and insert a drip tray. Position a lightly oiled grill rack over the coals and drip tray. Cook over medium heat over the drip tray for 45 minutes– 1 hour, covered with a lid or tented heavy-duty foil. Brush with oil occasionally during cooking. When cooked, sprinkle with the remaining parsley to garnish.

VARIATIONS
• Omit the goat's cheese and add 115g/4oz finely chopped mushrooms and 1 grated carrot.
• Substitute feta cheese for the goat's cheese and raisins for the pine nuts.
• Substitute smoked mozzarella for the goat's cheese and substitute pistachio nuts for the pine nuts.
• Use red and yellow (bell) peppers preserved in olive oil instead of sun-dried tomatoes.

Energy 400kcal/1659kJ; Protein 14g; Carbohydrate 19g, of which sugars 7.3g; Fat 30.4g, of which saturates 9.2g; Cholesterol 82mg; Calcium 115mg; Fibre 2.4g; Sodium 345mg.

SUMMER VEGETABLE KEBABS

THERE'S NOTHING NEW ABOUT THREADING VEGETABLE CHUNKS ON SKEWERS, BUT THIS METHOD OF TOSSING THEM IN A SPICY OIL AND LEMON JUICE MARINADE MAKES ALL THE DIFFERENCE. SERVE THEM WITH THE HOT AND CREAMY DIP AND YOU'LL HAVE VEGETARIAN GUESTS ASKING FOR MORE.

SERVES FOUR

INGREDIENTS
  2 aubergines (eggplants), part peeled
    and cut into chunks
  2 courgettes (zucchini), cut
    into chunks
  2–3 red or green (bell) peppers,
    seeded and cut into chunks
  12–16 cherry tomatoes
  4 small red onions, quartered
  60ml/4 tbsp olive oil
  juice of ½ lemon
  1 garlic clove, crushed
  5ml/1 tsp ground coriander
  5ml/1 tsp ground cinnamon
  10ml/2 tsp clear honey
  5ml/1 tsp salt
For the harissa and yogurt dip
  450g/1lb/2 cups Greek (US strained
    plain) yogurt
  30–60ml/2–4 tbsp harissa
  small bunch of fresh coriander
    (cilantro), finely chopped
  small bunch of mint, finely chopped
  salt and ground black pepper

COOK'S TIP
Make sure you cut the aubergines, courgettes and peppers into fairly even-size chunks, so that they will all cook at the same rate.

1 Prepare the barbecue. Position a lightly oiled grill rack over the hot coals. Put all the vegetables in a bowl. Mix together the olive oil, lemon juice, garlic, ground coriander, cinnamon, honey and salt, and pour over the vegetables.

2 Using your hands, turn the vegetables gently in the marinade, then thread them on to metal skewers. Cook the kebabs over high heat, turning them occasionally, until the vegetables are nicely browned all over.

3 Meanwhile, make the dip. Put the yogurt in a bowl and beat in the harissa, making it as fiery in taste as you like by adding more harissa. Add most of the chopped coriander and mint, reserving a little to garnish, and season well with salt and pepper.

4 While they are still hot, slide the vegetables off the skewers and dip them into the yogurt dip before eating. Garnish with the reserved herbs.

Energy 392kcal/1630kJ; Protein 9.2g; Carbohydrate 25.4g, of which sugars 17.9g; Fat 28.8g, of which saturates 3.2g; Cholesterol 0mg; Calcium 110mg; Fibre 5.5g; Sodium 19mg.

CASSAVA AND VEGETABLE KEBABS

SO MANY VEGETABLES ARE SUITABLE FOR COOKING ON THE BARBECUE AND THIS RECIPE INCLUDES AN ATTRACTIVE AND DELICIOUS ASSORTMENT OF AFRICAN VEGETABLES THAT ARE MARINATED IN A SPICY GARLIC SAUCE. SERVE THE VEGETABLES ACCOMPANIED BY A CREAMY BEAN DIP, SUCH AS HUMMUS.

SERVES FOUR

INGREDIENTS
    175g/6oz cassava
    1 onion, cut into wedges
    1 aubergine (eggplant), cut into
      bitesize pieces
    1 courgette (zucchini), sliced
    1 ripe plantain, sliced
    ½ red (bell) pepper and ½ green
      (bell) pepper, seeded and sliced
    16 cherry tomatoes
    rice or couscous, to serve
For the marinade
    60ml/4 tbsp lemon juice
    60ml/4 tbsp olive oil
    45–60ml/3–4 tbsp soy sauce
    15ml/1 tbsp tomato purée (paste)
    1 green chilli, seeded and
      finely chopped
    ½ onion, grated
    2 garlic cloves, crushed
    5ml/1 tsp mixed (apple pie) spice
    pinch of dried thyme

1 If using wooden skewers, soak eight in water for 30 minutes. Peel the cassava and cut into bitesize pieces. Place in a large bowl, cover with boiling water and leave to blanch for about 5 minutes. Drain well.

2 Place all the prepared vegetables, including the cassava, in a large bowl and mix with your hands so that all the vegetables are evenly distributed.

3 Blend the marinade ingredients in a jug (pitcher) and pour over the vegetables. Cover and leave to marinate for 1–2 hours.

4 Prepare the barbecue. Position a lightly oiled grill rack over the hot coals. Thread the vegetables, with the cherry tomatoes, on to the wooden or metal skewers and cook over high heat for about 15 minutes until tender and browned. Turn the skewers frequently and baste them occasionally with the marinade.

5 Meanwhile, pour the remaining marinade into a small pan and simmer on the grill rack for about 10 minutes to reduce. Strain the reduced marinade into a jug. Serve the kebabs on a bed of rice or couscous, with the sauce on the side.

Energy 167kcal/702kJ; Protein 3g; Carbohydrate 26.1g, of which sugars 7.6g; Fat 6.3g, of which saturates 1g; Cholesterol 0mg; Calcium 34mg; Fibre 3.3g; Sodium 7mg.

ROASTED RED PEPPERS WITH COUSCOUS

COUSCOUS MAKES A GOOD BASIS FOR A STUFFING, AND IN THIS RECIPE IT IS STUDDED WITH RAISINS AND FLAVOURED WITH FRESH MINT. CHARRED PEPPERS MAKE THE COMBINATION OF FLAVOURS TRULY SPECIAL AND THE PEPPERS ARE SIMPLE TO COOK IN THEIR FOIL PARCELS.

SERVES FOUR

INGREDIENTS
6 red (bell) peppers
25g/1oz/2 tbsp butter
1 onion, finely chopped
5ml/1 tsp olive oil
2.5ml/½ tsp salt
175g/6oz/1 cup couscous
25g/1oz/2 tbsp raisins
30ml/2 tbsp chopped fresh mint
1 egg yolk
salt and ground black pepper
mint leaves, to garnish

1 Carefully slit each pepper with a sharp knife and remove the core and seeds. Melt the butter in a small pan and add the chopped onion. Cook until soft but not browned.

2 To cook the couscous, bring 250ml/8fl oz/1 cup water to the boil. Add the oil and salt, then remove from the heat and add the couscous. Stir and leave to stand, covered, for 5 minutes. Stir in the onion, raisins and mint. Season well and stir in the egg yolk. Prepare the barbecue. Position a grill rack over the hot coals.

3 Use a teaspoon to fill the peppers with the couscous mixture to about three-quarters full (the couscous will swell while cooking). Wrap each pepper in a piece of oiled baking foil.

4 Cook over medium heat for 20 minutes, or until tender. Serve hot or cold, garnished with fresh mint leaves.

Energy 262kcal/1094kJ; Protein 5.8g; Carbohydrate 42.4g, of which sugars 18.9g; Fat 8.7g, of which saturates 4g; Cholesterol 64mg; Calcium 40mg; Fibre 3.9g; Sodium 53mg.

TOFU SATAY

SMOKED TOFU IS MARINATED WITH GARLIC AND SOY SAUCE BEFORE IT IS GRILLED WITH PEPPERS AND SERVED WITH A CRUNCHY PEANUT SAUCE. TOFU READILY SOAKS UP THE FLAVOURS OF A MARINADE OR FOODS IT IS COOKED WITH, SO YOU COULD ALSO SPREAD SOME MOISTENED HERBS ON TO THE COALS.

SERVES FOUR TO SIX

INGREDIENTS

 2 x 200g/7oz packs smoked tofu
 45ml/3 tbsp light soy sauce
 10ml/2 tsp sesame oil
 1 garlic clove, crushed
 1 yellow and 1 red (bell) pepper,
  cut into squares
 8–12 fresh bay leaves
 sunflower oil, for brushing
For the peanut sauce
 2 spring onions (scallions),
  finely chopped
 2 garlic cloves, crushed
 good pinch of chilli powder, or a few
  drops of hot chilli sauce
 5ml/1 tsp sugar
 15ml/1 tbsp white wine vinegar
 30ml/2 tbsp light soy sauce
 45ml/3 tbsp crunchy peanut butter

1 Soak 8–12 satay sticks in water for 30 minutes. Cut the tofu into bitesize cubes and place in a large bowl. Add the soy sauce, sesame oil and crushed garlic and mix well. Cover with clear film (plastic wrap) and marinate for at least 20 minutes.

2 Beat all the peanut sauce ingredients together in a large bowl, using a wooden spoon, until well blended. Avoid using a food processor to blend the ingredients, as the texture should be slightly chunky. Prepare the barbecue. Position a lightly oiled grill rack over the hot coals.

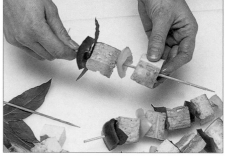

3 Drain the tofu and thread the cubes on to the satay sticks, alternating the tofu with the pepper squares and bay leaves. (Larger bay leaves may need to be halved before threading.)

4 Brush the satays with sunflower oil and cook over high heat, turning the sticks occasionally, until the tofu and peppers are browned and crisp. Serve hot with the peanut sauce.

COOK'S TIP

If you can only find plain tofu, leave it to marinate for 30 minutes to 1 hour for the best flavour.

VARIATION

Add mushrooms, cherry tomatoes and onion segments to the skewers if you like.

Energy 143kcal/593kJ; Protein 7.8g; Carbohydrate 6.2g, of which sugars 5.2g; Fat 9.8g, of which saturates 1.7g; Cholesterol 0mg; Calcium 350mg; Fibre 1.4g; Sodium 210mg.

ROASTED PUMPKIN <u>WITH</u> SPICES

ROASTED PUMPKIN HAS A WONDERFUL, RICH FLAVOUR ESPECIALLY WHEN CHARGRILLED WITH SPICES. EAT IT STRAIGHT FROM THE SKIN, EAT THE SKIN, TOO, OR SCOOP OUT THE COOKED FLESH, ADD A SPOONFUL OF SALSA AND CRÈME FRAÎCHE, AND WRAP IT IN A WARM TORTILLA.

SERVES SIX

INGREDIENTS
  1kg/2¼lb pumpkin
  60ml/4 tbsp oil
  10ml/2 tsp hot chilli sauce
  2.5ml/½ tsp salt
  2.5ml/½ tsp ground allspice
  5ml/1 tsp ground cinnamon
  chopped fresh herbs, to garnish
  salsa and crème fraîche, to serve

COOK'S TIPS
• Green-, grey- or orange-skinned pumpkins all roast well. The orange-fleshed varieties are the most colourful when it comes to cooking.
• It's worth scoring the flesh of the pumpkin slices in several places to get them to cook more quickly.

1 Cut the pumpkin into large pieces. Scoop out and discard the fibre and seeds.

2 Mix the oil and chilli sauce and drizzle most of the mixture evenly over the pumpkin pieces. Prepare the barbecue. Position a lightly oiled grill rack over the hot coals.

3 Put the salt in a small bowl and add the ground allspice and cinnamon. Sprinkle the mixture over the pumpkin.

4 Cook over medium-high heat for 25 minutes, basting occasionally and turning regularly until the pumpkin flesh is tender. Serve with the salsa and crème fraîche separately.

Energy 90kcal/371kJ; Protein 1.2g; Carbohydrate 4.2g, of which sugars 3.3g; Fat 7.7g, of which saturates 1.2g; Cholesterol 0mg; Calcium 49mg; Fibre 1.7g; Sodium 27mg.

SIDE DISHES & ACCOMPANIMENTS

It is well worth preparing some lighter dishes to complement
the rich flavours of the main courses. Beetroot with Fresh Mint
is the ultimate in light, salad-style refreshment, while
Cannellini Bean Salad is perfect with pitta bread.
Some of these sides, such as Vegetables in Coconut and
Ginger Paste, can also serve as mains if made in larger
quantities, and there is also a dazzling array of breads
and sauces on offer in this chapter.

SEARED MIXED ONION SALAD

THIS IS A FINE MIX OF FLAVOURS. ON ITS OWN, IT MAKES A GOOD VEGETARIAN SALAD, BUT IT IS ALSO DELICIOUS SERVED WITH GRILLED MEAT SUCH AS BEEF. COMBINE AS MANY DIFFERENT ONIONS AS YOU WISH; LOOK IN ETHNIC MARKETS TO FIND A DIVERSE SELECTION.

SERVES FOUR TO SIX

INGREDIENTS

6 red spring onions (scallions), trimmed
6 green spring onions (scallions), trimmed and split lengthways
250g/9oz small or baby (pearl) onions, peeled and left whole
2 pink onions, sliced horizontally into 5mm/¼in rounds
2 red onions, sliced into wedges
2 small yellow onions, sliced into wedges
4 banana shallots, halved lengthways
200g/7oz shallots, preferably Thai
45ml/3 tbsp olive oil, plus extra for drizzling
juice of 1 lemon
45ml/3 tbsp chopped fresh flat leaf parsley
30ml/2 tbsp balsamic vinegar
salt and ground black pepper
kuchai flowers (optional), to garnish

1 Prepare the barbecue. Spread out the onions and shallots in a large flat dish. Whisk the oil and lemon juice together and pour over the mixture. Turn the onions and shallots in the dressing to coat them evenly. Season to taste.

2 Position a grill rack over the coals to heat. Place a griddle or perforated metal vegetable basket on the grill rack over medium-high heat, rather than cook directly on the rack and risk losing onions through the gaps in the rack. Grill the onions in batches, for 5–7 minutes, turning them occasionally.

3 As each batch of onions is cooked, lift them on to a platter and keep hot. Just before serving, add the parsley and gently toss to mix, then drizzle over the balsamic vinegar and extra olive oil.

4 Garnish with a few kuchai flowers, if you like, and serve with warmed pitta bread and grilled halloumi for a vegetarian appetizer or with grilled meat or fish as a main course.

COOK'S TIP
When available, scatter the whole salad with a few kuchai flowers. These are the lovely blossoms of the evil-smelling Chinese chive. They are available all year round and are sold in Thai food stores.

Energy 117kcal/485kJ; Protein 2.7g; Carbohydrate 14g, of which sugars 10.1g; Fat 6g, of which saturates 0.8g; Cholesterol 0mg; Calcium 66mg; Fibre 3.1g; Sodium 9mg.

BAKED SWEET POTATO SALAD

WHILE YOU ARE BARBECUING YOUR MAIN DISH, BAKE SWEET POTATOES IN FOIL PARCELS AMONG THE COALS OF THE BARBECUE AND THEN CUBE AND TOSS THE FLESH INTO A CHILLI-SPICED SALAD FOR A WARM SALAD WITH A DIFFERENCE. IT MAKES A FILLING PARTNER TO BARBECUED MEATS AND FISH.

SERVES FOUR TO SIX

INGREDIENTS
  1kg/2¼lb sweet potatoes
For the dressing
  45ml/3 tbsp chopped fresh
    coriander (cilantro)
  juice of 1 lime
  150ml/¼ pint/⅔ cup natural
    (plain) yogurt
For the salad
  1 red (bell) pepper, seeded and
    finely diced
  3 celery sticks, finely diced
  ¼ red-skinned onion, finely chopped
  1 red chilli, finely chopped
  salt and ground black pepper
  coriander leaves, to garnish

1 Pierce the potatoes all over and rub the outside with plenty of salt and olive oil and then wrap each one tightly in a triple thickness of heavy-duty foil. Prepare the barbecue. Push the potatoes in between the coals heated to medium-high. Cook for 1 hour.

2 Combine the dressing ingredients in a bowl, season and chill.

3 In a large bowl mix the red pepper, celery, onion and chilli together. When the sweet potatoes are cooked, remove them from the foil packets and allow to cool for a few minutes. When just cool enough to handle, carefully remove the skin using a small, sharp knife.

4 Cut the peeled potatoes into cubes and add them to the bowl. Remove the dressing from the refrigerator, drizzle over the potato cubes and toss carefully so that vegetables are combined with the dressing. Season again to taste and serve, garnished with fresh coriander.

Energy 176kcal/749kJ; Protein 4g; Carbohydrate 40.4g, of which sugars 14g; Fat 1g, of which saturates 0.3g; Cholesterol 0mg; Calcium 115mg; Fibre 5.2g; Sodium 101mg.

BEETROOT WITH FRESH MINT

BARBECUED FOOD TASTES GOOD WITH SALADS, AND THIS BRIGHT AND DECORATIVE BEETROOT SALAD WITH A BALSAMIC DRESSING IS QUICK TO PREPARE AS WELL AS MAKING A GOOD ACCOMPANIMENT TO LEAFY SALADS. IT CAN BE PREPARED IN ADVANCE, WHICH IS ALWAYS USEFUL WHEN YOU ARE ENTERTAINING.

SERVES FOUR

INGREDIENTS

    4–6 cooked beetroot (beets)
    5–10ml/1–2 tsp sugar
    15–30ml/1–2 tbsp balsamic vinegar
    juice of ½ lemon
    30ml/2 tbsp extra virgin olive oil
    1 bunch fresh mint, leaves stripped
      and thinly sliced
    salt

VARIATIONS

• Add a chopped onion and some dill instead of the mint.
• To make spicy beetroot, add harissa to taste and substitute fresh coriander (cilantro) for the mint.

1 Slice the beetroot or cut into even-size dice with a sharp knife. Put the beetroot in a bowl. Add the sugar, balsamic vinegar, lemon juice, olive oil and a pinch of salt and toss together to combine.

2 Add half the thinly sliced fresh mint to the salad and toss lightly until well combined. Place the salad in the refrigerator and chill for about 1 hour. Serve garnished with the remaining mint leaves.

Energy 95kcal/399kJ; Protein 1.7g; Carbohydrate 10.2g, of which sugars 9.6g; Fat 5.6g, of which saturates 0.8g; Cholesterol 0mg; Calcium 21mg; Fibre 1.9g; Sodium 66mg.

VEGETABLES IN COCONUT AND GINGER PASTE

SWEET POTATOES AND BEETROOT TAKE ON A WONDERFUL SWEETNESS WHEN CHARGRILLED, AND THEY ARE DELICIOUS WITH THE SAVOURY ONIONS. ALL THE VEGETABLES ARE COATED IN AN AROMATIC COCONUT, GINGER AND GARLIC PASTE. SERVE THEM TO ACCOMPANY SIMPLY GRILLED MEAT.

SERVES FOUR

INGREDIENTS
  30ml/2 tbsp groundnut (peanut) oil
    or mild olive oil
  450g/1lb sweet potatoes, peeled and
    cut into thick strips or chunks
  4 beetroot (beets), cooked, peeled
    and cut into wedges
  450g/1lb small red or yellow
    onions, halved
  5ml/1 tsp coriander seeds,
    lightly crushed
  3–4 small fresh red chillies, chopped
  salt and ground black pepper
  chopped fresh coriander (cilantro),
    to garnish
For the paste
  2 large garlic cloves, chopped
  1–2 green chillies, seeded
    and chopped
  15ml/1 tbsp chopped fresh
    root ginger
  45ml/3 tbsp chopped fresh
    coriander (cilantro)
  75ml/5 tbsp coconut milk
  30ml/2 tbsp groundnut (peanut) oil
    or mild olive oil
  grated rind of ½ lime
  2.5ml/½ tsp light muscovado
    (brown) sugar

1 First make the paste. Process the garlic, chillies, ginger, coriander and coconut milk in a food processor, blender or coffee grinder.

2 Turn the paste into a small bowl and beat in the oil, lime rind and muscovado sugar.

3 Prepare the barbecue. Position a lightly oiled grill rack over the hot coals and place a wire vegetable basket on the grill rack to heat.

COOK'S TIP
Orange-fleshed sweet potatoes look more attractive than white-fleshed ones in this dish – and they are more nutritious.

4 Put the oil in a large roasting pan and add the vegetables and coriander seeds. Toss to mix. Transfer to the wire basket and cook over medium-high heat for 15 minutes.

5 Return the vegetables to the roasting tin, add the paste and toss to coat thoroughly. Add the chillies and season well with salt and pepper.

6 Grill the vegetables for a further 25–35 minutes, or until the sweet potatoes and onions are fully cooked and tender. Shake the basket regularly. Serve immediately, sprinkled with a little chopped fresh coriander.

Energy 284kcal/1194kJ; Protein 4.8g; Carbohydrate 42.4g, of which sugars 21.6g; Fat 11.9g, of which saturates 1.7g; Cholesterol 0mg; Calcium 106mg; Fibre 6.8g; Sodium 139mg.

LEMONY COUSCOUS SALAD

THIS IS A POPULAR SALAD OF OLIVES, ALMONDS AND COURGETTES MIXED WITH FLUFFY COUSCOUS AND DRESSED WITH HERBS, LEMON JUICE AND OLIVE OIL. IT HAS A DELICATE FLAVOUR AND MAKES AN EXCELLENT ACCOMPANIMENT TO GRILLED CHICKEN OR KEBABS.

SERVES FOUR

INGREDIENTS

275g/10oz/1⅔ cups couscous
550ml/18fl oz/2½ cups boiling
  vegetable stock
2 small courgettes (zucchini)
16–20 black olives
25g/1oz/¼ cup flaked (sliced)
  almonds, toasted
60ml/4 tbsp olive oil
15ml/1 tbsp lemon juice
15ml/1 tbsp chopped fresh
  coriander (cilantro)
15ml/1 tbsp chopped fresh parsley
good pinch of ground cumin
good pinch of cayenne pepper

1 Place the couscous in a bowl and pour over the boiling vegetable stock. Stir with a fork and then set aside for 10 minutes for the stock to be absorbed into the grains. Fluff up the couscous using a fork to separate the grains.

2 Trim the courgettes at both ends then cut into pieces about 2.5cm/1in long. Slice thinly and then cut into fine julienne strips with a sharp knife. Halve the black olives, discarding the stones (pits).

3 Carefully mix the courgettes, olives and almonds into the couscous so that they are well incorporated.

4 Blend together the olive oil, lemon juice, coriander, parsley, cumin and cayenne in a small bowl. Stir into the salad, tossing gently to mix the dressing thoroughly through the couscous and vegetables. Transfer to a large serving dish and serve immediately.

Energy 327kcal/1358kJ; Protein 6.9g; Carbohydrate 37.2g, of which sugars 1.6g; Fat 17.6g, of which saturates 2.3g; Cholesterol 0mg; Calcium 66mg; Fibre 1.9g; Sodium 425mg.

POTATO AND OLIVE SALAD

THIS DELICIOUS SALAD COMES FROM NORTH AFRICA. THE COMBINATION OF GARLIC, CUMIN AND LOTS OF FRESH CORIANDER MAKES IT PARTICULARLY TASTY AND YET IT IS QUICK AND SIMPLE TO PREPARE. IDEAL AS PART OF A SALAD SELECTION TO ACCOMPANY GRILLED MEAT, FISH OR POULTRY.

SERVES FOUR

INGREDIENTS

   8 large new potatoes
   large pinch of salt
   large pinch of sugar
   3 garlic cloves, chopped
   15ml/1 tbsp vinegar of your choice,
     such as a fruit variety
   large pinch of ground cumin or whole
     cumin seeds
   pinch of cayenne pepper or hot
     paprika, to taste
   30–45ml/2–3 tbsp extra virgin
     olive oil
   30–45ml/2–3 tbsp chopped fresh
     coriander (cilantro) leaves
   10–15 dry-fleshed black
     Mediterranean olives

1 Peel and chop the new potatoes into chunks. Put them in a pan, pour in water to cover and add the salt and sugar. Bring to the boil, then reduce the heat and boil gently for about 8–10 minutes, or until the potatoes are just tender. Drain well and leave in a colander to cool completely.

2 When cool enough to handle, cut the potatoes into thick slices and put them in a bowl.

3 Sprinkle the garlic, vinegar, cumin and cayenne or paprika over the salad. Drizzle with olive oil and sprinkle with coriander and olives. Chill before serving.

Energy 196kcal/822kJ; Protein 3g; Carbohydrate 24.5g, of which sugars 2.2g; Fat 10.2g, of which saturates 1.6g; Cholesterol 0mg; Calcium 42mg; Fibre 2.5g; Sodium 302mg.

CANNELLINI BEAN SALAD

TENDER WHITE BEANS ARE DELICIOUS IN THIS SPICY DRESSING WITH THE BITE OF FRESH, CRUNCHY GREEN PEPPER IN THIS DISH FROM ISRAEL. IT IS PERFECT FOR PREPARING AHEAD OF TIME AND TASTES GREAT AS A FIRST COURSE WITH PITTA BREAD AS WELL AS ACCOMPANYING MAIN COURSE DISHES.

SERVES FOUR

INGREDIENTS
  750g/1lb 10oz tomatoes, diced
  1 onion, finely chopped
  ½–1 mild fresh chilli, finely chopped
  1 green (bell) pepper, seeded
    and chopped
  pinch of sugar
  4 garlic cloves, chopped
  400g/14oz can cannellini beans, drained
  45–60ml/3–4 tbsp olive oil
  grated rind and juice of 1 lemon
  15ml/1 tbsp cider vinegar or
    wine vinegar
  salt and ground black pepper
  chopped fresh parsley, to garnish

1 Put the tomatoes, onion, chilli, green pepper, sugar, garlic, cannellini beans, salt and plenty of ground black pepper in a large bowl and toss together until well combined.

2 Add the olive oil, lemon rind and juice and vinegar to the salad and toss lightly to combine. Chill before serving, garnished with chopped parsley.

Energy 226kcal/947kJ; Protein 8.8g; Carbohydrate 27.6g, of which sugars 12.9g; Fat 9.6g, of which saturates 1.5g; Cholesterol 0mg; Calcium 92mg; Fibre 9g; Sodium 409mg.

CLASSIC PASTA SALAD

PASTA SALAD IS A POPULAR AND SUSTAINING ACCOMPANIMENT TO ALL KINDS OF DISHES. THIS VERSION CONTAINS BRIGHT GREEN BEANS AND CHERRY TOMATOES ON THE VINE, WITH PARMESAN, OLIVES AND CAPERS TO GIVE IT PIQUANCY. COOK THE PASTA AL DENTE FOR THE BEST TEXTURE.

SERVES SIX

INGREDIENTS
   300g/11oz/2¾ cups dried fusilli
   150g/5oz green beans, topped and
     tailed and cut into 5cm/2in lengths
   1 potato, about 150g/5oz, diced
   200g/7oz cherry tomatoes on the
     vine, hulled and halved
   2 spring onions (scallions),
     finely chopped
   90g/3½oz Parmesan cheese, diced or
     coarsely shaved
   6–8 pitted black olives, cut into rings
   15–30ml/1–2 tbsp capers, to taste
For the dressing
   90ml/6 tbsp extra virgin olive oil
   15ml/1 tbsp balsamic vinegar
   15ml/1 tbsp chopped fresh flat
     leaf parsley
   salt and ground black pepper

1 Cook the pasta according to the instructions on the packet. Drain it into a colander, rinse under cold running water until cold, then shake the colander to remove as much water as possible. Leave to drain and dry, shaking the colander occasionally.

2 Cook the green beans and diced potato in a pan of salted boiling water for 5–6 minutes or until tender. Drain in a colander and leave to cool.

3 To make the dressing, put all the ingredients in a large bowl with salt and pepper to taste, and whisk well to mix.

4 Add the tomatoes, spring onions, Parmesan, olive rings and capers to the dressing, then add the cold pasta, beans and potato. Toss well to mix. Cover and leave to stand for about 30 minutes. Taste for seasoning before serving.

COOK'S TIP
To round off the soft textures of this superb salad, buy a piece of fresh Parmesan from the delicatessen to shave into wafer-thin slices. This version of the cheese is a mature, softer version of the harder cheese used for grating and sprinkling over hot dishes.

Energy 376kcal/1579kJ; Protein 13.2g; Carbohydrate 43g, of which sugars 3.7g; Fat 18g, of which saturates 5g; Cholesterol 15mg; Calcium 212mg; Fibre 2.9g; Sodium 359mg.

BLUE CHEESE DIP

THIS DIP CAN BE MIXED UP IN NEXT TO NO TIME AND IS DELICIOUS SERVED WITH PEARS OR WITH FRESH VEGETABLE CRUDITÉS. THIS IS A VERY THICK DIP TO WHICH YOU CAN ADD A LITTLE MORE YOGURT FOR A SOFTER CONSISTENCY. ADD STILL MORE YOGURT TO MAKE A GREAT DRESSING.

SERVES FOUR

INGREDIENTS

150g/5oz blue cheese, such as
 Stilton or Danish blue
150g/5oz/²⁄₃ cup soft cheese
75ml/5 tbsp Greek (US strained
 plain) yogurt
salt and ground black pepper,
 plus extra to garnish

1 Crumble the blue cheese into a bowl. Using a wooden spoon, beat the cheese to soften it.

2 Add the soft cheese and beat well to blend the two cheeses together.

3 Gradually beat in the Greek yogurt, adding enough to give you the consistency you prefer.

4 Season with lots of black pepper and a little salt. Chill the dip until you are ready to serve it.

COOK'S TIP
If you like, add a handful of finely chopped walnuts to this dip, because they go wonderfully well with the cheese. It is advisable to grind the nuts in a food processor to avoid the dip being too chunky in texture.

Energy 206kcal/855kJ; Protein 12.1g; Carbohydrate 2.6g, of which sugars 2.6g; Fat 16.5g, of which saturates 10.7g; Cholesterol 44mg; Calcium 219mg; Fibre 0g; Sodium 473mg.

TOMATO KETCHUP

SWEET, TANGY, SPICY TOMATO KETCHUP IS PERFECT FOR SERVING WITH BARBECUED OR GRILLED BURGERS AND SAUSAGES. THIS HOME-MADE VARIETY IS SO MUCH BETTER THAN STORE-BOUGHT TOMATO KETCHUP, AND THE RECIPE WILL BE ENOUGH TO SERVE ABOUT 15 PEOPLE.

MAKES ABOUT 1.3KG/3LB

INGREDIENTS
2.25kg/5lb very ripe tomatoes
1 onion
6 cloves
4 allspice berries
6 black peppercorns
1 fresh rosemary sprig
25g/1oz fresh root ginger, sliced
1 celery heart and leaves, chopped
30ml/2 tbsp soft light brown sugar
65ml/4½ tbsp raspberry vinegar
3 garlic cloves, peeled
15ml/1 tbsp salt

1 Skewer each tomato on a metal fork and hold in a gas flame for 1–2 minutes, turning, until the skin splits and wrinkles. Alternatively, plunge the tomatoes into boiling water for 30 seconds, then refresh in cold water. Peel away the skins and remove the seeds then chop and place in a large pan. Peel the onion, leaving the tip and root intact, and stud it with the cloves.

2 Tie the onion in a double layer of muslin (cheesecloth) with the allspice, peppercorns, rosemary and ginger and add to the pan. Add the celery to the pan with the remaining ingredients.

3 Bring the mixture to the boil over a fairly high heat, stirring occasionally. Once it is beginning to bubble, reduce the heat and simmer for 1½–2 hours, stirring regularly, until the liquid has reduced by around half.

4 Purée the mixture in a food processor, then return to the pan, bring to the boil and simmer for 15 minutes. Bottle in clean, sterilized jars and store in the refrigerator. Use within 2 weeks.

Energy 586kcal/2509kJ; Protein 19.9g; Carbohydrate 116.3g, of which sugars 114.9g; Fat 8.2g, of which saturates 2.5g; Cholesterol 0mg; Calcium 329mg; Fibre 29.1g; Sodium 409mg.

THOUSAND ISLAND DIP

THIS VARIATION ON THE CLASSIC DRESSING IS FAR REMOVED FROM THE ORIGINAL VERSION BUT CAN BE SERVED IN THE SAME WAY — WITH GRILLED KING PRAWNS LACED ON TO BAMBOO SKEWERS FOR DIPPING OR WITH A SIMPLE MIXED SEAFOOD SALAD.

SERVES FOUR

INGREDIENTS
4 tomatoes
150g/5oz/²/₃ cup soft cheese
60ml/4 tbsp mayonnaise
30ml/2 tbsp tomato purée (paste)
30ml/2 tbsp chopped fresh parsley
4 sun-dried tomatoes in oil, drained
  and finely chopped
grated rind and juice of 1 lemon
red Tabasco sauce, to taste
5ml/1 tsp Worcestershire or soy sauce
salt and ground black pepper

1 Skewer each tomato in turn on a metal fork and hold in a gas flame for 1–2 minutes, or until the skin wrinkles and splits. Allow to cool, then slip off and discard the skins. Alternatively, plunge the tomatoes into boiling water for 30 seconds, then refresh in cold water. Peel away the skins. Halve the tomatoes and scoop out the seeds with a teaspoon. Finely chop the tomato flesh and set aside.

COOK'S TIP
Put together a colourful seafood medley – such as peeled prawns (shrimp), calamari rings and mussels – to accompany this vibrant and popular party dip.

2 In a bowl, beat the soft cheese, then gradually beat in the mayonnaise and tomato purée to a smooth mixture.

3 Stir in the parsley and sun-dried tomatoes, then add the chopped tomatoes and their seeds, and mix well.

4 Add the lemon rind and juice, and Tabasco sauce to taste. Stir in the Worcestershire or soy sauce, and salt and pepper to taste.

5 Transfer the dip to a serving bowl, cover and chill until ready to serve.

Energy 194kcal/805kJ; Protein 4.7g; Carbohydrate 5.7g, of which sugars 5.6g; Fat 17.1g, of which saturates 5.2g; Cholesterol 27mg; Calcium 11mg; Fibre 1.2g; Sodium 184mg.

BARBECUE SAUCE

THIS TRADITIONAL SAUCE CAN BE PREPARED IN ADVANCE, BOTTLED AND USED WHENEVER YOU FEEL LIKE HOLDING A BARBECUE, AS IT WILL LAST FOR SEVERAL MONTHS IN A REFRIGERATOR. SERVE IT WITH YOUR FAVOURITE BURGERS, SAUSAGES, GRILLED CHICKEN AND BARBECUED VEGETABLES.

MAKES ABOUT 900ML/1½ PINTS/3¾ CUPS

INGREDIENTS
    30ml/2 tbsp olive oil
    1 large onion, chopped
    1 garlic clove, crushed
    1 fresh red chilli, seeded and sliced
    2 celery sticks, sliced
    1 large carrot, sliced
    1 medium cooking apple, quartered,
      cored, peeled and chopped
    450g/1lb ripe tomatoes, quartered
    2.5ml/½ tsp ground ginger
    150ml/¼ pint/⅔ cup malt vinegar
    1 bay leaf
    4 cloves
    4 black peppercorns
    50g/2oz/¼ cup soft light brown sugar
    10ml/2 tsp English mustard
    2.5ml/½ tsp salt

1 Heat the oil in a large heavy pan. Add the onion and cook over a low heat for 5 minutes.

2 Stir the garlic, chilli, celery and carrot into the onions and cook for 5 minutes, stirring frequently, until the onion just begins to colour.

3 Add the apple, tomatoes, ground ginger and malt vinegar to the pan and stir to combine.

COOK'S TIP
Just add a little yogurt to the barbecue sauce to make a quick and easy dip.

4 Put the bay leaf, cloves and peppercorns on to a square of muslin (cheesecloth) and tie into a bag with fine string. Add to the pan and bring to the boil. Reduce the heat, cover and simmer for about 45 minutes, stirring the mixture occasionally.

5 Add the sugar, mustard and salt to the pan and stir until the sugar dissolves. Simmer for 5 minutes. Leave to cool for 10 minutes, then remove the bag and discard.

6 Press the mixture through a sieve and return to the cleaned pan. Simmer for 10 minutes, or until thickened. Adjust the seasoning.

7 Pour the sauce into hot sterilized bottles or jars, then seal. Store in a cool, dark place and use within 6 months. Once opened, store in the refrigerator and use within 2 months.

VARIATION
For Quick Barbecue Sauce, heat 20ml/2 tbsp oil in a pan and fry 1 finely chopped onion and 2 crushed garlic cloves until soft. Add a 200g/7oz can of chopped tomatoes, 30ml/2 tbsp tomato purée (paste), 15ml/1 tbsp soft light brown sugar, 15ml/1 tbsp Worcestershire sauce, a dash of Tabasco sauce, 30ml/2 tbsp vinegar and 15ml/1 tbsp English mustard. Simmer for 10 minutes and serve hot or cold.

Energy 723kcal/3036kJ; Protein 12.2g; Carbohydrate 114.3g, of which sugars 102.5g; Fat 29.1g, of which saturates 3.8g; Cholesterol 0mg; Calcium 243mg; Fibre 14.2g; Sodium 118mg.

SAFFRON BREAD SKEWERS

THIS ANTIPODEAN'S FIRESIDE FAVOURITE, CALLED DAMPER, IS ALSO A BIT OF A GIRL GUIDE TRADITION. IT'S A FUN THING FOR A LONG, LAZY BEACH BARBECUE. IT IS USUAL TO COOK DAMPER IN THE EMBERS OF THE FIRE, BUT ROSEMARY SKEWERS ARE A STYLISH ALTERNATIVE.

SERVES EIGHT

INGREDIENTS
24 rosemary spikes or wooden
  skewers (or 12 of each)
500g/1¼lb/5 cups plain
  (all-purpose) flour
25ml/1½ tbsp baking powder
250g/9oz/generous 1 cup plus
  30ml/2 tbsp butter
30ml/2 tbsp chopped fresh rosemary,
  plus 1 sprig
large pinch of saffron threads mixed
  with 15ml/1 tbsp boiling water
175ml/6fl oz/¾ cup milk
salt

1 Soak the rosemary spikes or wooden skewers in cold water for 30 minutes. Sift the flour, baking powder and salt into a large bowl. Rub in 200g/7oz/ scant 1 cup of the butter until the mixture looks like fine breadcrumbs, then add the chopped rosemary.

2 Strain the saffron water into the milk and add to the flour mixture all in one go. Mix to a paste with your hands and knead until the dough is smooth and elastic. Melt the remaining butter and stir it with the rosemary sprig to infuse it with the flavour.

3 Prepare the barbecue. Drain the skewers or rosemary spikes. Divide the dough into 24 equal pieces and twist one piece around each skewer or spike.

4 Position a lightly oiled grill rack over the hot coals. Grill the spiked dough over medium-high heat for 5 minutes, turning often, until cooked and golden. Brush occasionally with the rosemary dipped in butter and serve the saffron bread hot.

COOK'S TIP
If you're cooking a pan of soup *al fresco*, these breads taste terrific dipped in the soup.

Energy 456kcal/1905kJ; Protein 6.8g; Carbohydrate 49.8g, of which sugars 2.2g; Fat 26.9g, of which saturates 16.6g; Cholesterol 68mg; Calcium 119mg; Fibre 1.9g; Sodium 201mg.

SESAME BURGER BUNS

PUT YOUR HOME-MADE BURGERS INSIDE A TRADITIONAL SOFT BURGER BUN WITH A SESAME SEED TOPPING. SOFT BUNS ARE PERFECT WITH MEAT OR VEGETARIAN BURGERS AND ARE EASIER TO HOLD AND TO EAT THAN A CRUSTY ROLL. JUST ADD RELISH!

MAKES SIX

INGREDIENTS
- 500g/1¼lb/5 cups strong white bread flour
- 7.5ml/1½ tsp salt
- 25g/1oz butter, softened
- 5ml/1 tsp easy-blend (rapid-rise) dried yeast
- 15ml/1 tbsp sugar
- 150ml/¼ pint/⅔ cup lukewarm milk
- about 150ml/¼ pint/⅔ cup lukewarm water
- 10ml/2 tsp sesame seeds

1 Sift the flour and salt into a bowl and rub in the butter with your fingertips. Add the yeast and sugar. Mix well. Make a well in the centre and pour in the milk and the water. Stir the liquid into the flour from the centre outwards to make a soft dough.

2 Knead the dough on a lightly floured surface for 10 minutes then return to the cleaned bowl and cover with lightly oiled clear film (plastic wrap). Leave in a warm place until doubled in size (about 1 hour).

3 Knock back (punch down) the dough then divide into six equal pieces. Form into rounds and place on a greased baking sheet. Cover with lightly oiled clear film and leave to rise for 1 hour or until doubled in size.

4 Meanwhile, preheat the oven to 220°C/425°F/Gas 7. Brush the buns with a little milk and sprinkle with sesame seeds. Cook the buns for 15–20 minutes, or until golden brown. Cool on a wire rack.

COOK'S TIP
To use a bread machine, substitute the milk and water quantities with 300ml/ ½ pint/1¼ cups water and include 30ml/2 tbsp milk powder to the above ingredients. Put the ingredients in the bread machine in the order specified in the manufacturer's instructions. Set to a basic dough setting and then shape into buns and proceed as above.

Energy 352kcal/1488kJ; Protein 9.2g; Carbohydrate 68.6g, of which sugars 5.1g; Fat 6.4g, of which saturates 2.8g; Cholesterol 10mg; Calcium 166mg; Fibre 2.8g; Sodium 39mg.

GARLIC AND HERB BREAD

THIS IRRESISTIBLE GARLIC BREAD INCLUDES PLENTY OF FRESH MIXED HERBS. YOU CAN VARY THE OVERALL FLAVOUR BY USING DIFFERENT HERBS. PREPARE IT EARLIER AND HEAT IT IN THE OVEN WHEN YOU NEED IT, OR WARM IT UP ON THE GRILL RACK.

SERVES THREE TO FOUR

INGREDIENTS

1 baguette or bloomer loaf
For the garlic and herb butter
115g/4oz/½ cup unsalted (sweet) butter, softened
5–6 large garlic cloves, finely chopped or crushed
30–45ml/2–3 tbsp chopped fresh herbs (such as parsley, chervil and a little tarragon)
15ml/1 tbsp chopped fresh chives
coarse salt and ground black pepper

1 Preheat the oven to 200°C/400°F/ Gas 6. Make the garlic and herb butter by beating the butter with the garlic, herbs, chives and seasoning.

VARIATIONS

• Use 105ml/7 tbsp extra virgin olive oil instead of the butter.
• Flavour the butter with garlic, a little chopped fresh chilli, grated lime rind and chopped fresh coriander (cilantro).
• Add chopped, pitted black olives or sun-dried tomatoes to the butter with a little grated lemon rind.

2 Cut the bread into 1cm/½in thick diagonal slices, but be sure to leave them attached at the base so that the loaf stays intact.

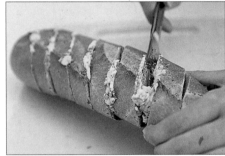

3 Spread the garlic and herb butter between the slices evenly, being careful not to detach them, and then spread any remaining butter over the top of the loaf.

4 Wrap the loaf in foil and bake in the preheated oven for 20–25 minutes, or until the butter is melted and the crust is golden and crisp. Cut the loaf into slices to serve.

COOK'S TIP
This loaf makes an excellent addition to a barbecue. If space permits, place the foil-wrapped loaf on top of the barbecue and cook for about the same length of time as for oven baking. Turn the foil parcel over several times to ensure it cooks evenly.

Energy 920kcal/3877kJ; Protein 22.1g; Carbohydrate 135.1g, of which sugars 7.2g; Fat 36.2g, of which saturates 20.8g; Cholesterol 82mg; Calcium 317mg; Fibre 6.3g; Sodium 1714mg.

RED ONION AND ROSEMARY FOCACCIA

MAKE THIS RICH AND TASTY ITALIAN BREAD WITH ITS TOPPING OF ROSEMARY AND RED ONION TO SERVE WITH YOUR BARBECUE FEAST. YOU COULD SERVE IT WITH A TOMATO, BASIL AND MOZZARELLA SALAD FOR A QUICK AND EASY FIRST COURSE WHILE YOU WAIT FOR THE COALS TO HEAT UP FOR BARBECUING.

2 Set the yeast aside in a warm, but not hot, place for 10 minutes, until it has turned frothy.

3 Add the yeast, the remaining water, 15ml/1 tbsp of the oil and the chopped rosemary to the flour. Mix all the ingredients together to form a dough, then gather the dough into a ball and knead on a floured work surface for about 5 minutes, until smooth and elastic. You may need to add a little extra flour if the dough is very sticky.

4 Place the dough in a lightly oiled bowl and slip it into a polythene bag or cover with oiled clear film (plastic wrap) and leave to rise. The length of time you leave it for depends on the temperature: leave it all day in a cool place, overnight in the refrigerator, or for 1–2 hours in a warm, but not hot, place.

5 Lightly oil a baking sheet. Knead the dough to form a flat loaf that is about 30cm/12in round or square. Place on the baking sheet, cover with oiled polythene or clear film and leave to rise again in a warm place for a further 40–60 minutes.

6 Preheat the oven to 220°C/425°F/ Gas 7. Press indentations into the dough with your fingers. Toss the onion in 15ml/1 tbsp of the oil and scatter over the loaf with the rosemary sprigs and some coarse salt. Bake for 15–20 minutes until golden brown. Serve the bread freshly baked or leave to cool on the baking sheet and serve warm.

SERVES FOUR TO FIVE

INGREDIENTS
450g/1lb/4 cups strong white bread
  flour, plus extra for dusting
5ml/1 tsp salt
7g/¼oz fresh yeast or generous 5ml/
  1 tsp dried yeast
2.5ml/½ tsp light muscovado
  (brown) sugar
250ml/8fl oz/1 cup lukewarm water
60ml/4 tbsp extra virgin olive oil,
  plus extra for greasing
5ml/1 tsp very finely chopped fresh
  rosemary, plus 6–8 small sprigs
1 red onion, thinly sliced
coarse salt

1 Sift the flour and salt into a bowl. Set aside. Cream the fresh yeast with the sugar, and gradually stir in half the water. If using dried yeast, stir the sugar into the water and sprinkle the dried yeast over the surface.

Energy 496kcal/2094kJ; Protein 11g; Carbohydrate 90.4g, of which sugars 3.8g; Fat 12.5g, of which saturates 1.8g; Cholesterol 0mg; Calcium 167mg; Fibre 4g; Sodium 496mg.

DRINKS & DESSERTS

People may not be expecting it, but they will usually find room for something sweet at the end of a barbecue feast! Designed to cleanse the palate while making use of the still-hot coals, the desserts here use a combination of caramelized or grilled fruit and sweet, toasted bakes. The sticky sweetness of hot, Honey-baked Figs is beautifully complemented by home-made Hazelnut Ice Cream, or if something lighter is required, try cooling classics such as Fresh Fruit Salad and Lemon Sorbet.

ALCOHOLIC FRUITY PUNCH

THE TERM "PUNCH" COMES FROM THE HINDU WORD PANCH (FIVE), RELATING TO THE FIVE INGREDIENTS TRADITIONALLY CONTAINED IN THE DRINK: ALCOHOL, CITRUS, TEA, SUGAR AND WATER. PUNCHES STILL COMBINE A MIXTURE OF SPIRITS, FLAVOURINGS AND A TOP-UP OF FIZZ OR JUICE.

MAKES ABOUT FIFTEEN GLASSES

INGREDIENTS

2 large papayas
4 passion fruit
300g/11oz lychees, peeled and pitted
300ml/½ pint/1¼ cups freshly
  squeezed orange juice
200ml/7fl oz/scant 1 cup
  Grand Marnier or other
  orange-flavoured liqueur
8 whole star anise
2 small oranges
ice cubes
1.5 litres/2½ pints/6¼ cups soda
  water (club soda)

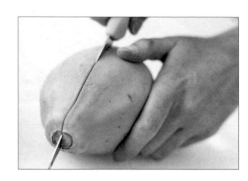

1 Halve the papayas using a sharp knife and discard the seeds. Halve the passion fruit and press the pulp through a sieve into a small punch bowl or a pretty serving bowl.

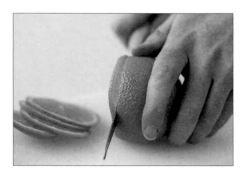

2 Push the papayas through a juicer, adding 105ml/7 tbsp water to help the pulp through. Juice the lychees. Add the juices to the bowl with the orange juice, liqueur and star anise. Thinly slice the oranges and add to the bowl. Chill for at least 1 hour, or until ready to serve.

3 Add plenty of ice cubes to the bowl and top up with soda water. Ladle into punch cups or small glasses to serve.

COOK'S TIP
This delightful punch also makes a fabulously alcoholic fruit syrup for a dessert of papaya halves stuffed with frozen yogurt or a fruit sorbet.

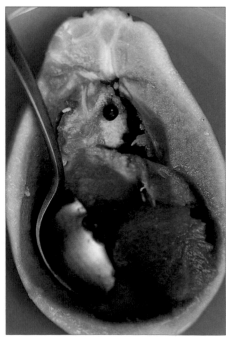

Energy 65kcal/274kJ; Protein 0.5g; Carbohydrate 11.6g, of which sugars 11.6g; Fat 0.1g, of which saturates 0g; Cholesterol 0mg; Calcium 10mg; Fibre 0.9g; Sodium 6mg.

APPLE-SPICED BEER

LIGHT BEER TAKES ON A WHOLE NEW DIMENSION IN THIS FUN AND FRUITY COOLER. DILUTED WITH FRESHLY JUICED APPLE AND FLAVOURED WITH GINGER AND STAR ANISE, IT'S A GREAT DRINK THAT IS REFRESHING AND LESS ALCOHOLIC THAN NORMAL BEER.

MAKES EIGHT TO TEN TALL GLASSES

INGREDIENTS
    8 eating apples
    25g/1oz fresh root ginger
    6 whole star anise
    800ml/1⅓ pints/3½ cups light beer
    crushed ice

1 Quarter and core the apples and, using a small, sharp knife, cut the flesh into pieces small enough to fit through a juicer. Roughly chop the ginger. Push half the apples through the juicer, then juice the ginger and the remaining apples.

2 Put 105ml/7 tbsp of the juice in a small pan with the star anise and heat gently until almost boiling. Add to the remaining juice in a large jug (pitcher) and chill for at least 1 hour.

3 Add the light beer to the juice and stir gently until the froth has dispersed a little. Pour the spiced beer over crushed ice in tall glasses, allow to settle again and serve immediately.

Energy 42kcal/178kJ; Protein 0.4g; Carbohydrate 4.8g, of which sugars 4.8g; Fat 0.1g, of which saturates 0g; Cholesterol 0mg; Calcium 6mg; Fibre 0.9g; Sodium 7mg.

NECTARINES WITH PISTACHIO NUTS

FRESH, RIPE NECTARINES STUFFED WITH A GROUND ALMOND AND PISTACHIO NUT FILLING ARE SIMPLE TO COOK IN FOIL PARCELS ON THE BARBECUE. MAKE THE PARCELS AHEAD AND GRILL THEM WHILE YOU EAT YOUR MAIN COURSE. WHEN OPENED, THE NECTARINES ARE IMMERSED IN A FRUITY LIQUEUR SAUCE.

SERVES FOUR

INGREDIENTS

  50g/2oz/½ cup ground almonds
  15ml/1 tbsp caster (superfine) sugar
  1 egg yolk
  50g/2oz/½ cup shelled pistachio
    nuts, chopped
  4 nectarines
  200ml/7fl oz/scant 1 cup orange juice
  2 ripe passion fruit
  45ml/3 tbsp Cointreau or other
    orange liqueur

1 Prepare the barbecue. Position a grill rack over the hot coals. Mix the ground almonds, sugar and egg yolk to a paste, then stir in the pistachio nuts.

2 Cut the nectarines in half and carefully remove the stones (pits). Pile the ground almond and pistachio filling into the nectarine halves, packing in plenty of filling, and then place them in pairs on pieces of double-thickness foil. Wrap them up, leaving a space at the top.

3 Pour the orange juice around the nectarines, then close the tops. Place on the grill rack over medium-high heat and cook for 25 minutes.

4 Cut the passion fruit in half and scoop out the seeds. Open the foil tops and add a little of the passion fruit to each parcel. Sprinkle over the liqueur. Cook for a further 5 minutes. Place the nectarines on serving plates and spoon the sauce over and around them.

COOK'S TIP
The sugar in the nutty stuffing should caramelize over the heat, creating a lovely golden-brown crumble effect.

Energy 272kcal/1135kJ; Protein 7.6g; Carbohydrate 20.7g, of which sugars 20g; Fat 15.4g, of which saturates 1.9g; Cholesterol 50mg; Calcium 62mg; Fibre 3.5g; Sodium 74mg.

HONEY-BAKED FIGS

TWO WILD INGREDIENTS — FIGS AND HAZELNUTS — ARE USED TO MAKE THIS DELECTABLE DESSERT.
FRESH FIGS ARE BAKED IN FOIL PARCELS WITH A LIGHTLY SPICED LEMON AND HONEY SYRUP AND ARE
SERVED WITH HOME-MADE ROASTED HAZELNUT ICE CREAM.

SERVES FOUR

INGREDIENTS

    finely pared rind of 1 lemon
    1 cinnamon stick, roughly broken
    60ml/4 tbsp clear honey
    8 large figs
For the hazelnut ice cream
    450ml/¾ pint/scant 2 cups double
      (heavy) cream
    50g/2oz/¼ cup caster
      (superfine) sugar
    3 large (US extra large) egg yolks
    1.5ml/¼ tsp vanilla extract
    75g/3oz/¾ cup hazelnuts

1 To make the ice cream, gently heat the cream in a pan until almost boiling. Meanwhile, beat the sugar and egg yolks in a bowl until creamy.

2 Pour a little hot cream into the egg yolk mixture and stir with a wooden spoon. Pour back into the pan and mix well. Cook over a low heat, stirring constantly, until the mixture thickens slightly and lightly coats the back of the spoon – do not allow it to boil. Pour the custard into a bowl, stir in the vanilla extract and leave to cool.

3 Preheat the oven to 180°C/350°F/ Gas 4. Place the hazelnuts on a baking sheet and roast for 10–12 minutes, or until golden. Leave the nuts to cool, then grind them in a food processor.

4 If you have an ice cream maker, pour in the cold custard and churn until half-set. Add the ground hazelnuts and continue to churn until the ice cream is thick. Freeze until firm.

5 To make by hand, pour the custard into a freezerproof container and freeze for 2 hours. Turn into a bowl and beat with an electric whisk or turn into a food processor and beat until smooth. Stir in the hazelnuts and freeze until half-set. Beat once more, then freeze until firm.

6 Prepare the barbecue. Position a grill rack over the hot coals. Remove the ice cream from the freezer and allow to soften slightly.

VARIATION
Use pecans instead of hazelnuts.

7 Put the lemon rind, cinnamon stick, honey and 200ml/7fl oz/scant 1 cup water in a small pan and heat slowly until boiling. Simmer the mixture for 5 minutes, then leave to stand for 15 minutes.

8 Using a sharp knife, cut the figs almost into quarters but leaving them attached at the base. Place them in pairs on pieces of double-thickness foil. Wrap them up, leaving a space at the top. Pour the honey syrup around and over the figs, then close the tops. Place on the grill rack over medium-high heat and cook for 15 minutes.

9 Arrange the figs on small serving plates, with the cooking syrup poured around them. Serve accompanied by a scoop or two of the ice cream.

Energy 909kcal/3770kJ; Protein 8.2g; Carbohydrate 48.7g, of which sugars 48.4g; Fat 77.1g, of which saturates 39.6g; Cholesterol 305mg; Calcium 206mg; Fibre 4.2g; Sodium 60mg.

CHARGRILLED PINEAPPLE

THIS IS A BOLD DESSERT, ATTRACTIVE TOO, IF YOU LEAVE THE GREEN TOPS ON THE PINEAPPLE.
HEATING PINEAPPLE REALLY BRINGS THE FLAVOUR TO THE FORE AND, WITH THE ICE-COLD GRANITA,
IT'S THE IDEAL FINISH TO A GLAMOROUS BARBECUE.

SERVES EIGHT

INGREDIENTS
 2 medium pineapples
 15ml/1 tbsp caster (superfine) sugar
 mixed with 15ml/1 tbsp water
For the granita
 15ml/1 tbsp sugar
 1 fresh long mild red chilli, seeded
 and finely chopped
 900ml/1½ pints/3¾ cups pineapple
 juice or fresh purée

COOK'S TIP
Chilli is a regular ingredient in fruit and citrus granitas, because it counters the sharp taste of the fruit.

1 To make the granita, place the sugar and chilli in a small heavy pan with 30ml/2 tbsp of the pineapple juice. Heat gently until the sugar has dissolved, then bring to a fast boil for 30 seconds. Pour the remaining pineapple juice into a large, shallow freezerproof container. The ideal size is about 25 x 14cm/10 x 5½in. Stir in the chilli mixture and freeze for 2 hours.

2 Fork the frozen edges of the sorbet mixture into the centre and freeze for a further 1½ hours until crunchy. Give it another fork over. Return it to the freezer, where it can stay for up to 1 week.

3 Prepare the barbecue. Thaw the granita for about 10 minutes in the refrigerator before serving, and fork it over to break up the ice crystals.

4 Cut each pineapple lengthways into four equal wedges, slicing right through the leafy crown. Remove the core from each wedge.

5 Heat a griddle on the grill rack over hot coals. Lower the heat slightly. Brush the cut sides of the pineapple wedges with the sugar mixture and grill for about 1 minute on each side, or until branded. Serve warm with the granita.

Energy 112kcal/482kJ; Protein 0.9g; Carbohydrate 28.4g, of which sugars 28.4g; Fat 0.4g, of which saturates 0g; Cholesterol 0mg; Calcium 34mg; Fibre 1.5g; Sodium 12mg.

CALVADOS-FLAMED BANANAS

SOFT AND CREAMY BAKED BANANAS, FLAMED WITH CALVADOS, ARE DELICIOUS SERVED WITH A RICH BUTTERSCOTCH SAUCE. THE SAUCE CAN BE MADE IN ADVANCE AND THE BANANAS ARE QUICKLY COOKED. HAVE A SENSIBLE PERSON IGNITE THE CALVADOS, WHICH MAKES A SPECTACULAR END TO A MEAL.

SERVES SIX

INGREDIENTS
115g/4oz/generous ½ cup sugar
150ml/¼ pint/⅔ cup water
25g/1oz/2 tbsp butter
150ml/¼ pint/⅔ cup double
  (heavy) cream
6 large slightly underripe bananas
90ml/6 tbsp Calvados

1 Place the sugar and measured water in a large pan and heat gently until the sugar has dissolved. Increase the heat and boil until the mixture turns a rich golden caramel colour. Remove from the heat and carefully add the butter and cream; the mixture will foam up in the pan. Replace it over a gentle heat and stir to a smooth sauce, then pour into a bowl and leave to cool. Cover and chill until needed.

2 Prepare the barbecue. Wrap the bananas individually in foil. Position a grill rack over the hot coals. Grill the wrapped bananas over high heat for 10 minutes.

3 Transfer the bananas to a tray, open up the parcels and slit the upper side of each banana skin.

4 Meanwhile, gently warm the Calvados in a small pan, then pour some into each banana. Put them back on the barbecue and wait for a few seconds before carefully igniting the Calvados with a long match. Serve with the sauce as soon as the flames die down.

Energy 359kcal/1501kJ; Protein 1.7g; Carbohydrate 43.7g, of which sugars 41.4g; Fat 17.2g, of which saturates 10.6g; Cholesterol 43mg; Calcium 29mg; Fibre 1.1g; Sodium 33mg.

TOASTED BRIOCHE SLICES WITH ICE CREAM

WARM AND SYRUPY-SWEET BRIOCHE SLICES FLAVOURED WITH ORANGE AND CINNAMON MAKE A DELECTABLE CONTRAST TO VANILLA ICE CREAM IN THIS UNUSUAL VARIATION ON THE TOASTED BUN THEME. FINELY GRATED LEMON RIND AND JUICE INSTEAD WILL WORK JUST AS WELL THE ORANGE.

SERVES FOUR

INGREDIENTS
  butter, for greasing
  finely grated rind and juice of
    1 orange, such as navel or
    blood orange
  50g/2oz/¼ cup caster
    (superfine) sugar
  90ml/6 tbsp water
  1.5ml/¼ tsp ground cinnamon
  4 brioche buns
  15ml/1 tbsp icing
    (confectioners') sugar
  vanilla ice cream, to serve

1 Put the orange rind and juice, sugar, measured water and cinnamon in a heavy pan. Heat gently, stirring constantly, until the sugar has dissolved, then boil rapidly, without stirring, for 2 minutes, until thickened and syrupy.

COOK'S TIP
You could also use slices of a larger brioche, rather than buns, or madeleines, sliced horizontally in half. These are traditionally flavoured with lemon or orange flower water, making them especially tasty.

2 Remove the orange syrup from the heat and pour into a shallow heatproof dish. Prepare the barbecue. Position a lightly oiled grill rack over the hot coals. Cut each brioche into three thick slices. Grill over high heat until lightly toasted on both sides.

3 Working quickly and using tongs, lift each hot brioche slice from the grill and dip one side into the syrup. Turn it syrup-side up on to a tray while you dip the remainder.

4 Lightly dust the tops with icing sugar then transfer the brioche slices back to the barbecue or grill rack. Grill for 1–2 minutes, or until the top is bubbling and the underneath is golden brown.

5 Transfer the hot brioche to serving plates and top with scoops of vanilla ice cream. Spoon the remaining syrup over them and serve immediately.

VARIATION
For a subtle difference in spiciness, substitute the same amount of ground cardamom for the cinnamon.

Energy 458kcal/1926kJ; Protein 9.1g; Carbohydrate 67.9g, of which sugars 45.8g; Fat 18.5g, of which saturates 10.2g; Cholesterol 1mg; Calcium 189mg; Fibre 1.8g; Sodium 253mg.

APPLE-STUFFED CRÊPES

WHILE THE COALS ARE STILL HOT AFTER THE BARBECUE YOU CAN HEAT UP TWO FRYING PANS AND COOK UP SOME LACE-THIN CRÊPES TO SERVE WITH GOLDEN FRIED APPLES. TOP THE CRÊPES WITH A DRIZZLE OF HONEY AND SOME CREAM AND THEY ARE SURE TO BE A POPULAR END TO THE MEAL.

SERVES FOUR

INGREDIENTS
   115g/4oz/1 cup plain
     (all-purpose) flour
   pinch of salt
   2 large (US extra large) eggs
   175ml/6fl oz/¾ cup milk
   120ml/4fl oz/½ cup sweet (hard)
     cider
   butter, for frying
   4 eating apples
   60ml/4 tbsp caster (superfine) sugar
   120ml/4fl oz/½ cup clear honey, and
     150ml/¼ pint/⅔ cup double (heavy)
     cream, to serve

1 To make the batter, sift the flour and salt into a bowl. Add the eggs and milk and beat until smooth. Stir in the cider. Leave for 30 minutes. Prepare the barbecue. Place a grill rack over the coals.

2 Heat a small heavy frying pan or flat griddle on the grill rack. Add a knob (pat) of butter and enough batter to coat the pan thinly. Cook the crêpe for about 1 minute until it is golden underneath, then flip it over and cook the other side until golden. Slide the crêpe on to a plate, then repeat with the remaining batter to make seven more. Set the crêpes aside and keep warm.

3 Core the apples and cut them into thick slices. Heat 15g/½oz butter in a large frying pan. Add the apples to the pan and cook until golden on both sides. Transfer the slices to a bowl and sprinkle with sugar.

4 Fold each crêpe in half, then fold in half again to form a cone. Fill each with some of the fried apples. Place two filled crêpes on each dessert plate. Drizzle with a little honey and serve at once, accompanied by cream.

COOK'S TIP
For the best results, use full-fat (whole) milk in the batter.

Energy 524kcal/2200kJ; Protein 8.3g; Carbohydrate 71.1g, of which sugars 49.2g; Fat 24.1g, of which saturates 13.8g; Cholesterol 149mg; Calcium 140mg; Fibre 2.1g; Sodium 71mg.

FRESH FRUIT SALAD

AFTER A RICH MEAL, NOTHING QUITE HITS THE SPOT LIKE A CLEAR-TASTING SALAD OF FRESH FRUIT. THIS SALAD HAS A PASSION FRUIT AND HONEY DRESSING THAT REALLY ACCENTUATES THE FLAVOUR OF THE EXOTIC FRUIT USED. SERVE IT WITH SCOOPS OF COCONUT OR VANILLA ICE CREAM, IF YOU LIKE.

SERVES SIX

INGREDIENTS
    1 mango
    1 papaya
    2 kiwi fruit
    coconut or vanilla ice cream, to serve
For the dressing
    3 passion fruit
    thinly pared rind and juice of 1 lime
    5ml/1 tsp hazelnut or walnut oil
    15ml/1 tbsp clear honey

COOK'S TIP
A clear golden honey scented with orange blossom or acacia blossom would be perfect for the dressing.

1 Peel the mango, cut it into three slices, then cut the flesh into chunks and place it in a large bowl. Peel the papaya and cut it in half. Scoop out the seeds and discard, then chop the flesh and put in the bowl with the mango.

2 Cut both ends off each kiwi fruit, then stand them on a board. Using a small sharp knife, cut off the skin from top to bottom. Cut each kiwi fruit in half lengthways, then cut into thick slices. Combine all the fruit in a large bowl.

3 Make the dressing. Cut each passion fruit in half and scoop the seeds out into a sieve set over a small bowl. Press the seeds well to extract all their juices. Lightly whisk the remaining dressing ingredients into the passion fruit juice, then pour the dressing over the fruit. Mix gently to combine. Leave to chill for 1 hour before serving with scoops of coconut or vanilla ice cream.

Energy 57kcal/240kJ; Protein 0.9g; Carbohydrate 12.4g, of which sugars 12.3g; Fat 0.7g, of which saturates 0.1g; Cholesterol 0mg; Calcium 21mg; Fibre 2.4g; Sodium 6mg.

LEMON SORBET

THIS SMOOTH, TANGY SORBET CREATES A LIGHT AND REFRESHING DESSERT THAT CAN BE SERVED AS IT IS OR TO ACCOMPANY FRESH FRUIT. IF YOU HAVE COOKED A RICH BARBECUE, THIS CLEAN-TASTING DESSERT MIGHT BE JUST THE RIGHT CHOICE TO END THE MEAL.

SERVES SIX

INGREDIENTS
200g/7oz/1 cup caster
(superfine) sugar
300ml/½ pint/1¼ cups water
4 lemons
1 large (US extra large) egg white
a little sugar, for sprinkling

1 Put the caster sugar and measured water into a heavy pan and bring slowly to the boil, stirring occasionally, until the sugar has just dissolved.

2 Using a vegetable peeler, pare the rind thinly from two of the lemons directly into the pan. Simmer for about 2 minutes without stirring, then remove the pan from the heat. Leave the syrup to cool, then chill.

3 Squeeze the juice from all the lemons and carefully strain it into the syrup, making sure all the pips (seeds) are removed. Take the lemon rind out of the syrup and set it aside until you make the decoration.

4 If you have an ice cream maker, strain the syrup into the machine tub and churn for 10 minutes, or until thickening.

5 In a bowl, lightly whisk the egg white with a fork, then pour it into the tub. Continue to churn for 10–15 minutes, or until firm enough to scoop.

6 If working by hand, strain the syrup into a plastic tub or a similar shallow freezerproof container and freeze for 4 hours, or until the mixture is mushy.

7 Scoop the mushy mixture into a blender or food processor and process until smooth. Whisk the egg white with a fork until it is just frothy. Spoon the sorbet back into its container; beat in the egg white. Freeze for 1 hour.

8 To make the sugared rind decoration, use the blanched rind from step 2. Cut into very thin strips and sprinkle with granulated sugar on a plate. Scoop the sorbet into bowls or glasses and decorate with the sugared lemon rind.

VARIATIONS
Sorbet can be made from any citrus fruit. As a guide, you will need 300ml/½ pint/ 1¼ cups of fresh fruit juice and the pared rind of half the squeezed fruits. For example, use four oranges or two oranges and two lemons, or, to make a grapefruit sorbet, use the rind of one ruby grapefruit and the juice of two.

Energy 133kcal/569kJ; Protein 0.7g; Carbohydrate 34.8g, of which sugars 34.8g; Fat 0g, of which saturates 0g; Cholesterol 0mg; Calcium 18mg; Fibre 0g; Sodium 12mg.

INDEX